A GOOD
BULLET

COMEDY, VIOLENCE AND ALL THE
TERRIBLE THINGS THAT MAKE US LAUGH

With Illustrations by Jack Whitehall

Published in 2013 by
Short Books
3A Exmouth House
Pine Street
EC1R 0JH

10 9 8 7 6 5 4 3 2 1

A CIP catalogue record for this book is available from the British Library.

ISBN 978-1-78072-169-9

Printed and bound in Great Britain by
CPI Group (UK) Ltd, Croydon, CR0 4YY

Cover design by Two Associates

Contents.

My Introduction to Me.

'What do you think makes people laugh,' I ask a friend of mine.

'Drugs,' he says, seriously.

He might be right. Only last week I went to a party where some comedians sat round a coffee table, discussing ethics and originality as they banged coke. That scene notwithstanding, this book is about why *I* think there's more than drugs to what makes me laugh.

A book about comedy will surely stand or fall on the author's sense of humour. Well, my favourite sitcom is *The Nanny*, an early nineties Fran Drescher[1] vehicle of

1 Fran Drescher is an actress and comedian from Flushing, Queens. Drescher's big-screen adventure began with a cameo in *Spinal Tap* and ended prematurely with *The Beautician and the Beast*, in which she plays a beautician (as, originally, she did in *The Nanny*) who melts the heart of an aloof comedy Milosovic, played by Timothy Dalton.
At this point, I should say that it's my editor's idea for this book to be footnoted. She was worried that you might not be fully cognisant with, for instance, Chesney Hawkes, who bobs up in a later chapter. 'You don't know Chesney Hawkes?' I asked her, incredulous. 'But he's the one and only!' Sadly, this didn't ring any bells either. My hand has been

endearingly sassy mediocrity. Make of that what you will. I'm a joke-writer, but this book doesn't contain advice on writing because I'm not in a position to give it. Leave that book to Armando Ianucci[2] or Julia Davis[3]. Nor is *A Good Bullet* about the comedy industry. Things that aren't comedies make me laugh; a lot of comedies leave me cold. Take *Miranda*. If I wanted to see a burly lady falling over, I'd watch women's rugby. Now, that's cruel and not true. So's a lot of this book. Why? Because I'm cruel. Whether what I say is true or not is up to you.

In his book *No Laughing Matter: Rationale of a Dirty Joke*, G. Legman[4] claimed that "a person's favourite joke

---

forced, therefore, principally to save Chesney's blushes.

My problem with footnotes was this: TV is in the habit of second-guessing the intelligence of its audience. Programme-makers are obsessed with references to books, films, people etc being 'too intellectual' (or 'too offensive') for the general public. This is a terrible habit; the art historian Claire Bishop has written that "an over-solicitousness that judges in advance what people are capable of coping with can be just as insidious as intending to offend them," and I couldn't agree more.

I was worried that selectively footnoting this book would look like I was second-guessing your intelligence. Also, I'd have fucked up – I'd maybe footnote Michel Foucault, but not in my darkest, most dystopian nightmares would I have dreamt that one day the name 'Chesney Hawkes' would mean literally *nothing*.

So I've decided to footnote everyone I mention by name. If the prolix bores you, just remember: I'm trying not to offend anyone.

2 Armando Iannuci – *The Day Today, I'm Alan Partridge, The Thick of It*. Bare tekkers.

3 Julia Davis wrote the spectacularly bleak *Nighty Night* and *Hunderby*, proving that comedy and laughter are not means and ends. They are a married couple of seething, vampiric sadomasochists – the standard relationship in any Julia Davis sitcom.

4 Gershon Legman (1917–1999) was an American joke archivist, cultural critic and collector of rare erotica. As a young Jewish immigrant,

is the key to that person's character." In the spirit of full disclosure, and with characteristic self-indulgence, I actually have two favourite jokes. This is the first:

There once was a bus conductor called Grahame. Grahame was a manic depressive; after some heavy losses at the dogs track, he'd hit the bottle, then hit the wife, then been hit with an even heavier divorce. One day, through a haze of vodka and meds, Grahame saw two boys vandalising the top deck of his bus. As he watched them key indecipherable tags into a window, something in Grahame snapped. The vodka/meds haze turning red, Gray hurled the kids – one by one and with defenestrative force – through the window and out into the oncoming traffic.

'For the callous murder of two young men, I have no choice but to sentence you to the electric chair,' the judge intoned.

'Bothered?' Grahame leered back from the dock.

'Not especially. However, the law states that I must grant a condemned man his final wish. Do you have one?'

'Yes, your Honour,' Gray replied. 'It has always been my wish to eat the Czechoslovakian banana.'

'Done,' the judge said, banging his gavel and sending

Legman was held down by his classmates while one of them wrote 'KOSHER' in "horse-shit juice" across his forehead, an event alluded to in *No Laughing Matter*, the second of Legman's two exhaustive studies of 'The Dirty Joke'. Legman is credited with inventing the vibrator. He was also big into origami while remaining sceptical of the Japanese, particularly their "fishlike sucking-in of the breath" when laughing.

a rookie policeman off to the shops. But it turned out that the good people of Czechoslovakia did not export these precious fruits. So the policeman caught a flight to Prague, a mysterious cobbled city of smoke-stained saints and spires. From there, he was directed to a tiny village into the very heart of the Czechoslovakian jungle.

'And what do you seek, my child?' a toothless old babushka hissed, once the policeman had crossed her grimy palm with silver.

'I have journeyed hither for the Czechoslovakian banana, O thou iron-plaited wise-woman,' the policeman replied, in his shaky restaurant Czech.

'You mean the Banana?'

'The banana.'

'No, the Banana. *We say it with a capital B.'*

'The Banana,*' he said again, a little testily.*

'Well, we sold the last one yesterday. Come back for the next harvest… in twelve years,' the crone called back to him, as her canary-yellow caravan lurched off back through the graveyard.

The judge was annoyed, of course, but the law's the law. And so Grahame spent twelve comfortable years on death row. He took up a number of courses, discovered God, and entered a prison marriage with a handsome Filipino firebug.

After the allotted time, the policeman (now a detective inspector) returned to the village in Czechoslovakia. The old woman led him to the jungle clearing in which the Banana grew. There, the policeman's heart sank. The Banana was at least twenty feet long and seven feet wide.

There was no way he could carry it all the way back home by himself.

Twelve years later, and the judge was dead, shot by his wife after his sordid 'other life' literally tumbled out of the closet. His wife had returned from the clinic unexpectedly, desperate to find those missing photos of her recently-deceased only daughter. She'd remembered an old album on the top shelf of their wardrobe, and was opening the door when Manuel scampered out, wearing a schoolgirl's uniform. The wife screamed – Manuel was the spit of her daughter – and dived under the bed for the shoebox in which her husband kept his gun. Then the judge himself walked in, dressed in heels, miniskirt and fox-fur merkin, and waving a pre-lubed cane. His wife didn't think twice.

The policeman, meanwhile, had made Chief Constable, but he hadn't got to where he was today by letting cases go unfinished. After much palm-crossing, he triumphantly returned to Grahame's prison with the Czechoslovakian Banana slung between two police Chinooks.

Having bid adieu to the cherry-lipped Filipino, Grahame was content to meet his Maker. It took him about three weeks to eat the Banana. He'd barely swallowed the last bite when the impatient policeman whisked him off to the electric chair.

No one was there to watch Grahame die, his victims' families having long since lost interest in the whole tedious story. Only the policeman was present – he'd shotgunned flicking the switch.

'Have you got a Rennie?' Grahame asked the policeman. 'I think I've got indigestion off all that banana.'

'It's pronounced Banana,*' the policeman growled, flicking the switch. A thousand volts flew through Grahame's body with an almighty explosion. But as the smoke cleared, the policeman saw that Grahame was somehow still alive.*

'Banana?' Gray said, as if nothing had happened.

'No, Banana,*' the policeman growled, twisting the voltage dial into the red, then flicking the switch. A million volts flew through Grahame's body with an almighty explosion. But Grahame* still *was not dead.*

'Banana? Is that right?' Grahame said again.

'It's Banana*!* Banana*!* Banana*!' the policeman cried. A billion volts flew through Grahame's body with an almighty explosion.*

'Well, it was delicious, however you say it,' Grahame said, smacking his lips.

The policeman sighed and whipped out a lethal injection. But before driving the needle into Grahame's bulging jugular, he asked the condemned man one last question: 'how come you survived all that electricity?'

'Well,' Grahame said, using a toothpick to jemmy the last chunks of banana from his teeth. 'To tell you the truth…'

'Yes?'

'To tell you the truth, I've always been a bad conductor.'

My other favourite joke is this:

What's brown and rhymes with Snoop?
Dre.

I'm a joke-writer because one of my friends, Jack Whitehall[5], is a comedian. We became friends when we were fourteen through a mutual love of *The League of Gentlemen*[6], though the first time we spent any quality time together, he spat in my face and I punched him in his. But, hey, that's boarding school.

Friends create a shared sense of humour. It's a way of growing closer, and of excluding outsiders from the relationship. The intimately abusive tone, the points of reference, the callbacks, stupid voices, one-liners, insults and punches – these script the performance of a friendship. It's a powerful language, and one which mocks and celebrates its speakers. You laugh with and at friends. You tease them; you're merciless because you know them and they know you enough to let you get away with it. A shared sense of humour is as intimate as the names (cruel, loving, exclusive) we give to our lovers.

Jack and I use our private code commercially. But we've discovered that the jokes we write which we find funniest are almost always the ones no one else laughs at. The most intimate elements of our humour still refuse to be made inclusive. And the day those elements do become accessible, I imagine we'll no be longer friends, only colleagues.

I should point out that Jack doesn't find either of my

5 Jack Whitehall is a comedian and actor who stars in *Bad Education* and *Fresh Meat*.

6 The never-bettered show written by Jeremy Dyson, Mark Gatiss, Steve Pemberton and Reece Shearsmith. Jeremy script edited *Bad Education*, and I was also lucky enough to write some sketches for his show, *Psychobitches*. Meeting him, I still get star-struck.

two favourite jokes funny. I laugh alone a lot. Who needs friends when you've got a Czechoslovakian banana?

But I was trying to be funny before I met Jack. To begin with, I'm fat and short-sighted. Like other fat, short-sighted people, I was bullied at school. Then I discovered the way to beat a bully is to ridicule them harder and faster than they can ridicule you. Being funny was pragmatic; I was taught the reflexes by my fear of humiliation. I sparred with anyone who took me on. Sometimes I tried my hand at out-boxing, keeping my opponent at bay with long, powerful punches. Other times I swarmed them with a flurry of hooks and jabs. The one thing I never learned at school was when to *stop* punching. That and French.

I became (and become) the bully. The power goes to my head. After all, language is the only realm in which I'm – if not the fittest – then at least not the shittest.

Comedy being Darwinian, I also discovered the other cliché: girls like funny boys, even if they're fat. Jokes compensated for my otherwise catastrophic levels of unattractiveness. My brand of violence became a way of asking for love: I'd savage myself until the girl laughed and said I didn't deserve the savaging. So, at school, I joked my way out of the following (chronological) shortcomings:

- Not being a Power Ranger.
- Not being good at sport.
- Liking Warhammer.
- Going through a phase of forgetting to wear pants on days when I was definitely going to have to take my

trousers off. For PE, if not for the PE teacher, a burly Welshman who was having an affair with my – and his – sour-faced geography mistress (and why are geography teachers all such *husks*?)

- My mother not letting me use Lynx deodorant, even though Voodoo was super-cool.
- Smelling.
- Wearing awful clothes.
- Not having a mobile phone.
- Getting a mobile phone that wasn't the green Nokia phone that was sort of like the one in *The Matrix*.
- Getting the green Nokia phone that was sort of like the one in *The Matrix*, only to discover that its factory settings did not include a load of fit girls' numbers.
- Going to boarding school.
- Still wearing awful clothes.
- *Still* being pubeless.
- Not really liking UK garage.
- Really liking Seal.
- Being too afraid to smoke weed.
- Smoking weed and pissing myself like I fucking *knew* I would.
- Experimenting with bracelets.
- Getting caught wanking like a shipwrecked rabbit over a photo of the pregnant Davina McCall because, as I explained at the time, it was all I had to hand. I'm not a pregnant fetishist. Pregnancy freaks me out. I don't want to bend a woman over a barrel of my own construction. I don't want to cooper stretch-marks. (I lost my audience with that riff on barrel-making, and deservedly so.)

- Being the only boy in my English and Drama classes.
- Fancying my best friend. Not Jack, though for six years he thought I was gay and I thought he was gay. That's how well we talk about our emotions.
- Still liking Warhammer. As any hustler will tell you, don't hate the playa, hate the game.

Jokes allow me to express the shame I feel for existing. Like I'm a usurper: I don't deserve my family, my friends, or my indistinct and scattered abilities. I have been privileged by life, of that I'm sure. Only, I'm not sure I *want* life. I don't know if I can rest here; brutal and banal one minute, impossibly beautiful the next, it gutters around me like a hotel's neon sign at night. I have no way of apologising for my lack of ease with myself and with the world, other than by making people laugh at me and it. And if that sounds grandiloquent, that's because it is.

The moment I realised all this (give or take – maybe not that bit about the sign) was at my primary school. I'd faked an illness to get out of a physics class. My father picked me up but my acting skills let me down. Busted, I wrote him a sketch to say sorry. The sketch was about a perverted priest (I was precocious, if by 'precocious' you mean sinister) and I read it to him while we ate fish and chips at a cafe that has since been closed down, and my dad and I know why: when we were leaving, we held the door open for a cockroach that was sauntering in (because, if you can survive a nuclear holocaust, you're likely to saunter). I assume that cockroach was just fashionably late to the diseased party the cafe was throwing for the family Blattaria, because after eating there I spent the next couple of days throwing up at school, too embarrassed to call my parents. And there's a moral there, as much to do with hygiene as writing.

I'm not a comedian. I don't have the naked detachment comedians need to perform in front of people, a detachment which isn't dissimilar to that required to use a urinal. Not that I mind exposing myself. When I'm in my comfort zone, I can be *too* honest. Does it benefit my book (or you) to admit that, though I have a thoroughly mediocre penis, I have balls big enough to border on the unsightly? No. Then why ram another of my shortcomings down your throat? Because you *might* confuse self-laceration for emotional maturity, and babes love a mature guy, meagrely-knobbed or otherwise.

Contrast that to this. There are three urinals: 1, 2, 3. A quick analysis shows that, by standing at 2, you're easily visible from both flanks. Plus, if two more men take up positions at 1 and 3, you're unable to perform the classic 45° privacy pivot away from one co-micturant without appearing to present yourself to the other. The natural inclination, therefore, is to take either 1 or 3.

But here's the problem: if you take 1, some bloke might still take 2 *even if 3 is unoccupied*. Thence the nightmare. There's the initial silence, spent staring at the wall as you try to forget that this monster's listening to you as much as you are to him. Then the hiss of his piss before yours! Oh right, *he's* OK – you're the one with the hang-ups, mate. If you're lucky, it'll trigger your pee in an awkward concordance. If you're unlucky, you'll seize up. It's a lottery. What's more, 2-takers aren't shy. You'll have to stomach the spit, the fart, the burp, possibly a hacking cough, and – worst of all – the ridiculous, self-aggrandizing shake. Am I in Chaucer? Must I take an ass to Canterbury? Then leave me out of your earthiness.

Are 2-takers having a laugh? Are they trying to freak you out? Show off (though the assumed correlation between confident pissers and the well-endowed doesn't hold that much water)? All I know is that their cloacal machismo makes me feel violated. It makes me want to proclaim, 'this is my body, and these are my rights! My great-grandfather didn't chain himself to the railings of Parliament. He didn't throw himself under the King's horse.' But I don't. I just use a cubicle instead. Which, in this metaphor, serves as a writer's room.

So I'm a joke-writer rather than a comedian because I'm uncomfortable about performing in front of men, either in comedy clubs or toilets. Obviously there's a huge cross-over between the two categories. Writers and comedians, I mean, not toilets and comedy clubs (though there's always Jongleurs). Jack, for instance, writes and performs. That he employs a joke-writer surprises a few people who don't think he's *got* any jokes, so what this writer's contributing is anyone's guess. More people are surprised for a different reason. We like to imagine that comedians are spontaneous. Most of them are not.

Stand-ups will tell a good joke hundreds of times. They'll stop only when it's been on telly because – if an audience sees them perform it 'live' after that – the illusion of spontaneity will die. Why the audience *needs* spontaneity is maybe to do with our egos. We want to be the joke's first and only audience. We crave its virginity. If my extensive research into pornography is anything to go by, comedians are whores with a vial of red paint to break between their thighs, and the audience are businessmen, probably from Japan. It's as simple as that.

It's not, but the idea that comedians prepare material does genuinely startle people. Which is bizarre, if for no other reason than there's now an awful lot of money at stake. Michael McIntyre[7] doesn't book a fifty-eight date stadium tour only to bound on stage trusting to luck. Sure, his brand of humour *looks* effortless, but observational comedy is notoriously tricky to nail. It requires you to witness things differently. To detach yourself. To put a fresh spin on things we've seen before. That's why McIntyre – a famous perfectionist – will spend months of trial, error, sweat and tears observing all of Lee Evans'[8] DVDs. It's a juggling act, it really is. Or it would be if Lee Evans juggled.

Why do people mock Michael McIntyre? Because his popularity enforces an idea of what comedy 'should' be. That makes him an orthodoxy, and orthodoxies threaten art. But who am *I* to judge him?

Well, I'm a terrible person. In August 2010, Sally Stott[9] wrote the following one-star review of a play of mine at the Edinburgh Festival:

---

7 Michael McIntyre, babbling brook of first-world problems.

8 Lee Evans, the sweaty first superstar of stadium comedy.

9 Sally Stott is a journalist. And what a savage review! But, to quote Youssou N'Dour, "nothing's in vain."

> I'm frequently amazed by the awful things audiences laugh at when they think they should. Here they initially find rape, Parkinson's disease, stoning and the phrase 'I want to bruise a woman's tits' hilarious, before giving up pretending to understand this pseudo-intellectual, but mostly pretty dubious, new play written and performed by Freddy Syborn.
>
> Somehow Syborn has managed to persuade three decent actresses to join him in his indulgent theatrical vision, which offers a fast-paced yet largely unwelcome insight into a multitude of horrendous prejudices – which I can only hope he doesn't also subscribe to in real life.

However bad this book turns out to be, I doubt I'll get a worse review than that. Not that I'm asking you to give it a go.

Stott's review has been invaluable to me. It's asked the questions that I hope – in a meandering and largely impenetrable way – to address in this book. Should jokes shock? Or, as I'd contend, is it possible for them *not* to shock? Can you force people to laugh against their will? Do you have a duty to make your audience understand *why* they're laughing? And why do we enjoy violence?

Maybe it's useful to explain the dubious, pseudo-intellectual play in question. It was called *Anatomy Act.* In it, three actresses and I played different impulses or currents of thought in my brain: fear, ego, confession and fact. I was inspired by Claude Shannon[10], a computer scientist who, in the 1940s, defined what was sent through telephone wires as either information or noise. Information is the content of a message. Noise is the stuff that makes that information unreliable or nonsensical.

As Shannon imagined it, 'information' is a material with no intrinsic value, quantified in bits (now bytes), and threatened on its journey from its source to its endpoint by meaningless noise. So, in my play, my brain was given four rival material bodies; we threw a barrage of scenes, sketches, science and sexual fantasy at the audience, who had to work out what was noise, and what was the painful truth.

I wanted to make the audience laugh *at* me, not because "they [thought] they should", but because they shouldn't. Take the line Stott quotes about bruising tits. As the embodiment of the violent male ego, 'I' was childishly excited by the thought of damaging a female body. My glee interrupted a mature, rational passage of dialogue. The three parts of my brain played by women stared long and hard at me; under their gaze, I crumpled, ashamed. In doing so, I wanted to offer up this vicious part of myself to mockery.

---

10 Claude Shannon (1916–2001) was an American mathematician and electronic engineer. He worked as a cryptographer in the Second World War – briefly collaborating with Alan Turing – before making his name with a paper called *A Mathematical Theory of Communication* (1948). In the introduction to *A Mathematical Theory*, Shannon writes that "the semantic aspects of communication are irrelevant to the engineering problem"; noise could be controlled if the engineer understood the statistical probabilities of certain messages being chosen from sets of other messages. Not being an engineer, however, I can only understand Shannon's ideas with semantic analogies, and even then in an 'impressionistic' (i.e. inaccurate) way.

All jokes victimise. There's nothing wrong with a little victimisation as long as the right person gets victimized. We *naturally* laugh at things that are tasteless, thoughtless or ill-timed. A 'funny' photo that went round the Internet four years ago shows a platform in Stockwell tube station. It's the same platform on which the police shot Jean Charles de Menezes[11] for the crime of wearing a heavy jacket in summer. The photo shows that a poster's been put up since, advertising the movie *Righteous Kill*. The tagline? "There's nothing wrong with a little shooting as long as the right people get shot." Which is also, of course, the first lesson rookies get taught by the Met (for the record, the second is how to harass black men, and the third is how to close ranks when lawyers/journalists/victims' families start sticking their oar in).

In *Anatomy Act*, the story I was trying to tell was a true one. When I was eighteen, I saw a girl for about four months. She was very intense, she could be very funny, and it became very clear that she was suffering from serious mental health problems. She broke up with me just before I went off on my gap year. I dealt with the pain by detaching myself from her. I allowed myself to really, bodily, think of her only once, on a road swarming with

11 Jean Charles de Menezes (1978–2005) was living in the same block of flats as the suspected perpetrators of the attempted terror attacks which took place two weeks after London's 7/7 bombings. Menezes – a Brazilian – was identified by the police on the basis that the real suspects were East African, and that Menezes' eyes looked "Mongolian." North Asia, East Africa and South America – it's all the same thing, apparently. Menezes did not resist arrest, but the police still shot him seven times in the head.

crabs, crabs scuttling from sea to land, land to sea, so that the road swam, breathed, breathed, swam orange with bodies, buckling under the weight of my feet. I thought of her then. I thought of her because she'd given me crabs. And I was stopped from aching because I found it funny.

After I came back, I bumped into a friend of hers in the street. I told them I'd like to see her again and the friend looked shocked. So shocked I laughed. 'Does she hate me *that* much?' No. She's dead. 'Sorry?' She's dead. 'Sorry?' She's dead. 'Sorry. I'm sorry.'

The *noise* of my response, its disbelief, its self-preservation, its obsession, anger and empathy, its fear and desire and coldness and love, memory's ruthless free market, this dark, dark shape falling from a blue sky, like a piano about to crush a cartoon – I felt too vivid, 2-D, childish and shrill. As you can see, all I have is adjectives. *Anatomy Act* was about that insufficiency, where once the fear of insufficiency, of my sudden inability with words – the very source of my strength – had me kept me silent. I told no one I loved about her death for four bad years.

She didn't kill herself over me. She took too many drugs. She believed too many things. Anyway, *Anatomy Act* wasn't about her. Pathos is simple and it would have been grotesque to exploit her memory. I chose to write about that little bit of me that wanted to be the cause of her death. The selfishness of W.H. Auden[12]:

12 W.H. Auden (1907–1973) was a British poet, the best of his generation. Disdaining the Second World War's "nightmare of the dark", Auden left Europe for America in 1939. Later, he made a partial return for the sake of a sinecure at Oxford. It was here that a friend of mine once had

The error bred in the bone
Of each woman and each man
Craves what it cannot have
Not universal love
But to be loved alone.

I used to ask for love with violence. *Anatomy Act* tried to examine this contradiction, having felt real violence done to someone I'd loved. I wanted to reject my comedy; to make criticisms of myself and let them stand, without asking for sympathy.

As I write this, I hear that another friend of mine, Jessie, has committed suicide. Another piano. I wonder how many the sky has left to rain.

Grief makes people talk a lot of bullshit. Maybe that's bullshit, all of what I've just said. The problem is that everyone tries to be comforting, and the truth is seldom a comfort. As such, no one really believes what they're saying, or at least I hope they don't. 'She's smiling down on us.' That seems unlikely; she smiled too little on earth.

When I heard about Jessie, I thought back to her last email. She'd been sitting on a Californian beach, watching The Roots[13] "killing it" (as she and I'd seen them kill it two years previously), drinking Mexican beer, smoking a joint, and there's me reading this in the rain of another

---

lunch with Auden and some of their mutual acquaintances. Apparently, the poet delighted in telling long, rambling stories, wilfully boring the pants off everyone.

13 The Roots are a hip-hop band from Philadelphia, formed by Black Thought and ?uestlove in 1987.

wasted June and thinking that *my* life was terrible. Now, the vividness of her voice makes me laugh; my mistaken self-pity makes me laugh; the disjunction between what she said and what she was shortly to do makes me laugh. Is that inappropriate?

The tone people use at funerals is measured, decent, clear, correct, timely and respectful and, as such, has nothing to do with life. It weighs out love, sorrow and hope like livers on a scale; it changes gloves to give you change. This is the acceptable voice of pain. Violence and laughter are its unacceptable alternatives.

I remember my father trying to write his mother's eulogy on the day of her funeral. We were late and the printer had run out of ink. But my father *had* to speak, though – faced with the prospect of failing to – he couldn't say anything. All he could do was kick the desk the computer sat on. He kicked it hard enough, in fact, for his foot to split its wooden sides. My sister and I were so shocked that we laughed at him, and this laughter calmed him enough to write the speech out by hand. But then the priest conducting the funeral made a mistake, reading on past the eulogy. The text being sacred, this mistake could not be corrected. Then my father tried to speak at the drinks afterwards, but he was drowned out by the hubbub of pensioners moving on in the direction of canapés. So my grandmother was denied her eulogy. Though I consider it still to be that hole her son kicked in the wood.

*

Why didn't Sally Stott find my play funny? Maybe it was awful. Maybe, in her eyes, it was a cheap poster stuck thoughtlessly to the site of a tragedy. Maybe she's a tad judgmental. She's certainly the only journalist I've heard of who's provoked burlesque dancers to march in protest against her. In 2010 (her *annus mirabilis*), Stott accused them of behaving like sex workers. In her review of *Circus Burlesque*, she said that no "enlightened person" – by which she means herself – could enjoy the show because, amongst other crimes against womankind, the female writer/performer wore cheap underwear and the dancing was "not even retro." Not even retro, you say? Well, count *me* out.

But Stott's review is the risk I run. Jokes bind the comic to their audience. As such, if I choose to tell aggressive jokes, I have to accept an equally aggressive reaction. And I continue to try telling that kind of joke because I'm interested in the way laughter is the product of neurosis, prejudice and fear.

I experience every terrible thing with one eye on how and why the situation is funny. This is the joke-writer's 'get out of jail free' card, as well as their jail. Everything's material, so nothing matters. I'm material. Nothing I do or say or feel matters. Hey ho.

But if *nothing* matters, why make more than six hundred people laugh at the mental breakdown I'd suffered in silence? Why put myself or anyone else through *Anatomy Act*? Because honesty has a value. Witnessing honesty has a value.

If silences were violences, I'd be locked away. I've beaten people black and blue with what I couldn't say.

The unspeakable monsters you. Everything must be faced, and everything must be paid for. Reliving on stage the worst moments of my life neither numbed nor wounded me – it gave me a chance to outlive them. The process healed me precisely because I'm not a performer, because I was never comfortable, because there was no privacy.

I'm not saying that the motives behind *Anatomy Act* belie some universal truth about writing. But the play made me learn things about myself, and these may ring true-ish with other comedians and joke-writers. These things also inform the perspective from which this book is written. So essentially this has all been a very egotistical disclaimer.

To laugh at tragedy is not to belittle it. To find someone's death funny is not, I believe, to lessen their loss. Comedy is capable of tragedy's seriousness and beauty. Comedy can also say more than any art form about the ordinary experience of life, that of defeated understanding, of disappointment, absurdity and shame. What I'm trying to do now is understand why that is.

I'd like to dedicate this book to my sister, George, for being the funniest person I know; to Alice, for being the most beautiful; to Harriet, for her faith in our work together; to Florence, because she'd kill me if I didn't; and to Jessie, though she deserves so much more.

A man goes to the doctor and says, 'Doctor, I think I'm deaf.'
And the doctor says, 'What?'
HA
HA
HA
HA
HA
HA

That's very offensive to doctors.
We're not all deaf, you know.
But they wouldn't know because they never listen.
Deaf bastards.
They wouldn't say that about Muslims.

That's the funniest joke I've ever heard. It's not blue, it's not offensive... literally anyone could find it funny.

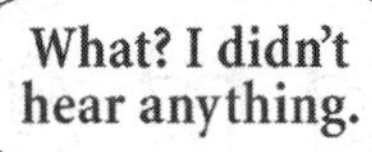
What? I didn't hear anything.

Deaf cow.

Comedy. Division.

I've started with me because the thing most people say about comedy (with a sagacity that's blind to the fact that the same truism applies to everything else) is that it's subjective. Paradoxically, let's accept that this is objectively true. I say paradoxically, because – with God's death as relevant to me as that of some bewhiskered Victorian forebear – objectivity is impossible. In my opinion.

Having said that, comedy is actually objective. Or at least it thinks it is. To clarify, comedy's essential dynamic is that of pointing out to one person or group of people the mistakes of others. However mild the observation (why do supermarkets think self-checkout machines are more efficient than traditional tills when they're probably not? LOL), jokes are not sympathetic.

God (when he was alive) didn't find much funny. He only promises to laugh, and even then only twice: in Psalms 2:2–4, where he'll "laugh at" some heathens who are annoying him, and in Psalms 37:13, where again he'll "laugh" at the wicked man whose "day is coming". What's so funny? The fact that these heathens haven't backed the right horse. When they die, they'll realise their mistake – at the exact moment it becomes impossible for them to avoid the consequences. Judgement Day is the punch-line.

This is the holy equivalent to slapstick, when a man sits down on the space he thought was occupied by a chair, only to realise – by hurting himself – that the chair's been moved by some providential hand. The man's mistake is only comic if the audience *knows* that the chair is not there prior to the fall. If they don't, if they're not on the side of providence, then they'll be as bewildered as the hapless pratfaller himself and the whole sorry episode switches genre to become tragic.

Comedy is a higher perspective. That the highest seats in a theatre are referred to as the gods is either no coincidence, or one that suits my argument very well.

Mark Twain[14] thought that "the secret source of humour is not joy but sorrow; there is no humour in heaven," but that doesn't stop God laughing at others' pain. His pleasure conforms to the philosopher Thomas Hobbes'[15] definition of laughter: "a sudden glory" felt

14 Mark Twain (1835–1910) was the handsomely-moustached American author who wrote *Huckleberry Finn* and *The Adventures of Tom Sawyer.* As a peculiar child, I always envied Tom Sawyer for being able to attend his own funeral. It was Twain who said that "if Christ were here now there is one thing he would not be – a Christian."

15 Thomas Hobbes (1588–1679) was an English political philosopher. Hobbes thought human beings were essentially self-serving; without a social contract, "a war of all against all" would make our lives

when we the laugher perceive "some eminency in ourselves by comparison with the infirmities of others." If they'd only listened to God, then the heathens wouldn't be in this hellish supermarket, trapped by all the unidentified sins in their damned self-checkout machines. But no prayers can help them now. To paraphrase the terraces, "they're shit, and they know they are | They're shit, and they know they are." And they must be *made* to recognise this. Their infirmities must be agonisingly obvious. Only then, as Thomas Aquinas[16] imagines in his page-turner the *Summa Theologica*, will God and his angels split their sides.

Sixteenth-century French theologian and roflcopter pilot John Calvin[17] approved of "laughter at the tears of our enemies, provided that it be not too lavish, but moderate and temperate and, for that reason, holy and approved by God." Calvin: the guy who gave the world Calvinism, in which the winners and losers are preordained (no matter how good or bad they actually are)

"solitary, poor, nasty, brutish, and short." Tom Waits quotes that last bit in *Come On Up To The House*, a song which takes a pragmatic approach to misery: "come down off the cross | We could use the wood."

16 As a young man, St. Thomas Aquinas (1225–74) told his parents that he was running away to become a Dominican priest. Unfortunately, Mr. and Mrs. Aquinas wanted him to become a Benedictine abbot, so they kept their son captive for two years in the family castle. At one point, his brothers even hired a prostitute to corrupt the saintly young tearaway, but Thomas kept her at bay with the help of a hot poker and some angels. It's your classic boy-meets-God coming-of-age story.

17 John Calvin (1509–64) was a French pastor. Calvin loved nothing better than a quiet evening in front of the fire of heretics whom his denunciations had condemned to death.

by the hidden agenda of a cruelly unaccountable god, *X Factor*-style. And it's this kind of thing that makes me – when asked by some believer if I've ever thought about being a Christian – itch to reply, 'yes, but in the way that I wonder what it would be like to be in a wheelchair, and only then because I'm curious if you can have sex or not'?

Anyway, clearly the vast majority of comedy today is not *consciously* to do with death. Michael McIntyre doesn't start a routine with the old observational standard of 'have you ever noticed that dying is the one thing everyone does but which no one wants to do?' He doesn't do this because that question would take him out of his comfort zone and put him in something that he's not so good at: a train of thought worth having. He also doesn't do this because mortality does not sell out the O2. Death is not the crucial ingredient to a good night out. Given the choice between acknowledging your senescence and a shot of sambuca, not a lot of people say 'go on then, show me the skull beneath the skin.'

But I say *consciously* because that religious dynamic is still very much intact. Comedians are still excluding people who don't think like them, who don't share the same experiences. For instance, I assume (though I couldn't be bothered to check) that Michael McIntyre has a joke about the school run. I also assume he makes the observation that, on the school run, it's annoying to be stuck in traffic because you're running late. Plus you're in a car with kids and – as we all know – children say the funniest things.

This joke, if it exists, is exclusive. Though we the Great British public think, 'oh I know exactly what he means, it's like he's taken the words out of my mouth and spun them into pure gold, the chuckling alchemist', McIntyre's material is tragically perplexing to the following social outcasts:

- People who – whether due to barrenness, isolation or choice – have no children, because they don't need to do the school run.
- Parents serving a driving ban, because they can't do the school run.
- Blind people, parents or otherwise, because they can't drive.
- Lower-income and/or busy families, because their children will catch the train or the bus.
- School bus drivers, because they don't give a shit if they're late. It's not their problem.
- Children, because being late to school is a positive.
- Patient people, because they're not bothered by a minor delay on the road to educating their kids.
- Convicted paedophiles, because their contact with children has been legally precluded.

Now, no one would admit to enjoying a joke that says 'fuck you' to the blind. But this doesn't stop McIntyre (possibly) steamrollering over their feelings in a steamroller he could in theory be licensed to drive, but which – due to strict industrial standards – his victims never could. Nor does it stop us from laughing, thanks to what Henri

Bergson[18] calls "a temporary anaesthesia of the heart", a lack of feeling that lets us find others' misfortune funny.

Every joke has a victim and that's just a fact. This victim will fall into one of three categories. They could be the subject of the joke: the Irishman, the blonde, the celebrity, the mother-in-law, the person knock-knocking. They could be the joke's target: the included audience or the excluded other, whichever's being mocked. Or they could be the joke-tellers themselves: wasn't I an idiot to pursue this course of action? But this isn't to make the false distinction between laughing *at* and laughing *with*. Every laugh does both. We laugh *at* the victim and *with* our fellow victimisers, whoever they are.

Comedy thrives on the schadenfreude of human error. For Bergson, seeing the person as a faulty machine was funny. By prioritising the body's physical failures, its short-circuits, he became the second-cleverest champion of the fart joke after James Joyce[19]. Now, I love physical comedy – I love a fart – but I think it's *thought* that we find funniest.

When he goes to a cut-price furniture sale, Mr. Bean buys too much to carry, so he's forced to drive his Mini

18 Henri Bergson (1859–1941) was French, and a Nobel Prize-winning philosopher. He wrote *Laughter: An Essay on the Meaning of the Comic*, which Wikipedia says is "idiosyncratic", though it "needs a quotation to verify" this adjective.

19 James Joyce (1882–1941) was an Irish novelist whose experiments with language ended up with his last novel, *Finnegans Wake*, being written in a kind of lyrical, smutty Esperanto. After his death, Joyce's wife, Nora, was asked about some of the authors the couple'd known in Trieste-Zurich-Paris. "If you've been married to the greatest writer in the world, you don't remember all the little fellows," she replied.

home with an armchair strapped to its roof. Taken out of context, this might be an amusing image in and of itself. It's more than amusing - it's *comic* - because it's a painful, dangerous situation created by a thought process.

Mr. Bean is greedy to the point of absurdity, but only because he's *imitating* social convention. In this, he's an example of what Susan Sontag[20] describes as "the subject of comedy." Bean suffers "the extremes of disrelation," either "underreacting or misreacting according to the norms of feeling." He gets greed wrong. He gets Christmas wrong. He's an outsider, trying and failing to be like us. Together in our eminency, we laugh at him. But his failure also suggests that within greed and within Christmas lie absurdities we've either overlooked or normalised. So we also laugh at our own infirmities, reflected back at us by Mr. Bean.

Bean's not actually greedy. He's mimicking the avarice he sees all around him, just as he imitates a man eating a sandwich, say. That he's a copy excuses him from censure. It excuses us, too, because copies don't feel like the real thing, merely simulate external appearances. Bean is an automaton, our comic clone, the clown. And even if some clowns refuse to forgive their audience for their infirmities, all clowns forgive us for laughing at them. If they didn't, would we forgive them for laughing at us? Performer and

20 Susan Sontag (1933–2004) was an American writer and critic. She was one of the first people to write about pop culture seriously and well. I can read her essays all day. In fact, this book is basically me failing to imitate Sontag, so maybe put it down and read *Against Criticism* instead.

audience are symbiotic: they free each other from the norms of feeling.

We find Mr. Bean funny because we think his feelings are imitative and that his thought processes aren't normal, and because we believe that our feelings are genuine and our thought processes are normal. More, that normality is both the antithesis of absurdity and qualitatively its superior. But 'normal' people identify with the absurd. If they didn't, absurdity wouldn't be funny. Nor is absurdity something to stigmatise. The Human Rights Act is absurd, but that doesn't mean that it's wrong, or that we should give up believing in its principles. Absurdity is illogical, yes, but the conditions and beliefs we call 'normal' are not the products of logic. As the 'anti-psychiatrist' R.D. Laing[21] wrote in 1967, "normal men have killed perhaps 100,000,000 of their fellow normal men in the last fifty years." Is it, then, that normality is antithetical to sanity?

Laing wrote punch lines ("life is a sexually transmitted disease and the mortality rate is one hundred percent") to make us see our situation from a new perspective. 'Punch line' was first used in New York around 1912–13 to describe elements of music and drama. The phrase came to be associated with comedy perhaps thanks to the character Punch, of '… and Judy' fame (and not to be confused with Richard, who may or may not be as prone to domestic violence and/or sausages). The name 'Punch' originated with the often violent *commedia dell'arte*

21 R.D. Laing (1927–89) was a Scottish psychiatrist. In his opinion, insanity was the only rational response to an insane world. He was pretty rad.

character 'Pulcinella'; though the Italian 'pulcino' refers to his bird-like nose and chin, its Anglicisation surely has to do with brutality. And while the Italians may not use 'punch' the way we do, they do call jokes 'battuta', which means a blow or beating. Punching makes people laugh. The mechanics of comedy are shocking, above and beyond the specific content of a joke.

G. Legman's *Rationale of the Dirty Joke* catalogues the 'horror stories' that groups of people tell to shock, revolt and amuse one another. To understand why we do this, Legman quotes a story told by Sir Walter Raleigh's[22] son, Aubrey. It seems that Aubrey was being outrageous at a dinner party one night when Walter hit him with "a damned blow over his face." Aubrey, however, "rude as he was, would not strike his father, but strikes over the face the gentleman that sate next to him and sayd 'Box about: 'twill come to my father anon.'"

For Legman, Aubrey's story exemplifies the joker's psychology. Aubrey can't bring himself to hit Walter, his father and ultimate authority. So he transfers his humiliation, anger and pain onto an innocent bystander. Aubrey then disguises this transference as a game. A sociable cycle of violence is created by neurosis and

---

22 Sir Walter Raleigh (1554–1618) was an English explorer and sometime poet who spent his time carving up the New World, flirting with Elizabeth I, smoking, being imprisoned and having his head chopped off to appease the Spanish. It was then pickled and given to his wife. In his poem, *What Is Our Life?*, Raleigh calls existence "this short Comedy," though Lady Raleigh probably didn't laugh *too* heartily on receipt of her husband's face floating around like a death mask made of jarred gefilte fish.

played out in the name of fun. Punches fly. Doubtless Aubrey later retired to masturbate over his mother, but a Freudian reading (as Legman's is) does not entirely satisfy me. After all, aren't there plenty of jokes that *do* hit back at the source of injustice? Aubrey could've done more damage to Walter's prestige with his punch-line than with a punch.

Comedy has a social function above and beyond individual motive. Can I justify that bold statement, given the solipsism of my first chapter? Well, by 'social function', I mean that comedy can make us ask questions – why is that funny? Am I wrong to laugh? – and questions are good for society. Susan Sontag defines art as that which "nourishes our capacity for moral choice."

> Art performs this "moral" task because the qualities which are intrinsic to the aesthetic experience (disinterestedness, contemplativeness, attentiveness, the awakening of the feelings) and the aesthetic object (grace, intelligence, expressiveness, energy, sensuousness) are also fundamental constituents of a moral response to life.

In theory, we laugh as a result of a moral choice: whose side am I on, the victim or the victimiser? But laughter is uncontrollable, graceless. Historically, it's been associated with 'low' types of people: drunks, bawds and prostitutes. This is because, far from encouraging contemplation, laughter destroys our civility.

In his *Treatise on Laughter*, the physician Laurent Joubert[23] describes how we laugh. The laugher's:

> mouth widens, the eyes sparkle and tear, the cheeks redden, the breast heaves, the voice becomes interrupted…the veins in the throat become enlarged, the arms shake, and the legs dance about, the belly pulls in and feels considerable pain; we cough, perspire, piss and besmirch ourselves by dint of laughing, and sometimes we even faint away because of it.

'Humour' as we know it is derived from the Latin *humor*, meaning liquid or moisture. Middle Ages medical theory invented the Cardinal Humours, four bodily fluids said to affect a person's character. Phlegm was associated with a calm, unemotional demeanour; yellow bile led to irascibility and choler; black bile made you melancholic; blood encourages optimism and good cheer.

"What piece of work is a man," Hamlet marvels, "how noble in reason! How infinite in faculties…in apprehension how like a god." This "paragon of animals" could be drained, lanced or leeched of their adjectival juices (gloom, malice, over-exuberance, cold). But pissing oneself laughing is to lose control over bodily fluids and forget civilised procedures. It's to become a beast.

"Some men, when they laugh, sound like geese hissing,

23 Laurent Joubert (1529–1582) was a French physician who spent much of his life fighting popular ignorance by writing medical advice in vernacular French, rather than in Latin or Greek. He published his *Traité du Ris* in 1576.

others like grumbling goslings; some recall the sigh of woodland pigeons, or doves," Joubert writes, while "for others it is like a horse neighing, or an ass heehawing, or a dog that yaps or is choking." These animal noises are the consequence of unkindness. For Joubert, "the common style of our laughter is contempt or derision," a feeling of superiority "over an ugly thing unworthy of pity." Maybe, though, this animal motif is a red herring. God has infinite faculties, but he still laughs at heathens.

There's a brutal (or, as Legman puts it, "filthy") dimension to comedy lacked by less *immediate* art forms. 'Immediate' means 'without mediation'. Laughter leaves you no space to breathe. A joke leaves you no time to think. There is no gap, no calming mediator, between a comedian and their audience. You can't negotiate with what's funny; you can't talk yourself down from laughing at morally offensive material if it *strikes* you.

Where, then, is the room for contemplation or attentiveness – if those are required for us to consider comedy as an art? Isn't a comic's energy and expressiveness bent on coercing you into agreeing with *their* moral choice, rather than letting you make your own? Sontag says that art transcends "judgement... [and] our facile labelling of persons and acts as good or bad." Where does that leave comedy? If, that is, you buy my thesis of God's slapstick, which you're welcome not to.

A painting of a beautiful person is not usually designed to make its viewer feel ugly. But a joke must *act on* its audience, at the audience's own risk. Not that we like to acknowledge this. Jokes don't tend to have an obvious aesthetic. Overly-crafted material is very hard to sell unless – as with Stewart Lee's[24] – an audience consciously takes pleasure in construction. This is because we expect the comedian to be spontaneous. Spontaneity is associated with honesty. Linguistic trickery is not. Aesthetics are a mediating factor, proof of an agenda, and most audiences find it unsettling to know they're being manipulated.

We find it funny to see a man realise that there is no chair. But comedy also puts its audience's own beliefs in danger. Mr. Bean's infirmities are our infirmities; to borrow a charming euphemism from the US military, comedy has blow-back. There's a type of truth that is only revealed through suffering. This suffering can help you understand yourself, but it can just as easily make you submit to someone else's impression of who you are and what the world is like. Comedy has something in common with torture.

In *The Shock Doctrine*, Naomi Klein[25] quotes an instruction manual given to CIA interrogators:

> There is an interval – which may be extremely brief – of suspended animation, a kind of psychological

---

24 Stewart Lee is the headline act of alternative comedy. I particularly love his routines about Joe Pasquale, the death of Princess Diana and *Top Gear*.

25 *The Shock Doctrine* is Naomi Klein's exposé of what has happened in countries forced to adopt a model of free-market democracy, the deregulated wet dream of (amongst others) Milton Friedman and the Chicago School of Economics. Klein's premise is that Western governments exploit social breakdown in order to present this model as a *fait accompli*, the only lifeline available to the shattered infrastructure in question.

> shock or paralysis. It is caused by a traumatic or subtraumatic experience which explodes, as it were, the world that is familiar to the subject as well as his image of himself within that world...At this moment the source is...far likelier to comply.

"The source" may or may not know something valuable. So the torturer becomes something of an electrical engineer: like Claude Shannon, their aim is to cut through the noise (of static, of screaming, of laughter) to the information concealed within.

Can torture be funny? For the torturer. Legman refers to an experiment conducted by Dr. Stanley Milgram[26] on forty test subjects. Milgram sat each in front of a control panel that could apparently deliver electrical shocks to a person in another room. Each subject was ordered to torture the unseen person, although in reality this 'other' did not exist. Of the forty, almost none refused to comply, and a significant number began laughing. Milgram writes that "on one occasion we observed a seizure [of laughter] so violently convulsive that it was necessary to call a halt to the experiment. The subject, a forty-six-year-old encyclopaedia salesman, was seriously embarrassed." His nobility of reason had been temporarily flooded by fluid.

---

26 Dr. Stanley Milgram (1933–84) was an American psychologist who wrote about this experiment in *Dynamics of Obedience*, published in 1961. He was inspired to carry it out by the trial of the Nazi Adolf Eichmann. Milgram's also to be thanked for the six degrees of separation theory and, as a consequence, Kevin Bacon's descent into self-parody.

The situation wasn't funny – though it could have been (for Milgram) if the 'torturers' themselves received the shock they meant for the other. So did these test subjects laugh at finding themselves in such a profoundly unethical, and advantageous, situation? The trial had a dog-eat-dog back-story; Milgram told the torturer that their victim was a friend of theirs, and their roles had been selected at random. Better him than me! In such an extreme instance of the victim-victimiser relationship, perhaps laughing is the natural response?

(Though wasn't the encyclopaedia salesman actually the *victim*? Milgram cut through the man's noise for deeper information. In which case, was the torture more fun for the victim or the victimiser?)

To take another instance, Charles Graner and Lynndie England[27] had a lot of fun photographing the inmates of Abu Ghraib. In one photo, a group of naked men look like they're giving each other blow jobs. The recipients are standing in a 'comical' way – comical, that is, because their leisurely, statuesque, hands-behind-head positions interrupt and contract the grim reality onto which they're juxtaposed. This disrelation or misreaction to their situation makes the men *theoretically* funny. Were it not for the hoods, that is.

There's nothing normally amusing about seeing someone suffering "a traumatic or sub-traumatic

27 Charles Graner and Lynndie England were the ringleaders of the abuse meted out to prisoners in Abu Ghraib, the prison in which the Ba'ath party had previously murdered hundreds of Iraqis. England served half of her three years' prison sentence. Graner got ten years, serving six and a half.

experience" when they neither submitted willingly to the experience (i.e. making them an audience member of sorts), nor were powerful enough to warrant abuse (i.e. making them a legitimate target). Torture is predicated on non-compliance. Comedy is not. Nor is comedy baselessly cruel, for the simple reason that most of us are not baselessly cruel. Whatever our cocktail of Cardinal Humours, we seldom find someone's *natural* condition laughable. Those scenes in Ricky Gervais and Stephen Merchant's[28] *Life's Too Short* that succeeded did so because the character 'Warwick Davis' chose the wrong course of action. Those scenes that failed did so because the actor Warwick Davis is a dwarf, whether he wants to be or not. Bad choices are the level at which we prefer to "box about". And this rule remains generally true, however dubious the material or its maker.

Take Jim Davidson's[29] character Chalky. Chalky is black and, unlike his patriotic creator, not especially intelligent. In one of his adventures, Chalky gets so stoned that he lies down in the middle of the road (which is black) at night (which is black) and is run over by a car (the colour of which is unspecified, though I fondly imagine it to be white). However, Chalky – a black man ironically named after a white educational tool – is not hurt because of his *biological* make-up. He didn't choose to be

28 Ricky Gervais and Stephen Merchant have written *The Office*, *Extras* and *Life's Too Short* together. Perhaps as a penance for his popularly-perceived cruelty, Gervais has also made the weirdly saccharine *Derek*.

29 Jim Davidson is a comedian of what could kindly be described as fluctuating popularity. Davidson's also currently in a certain amount of legal difficulty vis-à-vis Operation Yewtree.

black; his race isn't funny, because it's beyond his control. What we laugh at is Chalky's decision to get irie. We know Chalky's stoned because Davidson, that consummate performer, adopts not only a thick Jamaican accent, but also a slow, slurred delivery. So either Chalky is high, or he's just had a massive stroke. It's almost certainly not a stroke, though, because that would be a biological determination – a biological determination, moreover, associated with a high-pressure job and/or a rich diet, neither of which (and this is my projection here) Davidson would readily identify with Afro-Caribbean men. No, Chalky is stoned. He has *chosen* to partake. And it's this choice that Davidson lampoons. I think. Either that, or it's a race thing.

There's a reason laughter gets described as 'helpless'. It's an unresisting physical response to the imposition of a system of values. Joke-writers use emotive rhetoric in a way that politicians can only dream of, and they're far more likely to be believed because – however bizarrely – we expect politicians to lie and comedians to tell the truth. Now, Davidson is hardly Hitler[30] at Nuremburg. He's less well-dressed, and he can barely sell out the back room of a pub, let alone that fuck-off plaza – though it is tantalising to imagine Davidson's erstwhile *Big Break* colleague, snooker's John Virgo[31] (part owl, part peacock)

30 Adolf Hitler (1889–1945) was this bloke, right?

31 Pro snooker player John Virgo is 67! And yet it seems like only yesterday that he was lighting up all 222 episodes of the BBC's *Bullseye* rip-off, *Big Break*. Virgo potting trick-shots in those devil-may-care waistcoats of his is one of the defining images of my childhood.

serving as a Rudolf Hess[32] figure in this new world order. Nevertheless, Davidson proves that being exclusionary and prejudicial, not to mention unamusing, are in no way obstacles to becoming a successful comedian.

Today, Chalky's less likely to get a laugh. Black culture is more familiar to the majority than it once was. So too are the broader categories of race, gender and sexuality. This familiarity is constructive. As the Polish journalist Ryszard Kapuściński[33] says, "the self is only possible through recognition of the other." Seeing who we aren't clarifies, and criticises, who we are. That's not to say, though, that laughing at Chalky is impossible, or that society is inexorably improving.

'Our' identity of fifty years ago has assimilated what it once excluded. We're now offended on the other's behalf: we are, in part, offended for ourselves. But that's not to say we've stopped being threatened by otherness. The fault lines remain. They've just been internalised. That's why comedians have to use proportionately greater linguistic

32 Rudolf Hess (1894–1987) was Hitler's deputy and a sometime-victim of amnesia. In 1941, he flew solo to Britain, parachuting from his plane near Dungavel Castle in Scotland (where there now stands an immigration removal centre). Hess will therefore go down in history as the only man who's ever been *that* desperate to get to Scotland. He later formed Spandau Ballet with Tony Hadley.

33 Ryszard Kapuściński (1932–2007) was a Polish writer who specialised in what he called 'literary reportage'. Kapuściński's books are superb, though that's not an opinion shared by Wikipedia. The website complains that "nowhere in his writings does Kapuściński respond to or engage in any remotely sophisticated way" to his own "visceral Anti-Americanism." Kapuściński certainly reported with a poetic licence – something he admitted to throughout his career – though whether that makes him a Stalinist and bastard is another matter.

violence than they once did to expose them. And that's also why some people are taking a new kind of offence.

It's surely been observed by someone brighter than me that an irony of the West is this: the people who have the most security feel the least secure. So it is with our dominant class, Middle England, armed with its gaucheness and its snobbery and the way it prizes 'common sense' (read: DIY) over intelligence, as though B&Qs are more of an asset than libraries. Which they are, if the Tory party's policies are anything to go by. But, despite its domination, all it takes is a Welsh newsreader or a black actor or a lady vicar or any kind of Muslim for Middle England to lose its shit. Then up goes the battle cry of homogeny, the demand made by those content to be defined by boundaries as mutable as ethnicity, language and citizenship.

For all the bourgeois comics that play to stadia full of it, Middle England's truest voice can be heard in *Midsomer Murders*, the TV show in which acts of brutality are the stuff of a gentle Sunday evening. No wonder Middle England loves B&Q, one of the few companies that actively profits from serial killers (cable ties, hammers, saws, plastic sheeting if they're neat, and that's just the tip of a newly-decked iceberg honeycombed with young women).

Midsomer refuses the other. Its former producer, Brian True-May[34], told the *Radio Times* that his show was "the

34 Brian True-May left *Midsomer* shortly before the original Inspector Barnaby, played by John Nettles. Barnaby was replaced by his Brighton-based detective cousin, also called Barnaby. True-May was replaced by a cousin, also called True-May. Just as the second Barnaby

last bastion of Englishness" and as such has "no place" for ethnic minorities. Why? To comfort a demographic obsessed with the prospect of their own marginalisation. In the same interview, True-May claimed that "if you went in to Slough, you wouldn't see a white face there." Interestingly, he doesn't say "couldn't". There's a semantic difference, and it's to do with choice. 'Couldn't' suggests it's *objectively* impossible to see a Caucasian; 'wouldn't' suggests a *subjective* decision not to. I'd suggest True-May doesn't *want* to see evidence that contradicts his sense of victimhood, of his being surrounded.

'There's a sign at Slough train station that's written in Hindi! There's also English on it but signs aren't *meant* to be legible to as many people as possible, you noodle – and yes, I mean "noodle" to sting because it's foreign and foreigners use chilli. Signs are *meant* to be English. Because we're in *England*. And if we're not, why are Our Boys dying?' Brian True-May went on to say in a plaintive voice in the *Radio Times* in my head.

True-May's generation grew up on a diet of *Zulu*. In their imaginations, Britain is Rorke's Drift and they are the redcoats, fighting off a murderous, spear-chucking swarm of invaders. Middle England sees enemies everywhere, blithe to their own supremacy and in mourning for some Technicolor, semi-fictitious past. Middle England imagines itself to be the only target that's OK to attack in a room full of elephants. Only they're not white

---

continued to solve crimes, the second True-May continued to shoot black looks at foreign runners.

elephants. Oh no, they're probably African elephants or Indian elephants, because the politically-correct BBC homosexuals who cast the elephants in the room were afraid to use ordinary, decent English elephants because there might have been a tribunal.

Well, Middle England wants its own tribunal. In a twist as perverted as I hope Brian True-May's sex life is, this majority has started to adopt the language of a minority. It's done this to remain in a position of power, albeit a new kind of power: that (in theory) accorded to those who are marginalised.

Nick Griffin[35] sells the British National Party as a victim of "the pure, vicious bigotry of the British ruling elite," as typified by the BBC, which Griffin has also accused of being both hedonistic and pro-Sharia law. Why a hedonist would be in favour of the fairly prohibitive strictures of Sharia law is unclear. What *is* clear is why Nick gets silenced. He's part of what he calls an "ethnic minority." Which minority? "The English." And Huw Edwards[36] may be too busy snorting coke off Fiona Bruce's[37] burkha'd tits as she lies there teabagging the

35 Nick Griffin is the BNP's frontman. The band had a multi-million-pound summer '09 on the European festival circuit, but have since struggled to replicate their success in the hit parade. Griffin remains cagey about a rumoured Snoop Dogg-to-Lion-style reggae rebranding, though jahgriffin.co.uk has been registered as a domain name and Lee 'Scratch' Perry recently tweeted 'just wrapped on Heil The Selector #griffinkilledit!'

36 The 53-year-old Edwards was considered by some as 'too young' to front coverage of the recent Royal Wedding, many fearing the Welsh silver fox would refer to the Queen as "that bufting yat, fam."

37 Fiona Bruce is the wanton hussy who usurped Michael Aspel on

adhan-chanting, ket-guzzling Dimbleby[38] to see what's going on, but not Nick. Anyway, who needs 'facts' when the ruling elite have been silencing free speech for too long. So shout from the rooftops: Nick Griffin is a fat, handsy, one-eyed racist. What un-PC ribaldry! He may not 'factually' be any of those things, but don't worry – Nick loves being a victim.

Middle England also likes to ask for our sympathy, and no cultural form provokes its weird self-pity more than comedy. An example of this comes in Roger Lewis's[39] *Daily Telegraph* article about the comedian Frank Carson's[40] death. In it, Lewis thunders against Jimmy Carr[41], Frankie Boyle[42] and the rest of "these supercilious university graduates from nice homes who attempt to tell jokes." Jokes about ordinary, decent people, that is,

---

Antiques Roadshow. My friend's dad is also on *Antiques Roadshow* and thus briefly stars in the Affleck-Freeman action flop *The Sum of All Fears* (2002). In one scene, *AR* (as us 'tiquing pros call it) is on in a hotel room. An arms dealer prices a bomb as he watches my friend's dad evaluating Victoriana.

38 Dimbleby. Jonathan or David. Who gets teabagged by Fiona Bruce? You decide. (I started out on *Big Brother's Big Mouth* and the old instincts sometimes kick back in, like previously-ingested drugs resurfacing in the blood-stream.)

39 Roger Lewis is a journalist. Awkwardly, we share a publisher.

40 Frank Carson (1926–2012) was a comedian best known for his catchphrase "it's the way I tell 'em." A walking encyclopaedia of 'thick Irishman' jokes.

41 Jimmy Carr, taxpayer. Famously risqué on the topic of overweight women and gypsies, unless he's pretending to be left-wing on *10 O'Clock Live*.

42 Frankie Boyle. To paraphrase R.Kelly, Boyle's mind's telling him no, but his body's telling him yes, let's do one more rancorous tweet before bed.

because comics are now unwilling to offend Lewis's reactionary hypothetical, the "disabled single-parent Muslim lesbian on benefits."

Quite apart from the fact that Jimmy Carr and Frankie Boyle probably *are* willing to offend her, it's worth considering this improbable bogeywoman. Lewis imagines her to be untouchable, and in a totally different way to the untouchable in India. The Indian dalit is at the bottom of society; for Middle England, the "disabled single-parent Muslim lesbian on benefits" is at the very top of ours. But who would this Sapphic exemption, with her wealth of vulnerabilities, actually *be*?

- She's called Naima. I like this name because it's what John Coltrane's[43] first wife was called and I love the piece of music he wrote for her.
- Naima was born in the early eighties. Her parents are religious and liberal. They actively encourage her to study medicine.
- At university, she experiments with the usual things. As a consequence, she arrives at being a mother before she arrives at a full understanding of her sexuality.
- She chooses to keep the baby, a girl.
- The father, another medic, wants nothing to do with Naima or their daughter. He has a career to think about.

43 John Coltrane (1926–67). World-ending saxophonist; jazz has never recovered. Lewis Porter describes Coltrane's music by quoting D.H. Lawrence on Herman Melville: "*he records, almost beyond pain or pleasure, the extreme transitions of the isolated, far-driven soul, the soul which is now alone, without real human contact.*" Or, as Leroi Jones has it, "New Black Music is this: Find the self, then kill it."

- Though conscientious, the pressures of being a single parent mean that Naima drops out of university.
- With her parents unable to support both her and her baby, Naima claims and receives the benefits due a single parent in her situation.
- She gets a low-paid job at a supermarket. She works long hours and relies on her mother and her married sisters to help care for her child.
- One day, on the way back from this supermarket, she is knocked down by a car, Chalky-style. The doctors – and, as she lies in the back of the ambulance, Naima's delirious worry is that one of these doctors will turn out to be the father of her child – fear she won't walk again.
- Luckily, she can walk again, slowly, painfully, and with the aid of a stick.
- Disability benefits are soon boosted by unemployment benefits, as her job is now impractical thanks to her permanent injuries.

Now back living in her parents' cramped second-floor flat, her freedom in every way curtailed, does Naima deserve our mockery?

That's a different question to whether or not comedians should be *allowed* to try making us laugh at her. They should be. Silencing something gives it the power of taboo. Take Nick Griffin. Hundreds of people protested against his appearance on *Question Time* in 2009, trying to gag those ideas of his they felt to be dangerously contagious. If they'd succeeded, they'd have only increased Griffin's power as the 'forbidden' politician. Thankfully they failed, and *Question Time* revealed him to be what he is: an incoherent shambles.

Naturally, Nick – like any other comedian – blamed the room, complaining that "that wasn't *Question Time*, that was a lynch mob." And I suppose he'd know. If only he'd have taken tips from Ilias Kasidiaris[44], a politician belonging to Golden Dawn, Greece's anti-immigration far-right party. On the Greek equivalent of *Question Time*, Kasidiaris slapped a female MP, causing Golden Dawn's popularity to spike dramatically. Who knew Greeks were such suckers for the Punch and Judy vibe? Its third most popular party, Golden Dawn has become Greece's Lib Dems. Let's hope Golden Dawn break as many promises.

How Greek comedians cope with Golden Dawn is not something I know enough about. But here, for us, for now, freedom of speech gives hatred the rope it needs to hang itself. So why don't comedians attack Naima, even though they're free to? Because, to use an acting metaphor, Naima has very little *status*. She isn't powerful. She can't hurt us, making her an unsatisfactory victim. On a pragmatic level, therefore, Naima is crap material.

44 Ilias Kasidiaris defended his actions by quoting protocol 19.3 from *The Protocols of The Elders of Zion*, the fictional minutes from a fictional meeting between fictional nineteenth-century Jews conspiring to take over the world. *The Protocols* are a forgery described by the historial Norman Cohn as Hitler's "warrant for genocide." The American car manufacturer Henry Ford paid for the printing and circulation of 500,000 copies during America's own Greek-style meltdown in the 1920s. Wikipedia, meanwhile, tells us that – when he's not idly leafing through antisemtic pamphlets – Kasidiaris enjoys martial arts, writing and tango lessons.

Naima's weaknesses do create something of a Catch-22. If her victim status gives her the power to deflect victimisation, does that stop her being a victim? And if she is no longer a victim – if she has this power – then the silence surrounding her means that Naima begins to *resemble* a taboo. Comedians break taboos. Should they, then, break Naima? No. Naima's power is a figment of our imagination. She is the passive victim of 'our' neurosis. Middle England's insecurities have created a Wonderland in which Naima is able to threaten the able-bodied ethnic majority, armed only with her powerlessness. Political incorrectness gone mad!

With that in mind, why does it annoy Roger Lewis that comedians don't rip into those conditionings – the Islam, the disability, the fact that she has the temerity to prefer fucking women – that make Naima Naima? Because people like Lewis and, to a far greater degree, Charles Graner and Lynndie England lack empathy.

Empathy is not sympathy. Sympathy derives from feeling, empathy from thought; feeling *like* Naima is not productive, but thinking about her condition is. Empathy's a process by which we see ourselves in the other, the other in us. We imagine suffering *because*, rather than *as*, others suffer. The adverb 'as' is concerned with mimicking the scale of suffering. The conjunction 'because' is concerned with making coherent the reasons for suffering.

Empathy is self-interested. Reducing the pain of others reduces the possibility of suffering it ourselves. But it's also a tentative step towards making stuff better. And, weirdly, jokes often help most when they fail to make us laugh. It's when we're offended on Naima's behalf that we remember those our 'inclusive' society has excluded.

*

(Ancient) Greek comedies start with conflict and end with resolution. In *The Seven Basic Plots*, Christopher Booker[45] describes this conflict as being between two groups or individuals:

> One is dominated by some dark, rigid, life-denying obsession. The other represents life, liberation and truth. The issue is ultimately decided, of course, in favour of the latter.

We've been duplicating this generic arc ever since. Audiences like that the 'goodies' have truth on their side. We like knowing the outcome of the plot before it even begins. We also enjoy power being defeated. Comedy gratifies these fundamentally unrealistic tastes, but it's not necessarily a moral pleasure. The power it defeats doesn't need to be political. Nor does it need to be absolutely 'bad'. Comedy destroys its victims for having status, whether it's disguised as their pride, their skill, wealth, ambition or wit. That's why killing the comic themselves – destroying their authority – is sometimes the most sublime pleasure a comedy club has to offer.

45 Christopher Booker helped to start *Private Eye*. Booker now writes for the *Telegraph*, directing his ire at environmentalists, social workers and "the excesses of mad officialdom."

Comics have to operate within some kind of objectivity, whether or not they know it to be illusory. Some comedians 'tell it like it is' from a socially downtrodden but intellectually superior perspective. Other comedians 'tell it like it should be'. These are two sides of the same coin. For both narratives, truth and happiness are situated *beyond* reality, beyond life's constant obstacle. They're found in Klein's "suspended animation", in which "the world that is familiar to the subject as well as his image of himself within that world" vanish. Time stops. Happy endings seem possible. Comedy has a religious impulse.

Middle England hates it when this impulse gets turned on them. But if Middle England knew its history – and it doesn't – it would realise that this has always been comedy's real function. In the *Poetics*, Aristotle[46] says the word 'comedy' comes from the Dorians, whose "outlying villages" were called *kômai*, "the assumption being that the participants in comedy were called *kômôidoi* not from their being revellers but because they wandered from one village to another, being degraded and excluded from the city."

The ideal comedian is an outcast from the *polis*. Their victimising is a justifiable consequence of their own victimisation. A minority is able see the corpus it's a part of, but apart from, with a clarity denied the fully-integrated citizen. So in many ways the degraded, excluded Jim Davidson is the model comic. If only because I assume he's now living in his car.

---

46 Aristotle (384–322 BC) was Plato's student and Alexander the Great's teacher. A big dog.

The Russian critic Mikhail Bakhtin[47] defined two kinds of social experience. The first is "the official feast." "Laughter is alien" to this feast, which stands for "all that is stable, unchanging, perennial: the existing hierarchy, the existing religious, political and moral values." The Carnival, on the other hand, offers "a completely different, nonofficial, extraecclesiastical and extrapolitical aspect of the world, of man." The word "carnival" derives from the Latin for "putting away meat", and carnivals have been necessarily carnal ever since. But the agreement struck between officialdom and the populace – gorge, fast, gorge – isn't so much an example of a divided culture as it is of the symbiotic relationship between carnival, or fun, and authority. One relies on the other.

In 2006, I went to New Orleans for the first Mardi Gras after Hurricane Katrina. We stayed in Treme. Our louche hotelier told us that, before the hurricane, this area had been a no-go zone for people like us. We were safer now that the worst offenders had cleared out of the city, for fear of the re-housing process bringing them into contact with the police. Nevertheless, we had little reason to doubt the hotelier, given the quantity of stray

47 Mikhail Bakhtin (1895–1975) was a Russian literary critic and semiotician. Bakhtin's trademark is the concept of 'heteroglossia', or the 'multiple tongues' within a single language. *Rabelais and His World* began as a doctorate, submitted during the Second World War. However, Bakhtin's theory of the carnivalesque was taken as a veiled criticism of the Soviet 'official feast'. He was denied his doctorate, and the book took twenty years to be published. Rabelais, meanwhile, was a sixteenth-century French monk, satirist, scholar, author and bawd.

crackheads wandering in and out of his hotel.

Katrina exposed the racial fault lines dividing New Orleans and America. Fabricated reports of theft and rape were issued by the New Orleans police department and went largely unquestioned by the media. The hurricane itself had been waspish in its devastation. Up in the hills, the wealthiest remained untouched. By contrast, when we walked round St. Bernard, its shotgun houses lay still in ruins nine months after the flood. Apparently many of them still do – John Hillcoat[48] was able to film much of *The Road* on location in post-apocalyptic New Orleans.

In Nashville, a white college student told me she'd been shocked by how American news footage looked "third world", featuring as it did black people, their homes destroyed, pushing shopping trolleys full of junk through refugee camps. The "third world" stigma was the reason, locals claimed, that vans of Red Cross food had sat rotting outside the Superbowl though its temporary residents had run out of supplies. America wanted to believe in its supremacy, they said. Their lives were expendable to that belief; Red Cross aid given to Americans on American soil was taboo, regardless of the harm caused by that prohibition.

It's still amazing to see Kanye West[49] going off-script

48 John Hillcoat is an Australian director who frequently collaborates with Nick Cave on (amongst others) *The Proposition*, *Lawless* and music videos for Grinderman and the Bad Seeds.

49 Kanye West is the ludicrous rapper who replaced his bottom row of teeth with diamonds. West is also currently saddled with Kim Kardashian. If you don't know who Kim is, imagine what would

on live television to announce that "George Bush doesn't care about black people." He was co-hosting an appeal for money with the comedian Mike Myers[50]. The horrified double take Myers performs is the funniest thing he's ever done. It wouldn't have been, had West's hand grenade not hit home.

Over a million college kids came to party on Bourbon Street in 2005. In 2006, the crowds were much thinner, though the Girls Gone Wild bus had courageously set up camp in a nearby car park. It was a comfort to know that acts of God can only do so much; drunk young women will be exploited by web entrepreneurs come hell or high water. The musicians came back, too, and Bourbon Street was same as it ever was, everyone drinking hand grenades (made, unlike West's, of sugar and God knows how many spirits), chucking dollars at massively fat bluesmen or massively pneumatic strippers, eating cheeseburgers, buying shirts emblazoned with the city's mayor in a Willy Wonka get-up under the headline 'Ray Nagin's Chocolate City', strewing pearls from colonial balconies, flashing, fingering one another, buying strangers Jagermeister in an Austrian jazz bar genuinely called Fritzel's complete with large and bizarre framed photos of von Ribbentrop[51],

---

happen if an invading alien body snatcher took over an Evans mannequin, hollowed out the cranium, painted itself orange and then set out to destroy civilisation one sex tape at a time.

50 Mike Myers gave us *Wayne's World*, *Austin Powers* and a bizarre cameo in *Inglorious Basterds*. Myers is endearing for loads of reasons, not least his unswerving but misplaced faith in his ability to do British accents.

51 Ulrich Von Ribbentrop (1893–1946) was the Nazi ambassador to Britain before he became the German Foreign Minister. He helped

doing coke off their own soles, and mocking the evangelical Christians who used megaphones to accuse everyone, all of us, of being catamites.

Beyond the party, though, sulked streets whose flats and shops were empty. Our walk home was peppered with detritus: a smashed jukebox, a monkeypuzzle boulevard of upended church pews. It made me feel like Mardi Gras had become stable, unchanging, perennial, and that those were not human qualities. Like a new feast needed to be held in *these* streets, thronged with absence, or in the refugee camps out in the middle of nowhere. But I was an outsider. I probably didn't understand.

The other guest in our hotel was a wiry middle-aged woman who'd walked through the door to a whoosh of dry ice and the phrase 'tonight, Matthew, I'm going to be Patti Smith.'[52] She wore a top hat, referred to the sixties as "a different time, man" and had a great many conspiracy theories to do with the construction of levees. She was demonstratively 'cool' with our hotelier and his pals, doing street handshakes and addressing everyone as brother – everyone, that is, except us and our exploitative Anglo-Saxon vibe.

On the night of Mardi Gras, we got home at about 5 am. Patti was in the hotel, chatting idly of racial cleansing with the supremely bored hotelier. We wandered off to variously be sick, drink more or moon over photos of

---

broker the non-aggression pact with Russia. Von Ribbentrop was the first defendant to be hanged at the Nuremburg Trials.

52 Patti Smith is an American punk, poet and singer. She's probably best known for her amazing album *Horses* (1975).

absent girlfriends. A while later, I was engaging a stray crackhead in small talk when loud screams interrupted us. Patti was standing in the lobby, yelling the word 'nigger'.

It later transpired that the hotelier had told her about the Treme no-go zone. This seems to have been company policy, much in the way other hotels hand out maps of the local area. But Patti took offence. She was *sympathetic*, man. She's on *your* side. The hotelier asked what she meant by that. She meant black people. An argument broke out. The hotelier said she couldn't be on 'our' side because she was white. Patti protested: she felt *your* pain, which meant it was her pain too. He said she had no way of feeling like 'we' feel because 'we' don't exist – it's just "a million niggers in shit" (a catchphrase of his that was colourful in all kinds of ways).

Then she called him a racist. He asked how could he be a racist? She said that calling her 'white' was like her calling him a nigger. He took offence. She said he couldn't take offence because she was *quoting* an offensive word, not *using* it herself. He said nigger's nigger. She, perhaps unwisely, pursued the semantics of this.

"The real Patti Smith had a song called *Rock'n'Roll Nigger* and she's white. Does that make *her* a racist?" she barked.

"Yeah," the hotelier replied. Then, when he asked her to leave, she started calling him a nigger for real.

Watching Patti being first cuffed by two black policemen, then repeatedly slammed hard against the bonnet of a squad car, then thrown into its back seat, with her all the while shouting "nigger", I hastily made myself three rules of thumb:

1. Semantics have a time and a place.
2. Never fuck with American policemen.
3. When using the word 'nigger', always use the inverted commas hand gesture. You may look less cool singing the *Gold Digger* chorus at a Kanye concert, but the alternative risks him dissing you on live TV.
4. Some people don't want your sympathy.

Who was the victim? Patti, probably. Did she deserve her victimisation? Can two armed policemen be the victims of offensive language? Sticks and stones and all that, surely?

As I watched the hotelier (who, now I came to think of it, almost certainly sold crack) encouraging two policemen as they beat up a woman for repeatedly shouting an offensive word, I'd be lying if I said that I was wondering what the structural agreements were between carnival and authority, black and white. No one can be a structuralist the morning after Mardi Gras. What I *did* wonder was a slightly callous but not unrelated question: could this scene ever be funny?

Maybe, if the white person being beaten up was male – a nervy, posh dweeb like me – and if he'd accidentally said "nigger", then apologised, and was still apologising as the policemen kicked his head in. Or maybe if the policemen had, quite reasonably, asked why a hotel was full of crack addicts, turning the scene against the hotelier. Or maybe I should just get the fuck out of New Orleans.

To write or enjoy comedy, you have to understand the particular culture it's set in. Comedians can be outsiders. They can be immigrants. But they can't be wholly alien. This is for two reasons. The first is effectiveness: you can only mock what you know. The second is sensitivity: you should only mock what you are, or the club you belong to.

Jack and I researched our sitcom, *Bad Education*, by visiting a state school in Streatham, where we asked a teacher what insults his pupils use against each other. 'Well,' he replied, 'in my class, there's a kid whose parents come from the Congo. When the rest of the class want him to fuck off, they tell him to go sharpen his teeth.' There was a pause and then we explained that *Bad Education*'s not really the vehicle for *that* much reality.

And, yes, ours was a fairly colonial activity, delving into the dark heart of a London school for lexicographic rarities, but we had our comeuppance. In one classroom, we explained to the kids that I was a geeky, fat, four-eyed virgin. What, we wanted to know, would *you* call a geeky, fat, four-eyed virgin, in *your* patois, *your* language? A girl shrugged.

"Cunt?" she said, offhand.

Then the class went fucking *wild* shouting cunt at me, at Jack, at their teacher and each other, safe in the knowledge that this was kind of a obscenity-circus, the day-to-day ban on bad language having been rescinded for the nice, white telly people.

Comedy is a carnival in which ordinary prohibitions are lifted. Not all the way. There's no teeth-sharpening allowed from people like me or Jack. Quite apart from anything else, audiences are very good at detecting untruthful elements in a comic's act. It's unprofitable to pretend you have access to another world. But *generally* recognised types of violence, offensive language and sexual excess are all part of the free-for-all. Comedy forgives social misdemeanour. And society, by and large, forgives comedy, because it thinks they're in cahoots.

Like all transgression, comedy relies upon being seen by authority to resist authority. Comics need a Middle England to offend; Middle England needs to be offended. Boxing your neighbours is fun, but the boxers need to be feasting at the same table.

Frankie Boyle is an example of how a comedian can misjudge these table manners. It's worth mentioning two jokes of his that have provoked outrage. The first was told on Radio 4 in 2008. Of the Palestinian crisis, Boyle said: "I've got an analogy which explains the whole thing quite well. If you imagine that Palestine is a cake – well, that cake is being punched to pieces by a very angry Jew." The second was told on Channel 4 in 2010. Of Katie Price[53] and her handicapped son, Harvey, Boyle said: "*[this joke has been cut by a ludicrously over-cautious lawyer. Find it by googling 'Boyle+joke+Jordan+married+cage+fighter']*."

The first joke is legitimate because it mocks arbitrary analogies designed to distance us from a powerful group's treatment of a less powerful group. Perhaps Boyle should

53 Katie Price is a glamour model of varyingly pendulous charms.

have said 'Israeli' rather that 'Jew', but that word touches a nerve that arguably needs to be touched. The joke about Harvey Price, however, is misjudged. Though she exploits her family for money, that decision is Katie Price's alone. I can see the temptation of attacking the depressing *pietas* Price sells to trash magazines. But Boyle's mistake is to pick on the child and not the mother. Harvey is powerless; it's Jordan that craves and abuses her status. The joke's also not especially funny. That the BBC apologised for the Israel joke but Channel 4 didn't apologise for the Jordan joke, meanwhile, neatly illustrates the characteristic flaws of both broadcasters.

Boyle embodies the challenge successful British comedians face. They have to preserve an outsider's perspective at a time when the money is at an all-time high. I mention money because, if you're wealthy, you're implicitly part of the official feast, Ben Elton[54]. Other comedians lose their teeth, too, or they go out of the way to show they've still got them. This is an amplified version of the problem facing all joke-writers. Keeping perspective. Keeping it empathetic.

Can you tell a joke without being funny? You can definitely be funny without telling jokes. Laughter is first and foremost a sociable phenomenon and you seldom laugh

54 Ben Elton is the former left-wing firebrand. After Mrs. Thatcher was stabbed in the back, Elton continued to write comedy, but – like a star in the night sky – the light he gave off belied the fact that he was actually dead. Elton's recent output includes the hastily-cancelled Australian sketch show, *Live From Planet Earth*, and *The Wright Way*, an excruciating *Thin Red Line* rip-off based in a council's health and safety department.

at a constructed joke in a non-performative setting. In fact, people who use constructed jokes in conversation are cringe-worthy. It's like if you sleep with someone for the first time and they're doing all the tricks and you're left wondering where they *learnt* that? It's alienating. Technique makes you aware of the degree of artifice, of cultural duplication, at the heart of the two most natural relational activities: talking and fucking.

Nothing dates as badly as comedy because comedy is lyrical. Comedians may not be spontaneous, but their jokes live or die in the unmediated second. Timing is everything. Hitting the beat. Think how often you laugh when you catch someone's eye. You could be anywhere, at work, on the tube, in a lecture, a theatre, a church – anywhere other people carry out the serious business of their lives. All it takes is one second of eye contact – one beat – for everything to seem absurd. Why? Because you two *know better*. It's a judgement – can't they see what we see? You can share the moment with your best friend; you can share it with a total stranger sitting opposite you on the train.

Laughter negotiates new, spontaneous and dangerously intimate relationships between you and other people. Like today, I was in a grocer's when Olu, the woman at the till, handed me two oranges and a stick of ginger. The three objects lay there in her hand. I hesitated. I looked at the shape. She looked at the shape. We both burst out laughing.

I was holding money in my hand, but Olu was holding a change. The penis-thing flung us together in a kind of filthy suspension of the day-to-day, an obscene interruption of life. And it's interesting, but I don't think I'd have found it funny if Olu and I had been friends. Friendship would have robbed the scene of its risk; strangers, we put ourselves at each other's mercy.

To look at her, I'd guess Olu was of a type: a mid-sixties Nigerian lady, very neat, formally made up and, I assumed, a Christian, going on the crucifix which hung from her neck. But I didn't *know* anything about her beyond the name on her badge. All we had in common was a gleeful awkwardness created by the fear of how the other person might *judge* us for our laughter, our smut. This fear united Olu and me against the rest of the unseeing world. We belonged, briefly and romantically, to the sublime Fluke Penis Republic

Laughter is a moment produced by – but detached from – its time, like you're bubble-wrapping a moment against the journey and its slatted brutalities. I once took a train with a girl I was in love with. I was too much of a coward to say anything, and we both knew that, and that I never would. It was an overnight train, cutting through the wetlands of one unknown country into the wild hills of another, and she slept, her head on my lap. Keen not to get an erection, I started to count the beat of the rails and I counted till I knew I'd go insane with terror if I kept on. It wasn't infinity that scared me. It was a large finite number. There are only so many beats. That makes it harder to live, knowing you'd live and suffer and suffer and stop dead somewhere under bone-dulling breakers of worn and tiny regrets.

Today, Olu stopped me counting.

So it's no coincidence that 'comedy' is often understood as a live act. Nor is it coincidental that an improvisatory feeling helps it to succeed. Very few art forms *need* the active response of an audience. Only jazz prioritises being in the moment to the same degree. Like jazz, comedy obeys and defies the beat. But unlike jazz, or at least great jazz, comedy needs to sound *right*. Comedians crave your approval. They are caught between saying what they want to say and saying what you want to hear. It's a hard balancing act. Think how easy it is to backtrack if what you've said is met by disapproval; the average comedian is willing to recant everything for the sake of a feeling. The same joke is affirmed by laughter one night, only to be annihilated by silence the next. Galileo[55] needed the Vatican to force his renunciation. All a comedian needs to fall apart is one pissed heckler.

Laughter is a response to the unexpected. Accordingly, one of the easiest ways to manufacture a laugh is to shock for shock's sake. To say what's prohibited is comedy's greatest virtue, but also its greatest temptation. In this society, what's now unexpected is, amongst other things, a lack of (a show of) cultural understanding. To use a platform and a spotlight and a microphone to say intolerant things is shocking and often shockingly successful in that it *forces* people to respond.

55 Galileo Galilei (1564–1642) was an Italian astronomer and mathematician whose defence of the Copernicus' heliocentrism (i.e. that the earth turned around the sun, not the other way round) ran contrary to the Bible. The Catholic church accused Galileo of heresy. Galileo recanted some of his ideas, but was condemned to live under house arrest for the rest of his life.

Scott Capurro[56] is one of the most forceful comedians around. He's a misanthrope who told Time Out that "if at least parts of the crowd aren't shaking or angry by the end of my set, they haven't got their money's worth and I feel a bit dirty." Capurro's aim is to correct a prejudicial stereotype: he wants the crowd to realise that "'queers' can be something other than lonely, sexless, mincing, prissy, overweight, wall-eyed elves with one joke and no friends." Breathtakingly savage, Capurro doesn't excuse his behaviour by revealing 'the man behind the mask.' No sentimental, just-kidding coda or subtext is permitted to soften his act. In this, he's massively outnumbered by the many less intelligent and committed comedians who'll crack an Anne Frank gag then scurry back to shelter behind 'irony'.

The definition of irony is this: in Mexico, in a village called Tabasco, live the two last speakers of a language called Ayapaneco[57]. Manuel Segovia and Isidro Velasquez are both in their seventies and live about five hundred metres apart. However, they rarely speak to each other because "they don't have a lot in common."

The definition of irony is not this: saying something disparaging about Muslims and then raising an eyebrow, shaking your head at your own outrageousness,

---

56 Scott Capurro is an American stand-up operating mostly in the UK. The first time I saw him, he asked the girl I'd taken to the gig if her clitoris tasted of elderflower. She refused to answer either way, and sadly I never found out for myself.

57 The name 'Ayapaneco' is a colonial imposition. According to an article in the *Guardian*, Segovia and Velasquez call their language *Nuumte Oote*, meaning 'True Voice'.

or chuckling as if to say 'what am I like?' To which the answer is 'a little bit of a coward.'

Though hardly a barrel of laughs himself, Hegel[58] nailed the problem when he wrote that:

> the most tasteless things can move people to laughter, and they often laugh all the same at the most important and profound matters if they see in them only some wholly insignificant aspect which contradicts their day-to-day outlook.

The art of telling a good joke is knowing how and why you are victimising someone. It's an art that can be overridden by pragmatism, by pandering, by the fear of dying (if only on stage). Particularly if your priority is effect over cause, affirmation over meaning.

Hans Teeuwen[59] is a Dutch comedian who plays with our inherent tastelessness by annoying people in the name of free speech. He'll tell stories set in enchanted forests full of diseased talking animals, or sing a song dedicated to a mysterious Doctor Hemmington while writhing in and out of a fold-flat chair. This is not McIntyre territory. As such, Teeuwen's walk-out rate is astronomical, but I haven't seen him abuse anyone for leaving his show. Maybe this is because walking out requires either courage or indifference, and abusing courage is counter-intuitive,

58 Georg Wilhelm Friedrich Hegel (1770–1831) was a German philosopher of some rigour. To be honest, it's quite hard to summarise him in a footnote.

59 Hans Teeuwen is a comedian, absurdist and crooner.

abusing indifference a waste of time. Anyway, walk-outs are a natural corrective. The audience is free to leave; this freedom, when exercised, victimises their victimiser. For a comic to object to this, to sulk or swear, is to demonstrate exactly the characteristics they deplore in their audience.

Teeuwen tortures us. One joke begins with him imitating a casual, 'have-you-ever-noticed' relationship with his audience. He describes seeing a man in the street, who, it turns out, was "a Muslim." Or, rather, a "Mussssslom", Teeuwen's Dutch accent stretching this 'Muslim' on the rack of our growing discomfort. Then there's a beat. Teeuwen corrects himself. The man wasn't a Muslim at all. "He was a Jew." Or, rather, "a djuwww, a djuwwh, a real dejeewah." The comedian invites us to recognise the stereotype behind this expletive bluntness. Then there's another pause. Oh no, he wasn't a Jew. "He was a Christian, a Chreestiann, a Christeeenanan," Teeuwen says, his hands clasped in a prayer, his face screwed with menacing sentimentality. Then there's a third beat. Teeuwen smiles brightly. "What a pity that there is no God."

Though his punch line denies the existence of God, religion as such is not Teeuwen's target. Rather, it's the culture of fear surrounding certain words. Teeuwen doesn't say Buddhist or Hindu or Jain because, one, they're offshoots of separate traditions and, two, here they don't have the same, strong cultural associations as Muslims, Jews and Christians. Simply by *intoning* these identities, Teeuwen criticises the layers of unspoken prejudice that have built up around skin-deep, superficial differences

– as the framing device of sight and mistaken identity suggests, and which the various monotheistic denominations of the man confirm.

An excellent physical performer, Teeuwen's presence on stage is enough to make me laugh, but I laugh nervously. I'm uncertain as to what act I've let myself in for. Is this going to be a gig Roger Lewis enjoys? When I hear Teeuwen say 'Muslim', my mind turns to stonings, suicide bombers and burkas. Then, when I hear 'Jew', my first thought is the Holocaust, which is just *so* Route One. Then, when I hear 'Christian', I'm concerned. Is Teeuwen attacking a vague assumption of what I might or might not believe based on my nationality and race? That's not fair! Exclude me, include them, or include me and exclude them, but don't lump us all together!

My discomfort, my offence, stems from self-defence. More explicitly, that when I think 'you can't talk about Muslims!' or 'you can't talk about Jews!' or 'maybe you can talk about Christians? Are they Catholics? I'd laugh at Catholics perhaps,' what I'm really thinking is, 'can I laugh at these people *safely*? Can I be *excluded* from the consequences?' The laugh is not on some Naima-like outsider. The laugh is on me. My cultural cowardice is as precarious and impractical as Mr. Bean in an armchair on top of his Mini.

Teeuwen victimises those who seek exclusivity. There are certain people (let's call them believers) who demand to be excluded from debate. Their sick note? That 'we' shouldn't attack things we don't understand, i.e. their belief. And maybe we shouldn't. On the other hand, if I don't understand something, the natural impulse is to ask questions. So why humour believers, who are so desperately insecure that they confuse a question with an attack? Look at Scientology. Is there anything more suspect than an organisation refusing to submit to scrutiny? What are they afraid of? Laughter, I'd imagine, given that they basically believe in *Star Wars*.

A liberal society – one which treasures the ideal of free speech – is built on the founding lie of total inclusivity. But this society still needs to *exclude* somebody, otherwise how would its citizens truly understand the blessing of *inclusion*? It suits a liberal society, therefore, when a minority of others (or believers, or whatever) demand to be excluded from free speech's jurisdiction. That's why the authorities play along with minorities of all denominations and descriptions, reassuring each of them that they're special.

'Of course you must be excluded from the rough-and-tumble of free speech! We'd never want to hurt your feelings. Guys?' the liberal authorities say, looking sincerely into each other's eyes. 'No one talk about the [insert minority] ever again, OK? We now officially *respect* them'

Everyone's happy. The [insert minority] feels 'respected'. The authorities can pat themselves on the back, then play innocent when – at some convenient moment of crisis – they really start turning the fucking screws.

'*They* are to blame for everything that's wrong in *our* society. We respected the [insert minority] and they threw our values back in our face. And to think,' the authorities continue with a cuckolded bleat, 'that we *trusted* them!'

The [insert minority] is so readily accepted *as* The Enemy because the majority know so little about them. Being exempt from criticism, the minority are seldom discussed. And the authorities are blameless for turning the minority into a silent, opaque threat. After all, everyone's been so nice to one another! The irony being that, if the minority hadn't fallen into the trap of demanding 'respect', then they wouldn't have been excluded in the first place.

Is it possible to create a comic language that includes everyone? How do we justify the use of linguistic violence? If not, does comedy become little more than that experiment conducted by Dr. Milgram? Are comics doing nothing more than following the orders of their own, violent neuroses, shocking strangers in another room? Surely not, as long as the connection with the audience remains unbroken.

Those are tricky questions. Teeuwen asks them. More people need to. Though that's just my opinion. After all, what's a joke got to do with Aristotle, Bahktin or Hegel if it pleases people? Bertold Brecht[60] said that "nothing

---

60 Bertold Brecht (1898–1956) was a German playwright and director. He developed the 'Epic Theatre', eschewing sentimentality and the suspension of disbelief in favour of analysis, alienation and '*spass*', or intellectual fun. The Nazis drove him into exile and this proved to be his most productive period, in which he wrote *Mother Courage and Her Children*, *The Life of Galileo* and *Fear and Misery In The Third Reich*. After an unhappy spell in Hollywood, Brecht returned to East Germany to run the Berliner Ensemble with his wife and collaborator, Helene Weigel.

needs less justification than pleasure", though Missy Elliot[61] put it better:

> "Big Daddy Kane and Public Enemy, Salt N Pepa, Lite E, PMD, LC, Run DMC, KRS One, Rakim[62] – most of them artists used to dance and still get respected in the street… So if you want to be hard and ice-grill and Harlem-shake at the same time, whatever. Let's just have fun. It's hip hop, man. This is hip hop."

But is fun enough where comedy's concerned? Laughter is a weapon and both can destroy as well as construct. The plot of *Unforgiven* was set in motion by a prostitute giggling at a man's penis. And I know that's only a film, but I think it rings true, tangentially. Laughter can bring us closer together. Laughter can also drive us apart. It can't do one without the potential for the other. A laugh is like that penis-shaped vegetable cluster, tearing through the ordinary to slap us about the face. How do you handle power like that? How do you respond?

Comedians and joke-writers have to ask themselves, is comedy's only function to provoke laughter? If not, what are comedy's responsibilities – to itself and to its audience?

61 Missy 'Misdemeanor' Elliot: queen of hip hop, Adidas clothes horse and Little Mix collaborator. Spot the odd one out.

62 AKA a whole lot of hip hop.

Offence and obscenity, cunts.

"How do you crucify a spastic? On a swastika."

Comedian, magician, psychopath, Jerry Sadowitz[63] has been telling that joke for decades. I feel for it Ian Holm's[64] admiration for the Alien: "I admire its purity, unclouded by conscience, remorse, or delusions of morality." It's got the simplest structure a joke can have (other than a pun or a fart, which to my mind are roughly equivocal, without wishing to do the fart down), familiar

---

63 Jerry Sadowitz is unique. In his shows, the offence-quota reaches a critical mass at around the half-way mark. For the next ten minutes, being screamed at by a Scotch Fagin becomes intolerably boring, tiring and uncomfortable. But then you break through the wall, entering a euphoric final fifteen minutes in which no Madeleine McCann joke is too old or vile. It's like a spin class in Broadmoor.

64 Ian Holm starred as Ash, the creepy robot in Ridley Scott's *Alien*. Because he's not technically alive, Ash isn't on the Alien's food-chain. This allows him to sit back and admire the slathering, fanged, penis-faced killing machine as it gorges on his human colleagues.

to anyone who's ever pulled a Christmas cracker, hoping against hope that its contents will distract them – if only for a moment – from staring through the faces of their semi-sentient grandparents down the long, dark fudge-tunnel of time.

The 70s were full of puce-faced fat men with bugger's grips and frilly nylon shirts wheezing out similar question-answer gags like sweating, racist accordions. *What do you call a black milkman? Why did my mother-in-law think I was Jewish? When did the Indian get thrush?* Undoubtedly more innocent times. However, the structural linearity of the set-up/punch means that journeymen working the Embassy club could usually only hope to insult one or, at best, two types of victim per joke. Not Sadowitz. His choice of victim is offensive; the question he asks is offensive; the answer he provides is offensive – and all to different groups of people. His victims include the disabled, Christians, Jews and Germans, but in its multiplicity the joke actually creates a transcendent obscenity that includes us all.

To find Sadowitz's joke funny or offensive, I have to have in my head the image of a spastic. That's different from the image of a disabled person. I know that – as an able-bodied outsider to disability – I can only laugh at it if permitted to so by someone who lives that reality. But I also know that a spastic is a mad, capering, clumsy, flailing freak. He's not normal (not like me). He couldn't be crucified in a normal way (not like me). And this is Sadowitz's brilliance: he takes a prejudice I have against the disabled and literally nails it to the symbol of a party that took that same prejudice to its murderous conclusion.

I find this joke funny because it has the right to abuse me. Oddly, I also find it funny because the swastika/spastic combo reminds me of the pose Morecambe and Wise used to strike, legs and arms at jaunty diagonals. Perhaps I'm just peculiar. But the point is this: no one's offended by nonsense. You don't storm out of Noel Fielding's[65] set, you just grit your teeth, sit back and think, 'oh, a squirrel made out of cheese, isn't that harmlessly shit.' But Sadowitz, he's struck a chord on the most off-key heartstring I have.

'Getting' Jerry Sadowitz's joke makes you aware of just how much filth you have in your head. It's like newspapers writing "f***" and "c***". If anything, asterisks are *more* obscene than plain 'fuck' and 'cunt' because they force readers into complicity. The observer is bound to the observed and the asterisk is neurotic: what society won't admit to, it's made to think about under the stars of shame. Asterisks ask 'do you know what I mean?' Readers then have to admit that they do. More, they have to *produce* the words themselves. Either that, or play a weird little guessing game:

Man: Darling, is England's former captain John Terry[66] more likely to have called Anton Ferdinand a black

65 Noel Fielding is the co-creator of the *Mighty Boosh*.

66 John Terry, lion-hearted warrior, was found not guilty of racially abusing Anton Ferdinand by a jury. Confusingly, he was subsequently found guilty of the same crime by the FA. This was a sad day for everyone. The British court system outshone by football's most pathetic ruling body? #guttedmate.

shit, a black fuck or a black cunt? The *Telegraph*'s only written 'black' and then four asterisks, the ****s.

Woman: Well, Chelsea *were* going through a rough patch at the time, and QPR were once wily if workmanlike opponents, so JT will have been under pressure. But he's friends with Rio Ferdinand[67], Anton's brother, so he wouldn't be too offensive, would he?

Man: Black shit?

Woman: But there'd be no furore over a black shit, surely?

Man: Black fuck, you reckon?

Woman: Well, black cunt is a *bit* strong, even for England's Brave John Terry.

The point being that we're so wound up by 'obscenity' that we miss the truly obscene, even though it's staring us in the face. (I'm just spelling it out, in case any jurors from the Terry case are reading this book. Which is a long shot, given that they can't even read a set of lips.) Having said that, there's no need for a newspaper like the *Sun* to write obscenities. After all, I doubt anyone leaving a message on Milly Dowler's[68] answer phone was calling her a cunt.

As Stewart Lee asks, "if a tree says 'fuck, cunt, abortion, piss' in a forest, and no one is there to hear it, is the tree offensive?" In other words, are fuck and cunt

67 Rio Ferdinand, resurgent central defender and prank-artist.

68 Milly Dowler (1988–2002) was murdered by Levi Bellfield. *News of the World* journalists hacked her answer phone messages. This activity led the Dowler family to hope that she was still alive.

offensive in and of themselves, or will they one day lose their power to shock? Only if we have new obscenities to load with our revulsion. Because we'll need to scapegoat *something.*

The word 'scapegoat' – signifying, at first literally, an animal burdened with the sins of a community – has its origin in the Book of Leviticus. Surprisingly, it's worth quoting at length:

7 And [Aaron] shall take the two goats and present them before the LORD *at* the door of the congregation.
8 And Aaron shall cast lots upon the two goats; one lot for the LORD, and the other lot for the scapegoat.
9 And Aaron shall bring the goat upon which the LORD's lot fell, and offer him for a sin offering.
10 But the goat, on which the lot fell to be the scapegoat, shall be presented alive before the LORD, to make an atonement with him, *and* let him go for a scapegoat into the wilderness.

It's a good yarn, in which the scapegoat becomes nothing less than a four-footed *kômôidoi*, "degraded and excluded" by the authorities. The Hebrew 'azāzēl' was translated by William Tyndale[69] in 1530 as 'scapegoat' to suggest that a community can 'escape' its sins by projecting them onto an outcast. But this escapism cuts both ways. God's animal has its throat slashed; the

69 William Tyndale (c. 1494–1536) was the Protestant reformer who translated and printed an English-language Bible – a crime in the eyes of the Catholic Church. Tyndale was executed for heresy.

scapegoat is free to live in sin (and, whatever the sins of the Children of Israel, I doubt they much bothered the goat).

In *The Scapegoat*, René Girard[70] describes those sins societies want to escape. Like Jerry Sadowitz's jokes, they "transgress the taboos that are considered the strictest... they attack the very foundations of cultural order." But sins, jokes, are *required* to do this. There's a complicity between the transgressive individual and the crowd that needs to despise them. According to Girard, the mob "see themselves as completely passive, purely reactive...there is only one person responsible for everything" sick in their society. Theirs is a false innocence.

Though the word 'tragedy' comes from the Greek word for a 'goat-song', goats themselves have a very limited amount of tragic agency. A goat could poo somewhere inappropriate, bleat loudly, or perhaps molest a kid if it was a goat priest, but that's sort of it. Scapegoats, too, are burdened with a disproportionate role within the performance of social morality. We need villains. If Sadowitz stopped performing, we'd find someone else to be shocked by.

Scapegoating is a mark of dishonesty. At the Nuremburg Trials, Hitler became a scapegoat for others' culpability. It was pragmatic to accept this, regardless of just how many lawyers, doctors, teachers, policemen, scientists and soldiers it actually took to build and run

---

70 René Girard is a French historian and critic. Born in 1923, Girard has written 30+ books.

the Nazi state. Though that's not to scapegoat Germans – they were pursuing ideas that predated Nazism. Winston Churchill[71] was the vice-president of the First International Congress of Eugenics in 1912. Its agenda? The liquidation of individuals who didn't flatter society's self-image. To quote Jack Nicholson's[72] character in *The Departed*, "I don't want to be a product of my environment. I want my environment to be a product of me." And don't we all?

Passivity is convenient. I'm just a consumer! I have rights, not responsibilities! But no one is exempt from thinking about their position in relation to others' suffering. Just because I'm not a sweatshop foreman doesn't make my choice of trainers OK. Just because I only buy (rather than sell) Apple products doesn't mean that I shouldn't feel involved in the story of the Foxconn factory in China, where iPhones and iPads are made, where conversation between workers is forbidden, and where suicide rates rise in direct proportion to commercial demand.

When confronted by difficult or shocking material, we become Girard's mob. We blame someone else – in this instance, the joke-writer. *We* don't have microphones, *we're* not the ones spouting obscenities. But comedy is a performance; a performance needs an audience, an audience needs a performance.

---

71 Winston Churchill (1874–1965) won the Second World War, coined the phrase 'The Iron Curtain' and briefly sported a grass Mohican in Parliament Square.

72 Jack Nicholson. Lothario, actor, Lakers fan.

Heckler: Are you saying I can *never* legitimately object to a joke?

Freddy: No, but only if you *never* legitimately object to my balls. *[pumps fist]* Yes! Taxi for one.

Say you're a physicist and you're conducting an experiment (or whatever you do – I didn't listen at school, just read *Viz* under my desk, which meant that I sometimes had to explain why I found prisms funny). Classical physics defines the components of an experiment as either observer or observed. The scientist is the observer; the content being experimented upon (say, sound waves or one of those hilarious prisms) is the observed. But observer and observed leech. As the mathematician Alan Turing[73] wrote, "when we are dealing with atoms and electrons we are quite unable to know the exact state of them; our instruments being made of atoms and electrons themselves." Shouldn't we come to the same conclusion when considering the comedian and their audience, particularly

73 Alan Turing (1912–54) broke the Enigma code and possibly did more than anyone else to 'invent' the computer. He objected to the idea that machines could never be 'human' (or 'normal') and, therefore, that they did not have the right to life. So Turing set the machine these challenges: "Be kind, resourceful, beautiful, friendly, have initiative, have a sense of humour, tell right from wrong, make mistakes, fall in love, enjoy strawberries and cream, make someone fall in love with it, learn from experience, use words properly, be the subject of its own thought, have as much diversity of behaviour as a man, do something really new." We know a machine can't do all these things. Is this evidence of the machine's sub-humanity? Only if we imagine that human beings *can* do all these things. But *can* I do all these things? Can you? Alan Turing was chemically castrated by the British state; he died in unresolved circumstances a few years later.

when we, the audience, are presented with something we object to?

When the classical mathematician or the classical physicist got a result that didn't fit the laws they imposed upon an experiment, they assumed the result – and not the law – was at fault. It's as when we're offended: we blame the offender, never the lack of self-awareness we bring to the gig.

Only hypocrites get offended by comedians; when Frankie Boyle made a joke about her appearance, Rebecca Adlington[74] said that "I cannot say I don't laugh when a comedian tells a joke about someone else. So it would be hypocritical to turn around and say you can't joke about me." So why *are* audiences still shocked by Boyle's material? It's not like he got them watching under false pretences – his tours are called things like *I Would Happily Punch Every One Of You In The Face*. In theory, at least, his audience are just as happy to get punched.

Why? For the same reason you see a horror film. You want to be brutalised by the content. The more popular these films (and comedians) get, moreover, the more shocking they need to be. It's a question of supply and demand. As Catherine MacKinnon[75] says of the increase

74 Rebecca Adlington is an Olympic gold-winning swimmer.

75 Catherine MacKinnon is an American writer and professor of law. Her attitude towards pornography is a useful one to consider in the context of this chapter. For MacKinnon, obscenity is a moral judgement. To describe pornography as obscene, therefore, is to miss the point. The scenes being depicted should not be judged on the criteria of taste or offence, but on whether they render the subjects powerless. The loss of power is *political*.

of violence in porn, "greater efforts of brutality...[and] more and more violence" are "necessary to keep the progressively desensitized consumer aroused." The one thing the consumer *doesn't* want is to be confronted with the consequences of their appetite. If you eat Big Macs every day, you're unlikely to own a weighing machine. If you use a Mac, reading about Foxconn workers tumbling off factory roofs might prompt you to close the window.

In *Being and Nothingness*, Jean-Paul Sartre[76] describes an eavesdropper kneeling at a keyhole. This eavesdropper needs to remain undetected, the better to derive pleasure, surprise, outrage or information from what's being said. He's so focused on listening that he loses awareness of his surroundings. In his mind, he is silent, invisible. Then, behind him, he hears a floorboard creak. In that instant, he becomes aware of how he *looks* to someone else. He sees himself through another's eyes and all he can feel is shame.

Frankie Boyle's critics do one of two things in order to pretend that they're somehow above him. They say either that the shock factor has worn off (supply has failed demand), or – if they *are* shocked – that they've taken offence at the construction of his material, not its subject-matter. This second criticism is a little disingenuous.

76 Jean-Paul Sartre (1905–80) was a French writer most famous for being an existentialist (his neologism). Sartre wrote *Being and Nothingness*, his *Critique of Dialectical Reason*, and the three *Roads To Freedom* novels. Sartre's loyalty to the Marxist cause ruined his friendship with Albert Camus – Hutch to Sartre's Starsky. Sartre is buried with Simone de Beauvoir, his lover for more than half a century, in the Montparnasse cemetery.

People enjoy all kinds of clumsily-made, nonsensical bullshit. Look at the *Twilight* films. What people don't like is self-examination.

To use a much-publicised incident, if Sharon and Kieron Smith[77] – the parents of a child with Down's Syndrome – are in the front row (*the front row!*) of a Frankie Boyle gig, and he tells a joke about Down's Syndrome, the Smiths are *not* offended by his technical abilities. Though Sharon Smith said in a blog entry that "I expected dry, nasty, crude humour, yes, but...[his jokes] weren't even clever", she did not storm out because of an over-obvious set-up or a mistimed punchline, deviation from the rule of three or a callback that labours the point. Nor was she outraged by Boyle's being merely unamusing, though his jokes picked on Down's Syndrome as a natural condition and thus failed to be funny. Couldn't you argue (if you were particularly cynical and honestly only playing Devil's advocate) that Sharon Smith stormed out because she recognised in herself what she finds hateful in others: the pleasure taken in victimisation. It's only now *her* child's the victim that she and her husband see how they've previously taken part in "nasty, crude" victimisation themselves.

Sharon Smith was caught eavesdropping, and she didn't like what she saw. Terrifyingly, however, that's an

77 I don't want to slight the Smiths' intelligence. Kieron Smith is the author of *The Politics of Down's Syndrome*. In it, Smith describes how John Down – the man who first diagnosed the syndrome – used the words 'mongoloid' and 'mongol idiots' to describe people with it. These racist undertones, Smith suggests, are part of why Down's Syndrome is uniquely 'other' in the public imagination. Perhaps its otherness makes Down's Syndrome such an appealing topic for some comedians?

opinion shared by the *Daily Mail*'s online forum (minus the Sartre reference). As the *Daily Mail* online forum also wants to castrate benefit-scrounging homosexual Chinese imam-lizards with yo-yoing weight problems and a heroin habit funded by muggins here, I'm going back on my word. Are Frankie Boyle's critics right? Does *structure* alone have the power to offend?

Here's a blank page.

To everyone except the tree that's been pulped to produce it, that page is pretty inoffensive. But what if I tell you that I'm running a competition for the best drawing of the Prophet Muhammed[78]? All you have to do is draw him on that blank page, cut it out, pop it in the post to my home address (which – given the context – it may be wiser to withhold) and, who knows, *you* might be the winner! In that context, even an empty space can be distasteful and obscene.

Disgust is extremely relative. For Muslims, the drawing you've just done of the Prophet doesn't need to be offensive as non-Muslims understand it. No *Viz*-like big hairy balls, prehensile cocks, piss or Swastikas are needed to get those effigies burning. For Hollywood, nudity is prohibited. Never mind all the violence coursing through a PG-13 – as long as the combatants are fully-clothed, they can blow up whatever they like. This is because spectacular acts of aggression re-enforce America's image of itself. If America suffers aggression, it proves that America stands alone against the forces of evil; if America commits aggression, it proves America can overcome those forces. Consensual sex, on the other hand, is democratic, destabilising, unownable. Bill Clinton[79] was nearly impeached for getting a

78 Muhammed (the name on his driving licence was Abū al-Qāsim Muhammad ibn 'Abd Allāh ibn 'Abd al-Muttalib ibn Hāshim) died in 632. Muhammed founded Islam, conquered Mecca and united the Arab world.

79 Bill Clinton, horndog and saxophonist.

blow job; George W. Bush[80] (or Tony Blair[81], for that matter) had no such trouble in the aftermath of a costly, illegal and largely fruitless war. Which is ironic, given that Iraq's justification was sexed-up to the point where it dripped with more jouissance than a teenage boy's sock.

That empty page threatens us, not with its content, but with the possibility of violence. It's an asterisk – we project ourselves onto it. And while we're on the subject of *projection*, here's some offensive structuring for you. Let's say that the content of a movie is its story, its structure is its method of storytelling (cuts, music and so on), and its context is the audience watching it. I'd like to think about how an Austrian director, Michael Haneke[82], manipulates structure and context in a far more shocking

---

80 George W. Bush. Was his folksy witlessness a ruse to curry favour with American pondlife? Or was he genuinely a mentally subnormal puppet, a kind of piñata full of horseshit designed to keep everyone entertained while the military-industrial complex went to town? President Eisenhower coined the phrase 'military-industrial complex' in his 1961 farewell speech to the nation. "We must guard against the acquisition of unwarranted influence, whether sought or unsought, by the military-industrial complex," Eisenhower said, because "the potential for the disastrous rise of misplaced power exists, and will persist." George Bush's presidency was one result of this persistence.

81 Tony Blair. On Michael Parkinson's chat show, Blair confessed to consulting God on whether he should start the Iraq war. That clip has since overtaken Ollie Reed dancing for Michael Aspel in Channel 5's *The 100,000 Most Embarrassing Moments On A Chat Show Ever*. In the talking heads cueing up Blair's confession, Alex Zane said he almost shat himself laughing, Shappi Khorsandi looked embarrassed but resigned about the way her career's going, Tony Parsons asked for some money and Helen Lederer was utterly incomprehensible.

82 Michael Haneke. The best.

way than mere content ever could be, and about how he does so using cinematic asterisks.

The plot of Haneke's film(s) *Funny Games* is fairly straightforward. A happy, bourgeois family (mum, dad, son and dog) drive to their lakeside holiday home. En route, they stop at their friends' house. From the other side of a large electric gate, they see this other couple accompanied by two young men, dressed in nautical/golfing whites. The family drive on to their own gated home. The two young men pay them a visit. They break the father's leg. They kill the dog. They make a bet: mother, father and child will all be dead by morning. Then they win this bet with callously entertaining efficiency.

Am I too late to say 'spoiler alert'? Probably, but it doesn't matter, because the content of Haneke's film is essentially irrelevant. Yes, murder is an unpleasant business, but far from unique to *Funny Games*. What upsets audiences is the way Haneke tells it.

Funny Games begins with classical music. It's incidental in a technical sense, in that the music is being played *within* the scene, rather than imposed *over* it by an editor. We see that the family are playing a game in their car. The father plays the mother a piece of music. The mother has to guess what it is. She succeeds; they switch. They have a little laugh. Then the title 'Funny Games' flashes up, and thrash metal drowns out the incidental. It's the first of many 'funny' games, games which play with the rules of film as roughly as the killers do with the family.

Our victims are killed in anti-Hollywood order: first the golden retriever (think back to *Independence Day*[83] – however many millions perish, the dog must survive!), then the child, then the husband, then the wife. They're selected to die with games, and revealed to be dead with other games. When the mother is sent looking for her dead dog, one killer guides her with 'hot' and 'cold'; when she goes wrong, he turns to the camera and smiles, as if to say, 'what's she like?' Why does Haneke have him do this? As I understand it, to make it explicit that we're the beneficiaries of a cultural context in which our pleasure is prioritised over others' pain.

Funny Games doesn't *define* violence in a way that's easy for the viewer to understand. The killers change names indiscriminately, whereas (in the American version of the story) both father and son are called George. The killers also invent multiple motives for their psychopathic actions. They're drug addicts. No, they're homosexuals with terrible home lives. All we *do* know is that they enjoy tormenting their victims with variability, a trick Christopher Nolan[84] cribbed for the Joker's back-stories in *The Dark Knight*. In *Funny*

---

83 Roland Emmerich's *Independence Day* is an action film that stars Will Smith, Jeff Goldblum and Bill Pullman. I made my dad buy me a plastic toy based on the aliens who besiege earth and destroy the White House (the ultimate obscenity). However, *Independence Day* scared me so much that I couldn't even bring myself to open the packaging the toy came in, much less play with the thing. It remained a mint-condition nightmare under my bed.

84 Christopher Nolan's directed *Memento*, *The Prestige*, *Inception* and the Dark Knight trilogy. He's a structural engineer whose films fetishise kit while remaining absolutely sexless. Nolan has yet to make a dud.

Games, the only (counter-productive) clarity comes from the killers' white clothing, standing out against the night. Death is unknowable; its approach, all too apparent.

In a normal film, we know when to be afraid. Camera shots generally get more disorientating in the build up to an attack, then perceptibly longer, focusing on the foreground of a protagonist's terrified face, limiting our awareness of their environment just before something horrific bursts from its shadows. Then a knife goes in, there's a spurt of blood, and we're granted catharsis.

Haneke breaks these and most other unwritten rules filmmakers and their audiences have agreed between them over the century or so of cinema. For instance, films have scores, designed to tell us what's scary or moving or fun. They're usually overbearing: *The Dark Knight Rises*' soundtrack sounds like nothing more than a fat, angry man (me, maybe) running down about 4,317 short flights of stairs. But *Funny Games* has no score. Haneke told *Sight & Sound* that "I spend a lot of time on the [sound] mix – often rather more than on the image…it's the part of filmmaking I like best." His killers are announced not by violins and kettle drums, but by the dull, pocked whorl of a golf ball settling into a floorboard's warp. This sound makes me aware of the moving thing's inevitable cessation. And it makes me wonder, have the family noticed this board before? How many more invisible perversions are worn into the architecture?

Funny Games' soundscape is comparable to John Cage's[85] *4'33"*, a composition which famously contains no notes. When it's performed, the musicians sit in front of blank pages while the audience listens to itself. Shifting positions, whispered conversation, coughs, breath – the artist brings nothing to his creation other than his audience. Cage's intention is meditative. Haneke, too, makes us think about ourselves. He makes us think about how vulnerable we are in our own, sealed environment.

We're also denied the dubious pleasure of seeing a boy being shot. When George Junior is murdered, Haneke's camera is lingering on one of the killers making a sandwich. Maybe we'd have missed the murder, too – this popcorn's not going to eat itself. The killers then leave the house. Unfortunately, we can't leave with them. Instead, we're stuck in the room where the violence has taken place. In one long take, we see the mother vomiting,

---

85 John Cage (1912–92) was an American avante-garde classical composer. Cage's compositions became gestural; his single instruction to the musician performing the piece, *0'0"*, was "in a situation provided with maximum amplification, perform a disciplined action." In the first performance of *0'0"*, Cage writing that sentence constituted the action. In his 1957 lecture, *Experimental Music*, Cage said that "there is no such thing as an empty space or an empty time... try as we may to make a silence, we cannot." He described going into an anechoic chamber, "its six walls made of special material, a room without echoes." Cage says he "heard two sounds, one high and one low. When I described them to the engineer in charge, he informed me that the high one was my nervous system in operation, the low one my blood in circulation. Until I die there will be sounds. And they will continue following my death. One need not fear about the future of music."

hopping ridiculously around, extricating herself from the gaffer tape that the killers have tied her up in, then kneeling next to her emasculated husband. The relentless respect paid to the reality of these characters' feelings is a device to scapegoat us for making them the scapegoats of our escapism. To humiliate our appetites still further, she is stripped to her very ordinary underwear.

In contrast to the generic presentation of violence on screen, comedy is often filmed with long, wide takes which reveal everything to the viewer. This is why comedy suits being shot live in front of a studio audience (rather than drama, say). Furthermore, comedy prioritises the *consequences* of its characters' actions over the actions themselves. Think how *The Office* draws out every shot, leaving us in the horrendous moment *after* David Brent's misjudged jokes. Haneke is likewise uninterested in the joke (the act of violence) so much as its aftermath. His killers are Brent-like: excruciating, self-conscious, unfunny and unfair. We're entertained not by them, but by the all-too-visible destruction they leave in their wake.

Haneke's joke is that we play socially-conditioned games in the vain idea that violence will obey the same set of rules. The family greet their killers politely; sociability destroys them. Other structural agreements are broken, too. In one scene, the wife manages to shoot one of the killers. The other finds the TV remote, rewinds the film and stops her from getting hold of the gun. In the face of this inexplicable brutality, all the father can do is demand that the killers "at least watch [their] language around my son." An irrelevant request – given that a) his son is about to die, so what does it matter? and b) his tormentors are excessively polite – but one indicative of a social code of conduct ill-calibrated to gauge the truly obscene.

Is *Funny Games* funny? The first time you watch it, no. Jack and I sat in the cinema listening to our own screams for two unhappy hours. The second time you watch it (if you do watch it a second time), yes. It's like watching My Bloody Valentine[86] play their twenty minute noise piece, *The Holocaust*.

Bathetic title aside, this music – which sounds like a jet taking off, and which is so loud that venues are legally obliged to hand out ear plugs – challenges the audience's enjoyment as furiously as *Funny Games*. During the band's live set, *The Holocaust* irrupts from the bridge in another song, *You Made Me Realise*. When it finishes, and the band abruptly switch back to the final chorus of the newly-small, manufactured-sounding song, we're distanced enough to see our pleasure for what it is. I've seen them do this twice. The first time, I was aggravated and bored. The second time, somehow, it became funny, to see content so comprehensively destroyed. Why? Because, as with *Funny Games*, you made me realise.

*

86 My Bloody Valentine are a band of morose romantics who release new material every twenty years or so.

In the *Preface* to his Dictionary, Samuel Johnson[87] says he's "driven by the fear of evil." What evil? Entropy. Everyone has *always* agreed, the Greeks onwards, that the world is going downhill. The present scares us because we can't control it; whatever its horrors, the past is comforting, well-defined, the longer-dead the better. Even the Second World War gets romanticised – ordinary decent people didn't have to lock their doors at night when they were being blown to bits by the Luftwaffe. Every generation invents a socio-moral Big Bang at some point before their birth in order to bewail its heat as it becomes more and more diffuse, regardless of the fact that such an invention is clearly bullshit.

'Obscenity' is defined by the *Oxford English Dictionary* as "tending to deprave and corrupt." As Johnson figures it, time itself is obscene. As he says:

> We retard what we cannot repel, we palliate what we cannot cure. Life may be lengthened by care, though death cannot be ultimately defeated: tongues, like governments, have a natural tendency to degeneration.

Words are threatened *by* the body because they emanate *from* the body, that purling wide mouth of neurosis, that victim of time. Tongues sit in our heads

87 Dr. Samuel Johnson (1709–84) spent nine years writing *A Dictionary of the English Language*. He has been posthumously diagnosed with Tourette's, and was memorably played by Robbie Coltrane in *Blackadder the Third*.

like red, lecherous secrets; they age and grow gross and yet they're the instruments we have to play language. When they learn new licks, meanings change, and men lose control. This is why Johnson figures his project as palliative: loss is deathlikely inevitable as long as you associate (as men in authority do) change with forfeiture.

Death prompts denial and denial is funny. Descriptions of the body's ordinary experience were prohibited for centuries. And yet tongues are sexual tools and writing hands wipe arses; the bits of us issuing bans live in the closest proximity to the activities being banned. Michel de Montaigne[88] found this prohibition "amusing". It was ironic, he thought, that "the words which are least used, least written, and most hushed up should be best known." And why were they hushed up? Sartre's eavesdropper forgot himself in silence.

Simone de Beauvoir[89] was Sartre's lover. In *A Very Easy Death*, an account of her mother's dying, de Beauvoir gives the most incredible description of a taboo. She's with her mother in hospital when her mother says that "'I

88 Michel de Montaigne (1533–92) was a French writer and anecdotal sceptic. His father being deranged with humanism, young Michel spent three years of his childhood living with a random peasant family. After coming back to live in the family castle, his father saw to it that Latin became Michel's first language. A highly-decorated courtier and Mayor of Bordeaux, Montaigne revealed that "kings and philosophers defecate, and so do ladies." Forced into an arranged marriage, he fathered six daughters, only one of whom survived childhood.

89 Simone de Beauvoir (1908–86) was a French writer perhaps best known for *The Second Sex* (1949). She was an editor of *Les Temps Moderne* from the time Sartre and others created it until her death.

no longer have any shame.'" As such, Mme de Beauvoir no longer conceals her "bald pubis" from her daughter, who writes that:

> The sight of my mother's nakedness...jarred me. No body existed less for me: none existed more. As a child I had loved it dearly; as an adolescent it had filled me with uneasy repulsion... [it was] both repugnant and holy – a taboo.

De Beauvoir is "astonished at the violence" of her response to the sight of her mother's vagina. And it's not that her mother's broken a taboo. She *is* the taboo. Her "capitulation to being a body and nothing more" offends de Beauvoir. Shamelessness (an unattractive quality) presents the body undisguised, beyond psychological constraints or questions of taste – beyond all of civilisation's impositions. On the brink of death, de Beauvoir's mother is offensively, uncomplicatedly a living *thing*.

As there's 'bad' language, there's 'good' language, and 'good' language wants to be clean of our sinful life. So words are extracted from the human; slapped, cleaned, weighed; the connection to the bloody mess of their author is cut. Text is born. But, being inhuman, text doesn't *die*. Text even prevents part of its corporeal parent from dying too, by recording them. The word 'record' derives from the French for 'remembrance', with the Latin 'cor' meaning 'heart', and surrogate paper hearts are hoped to beat for a writer (or their mother) once their own has stopped.

How much more unsettling is it when a suicide leaves no note? Destroying your body is one thing, but refusing to have the last word? There's no trace of a still-living voice to offer explanation or absolution, which the bereaved require for their own self-preservation. It's shameless.

European colonialists in the nineteenth century were amazed to discover that sub-Saharan Africans did not generally make written records. Nor did they write contracts to designate the ownership of land, nor legal constitutions, nor names on a map. Practically the whole African continent was *res nullius*, a blank piece of paper. Colonialists like Henry Morton Stanley[90] and Pierre Brazza[91] scrabbled to draw and name its waterfalls, its rivers and lakes. Cecil Rhodes[92] went one further and

90 Henry Morton Stanley (1841–1904) was a British journalist turned colonial nation-builder, as well as a signal failure with women. In 1885, he began courting Dorothy Tennant, the model in Millais' painting '*No*' (in which a lady rejects a suitor's proposal). Stanley wrote to her from Pompeii, saying he'd like her to see the ruins because "interchanging of sentiments regarding the awful calamity would have seemed to increase one's pleasure and interest in the scene." S&M tourism? Work your chat, Stanley! Tennant turned down his proposal of marriage – life imitating art – before finally accepting him a few years and a lot of futile, murderous Ugandan escapades later. I doubt any of that's relevant, but I find it slightly endearing.

91 Pierre Brazza (1852–1905) was a French explorer with a pantomimic quality. "White men have two hands," Brazza would say to each African king he met. "The stronger hand is the hand of war, the other the hand of trade. Which do you want to shake?" The African ruler invariably shook the hand of trade.

92 Cecil Rhodes (1853–1902) was described by the British Colonial Office as "grotesque, clownlike…not to be regarded as a serious person." Sadly, not everyone agreed. He founded his own country (modern-day Zimbabwe) with two hundred pioneers: farmers, doctors, engineers, parsons, butchers, bakers and a Jesuit priest.

named himself a new country: Rhodesia. Quite a legacy he left himself.

Africans were seen as mute, and silence is amnesiac. As late as 1963, the Oxford don Hugh Trevor-Roper[93] was able to say that "perhaps in the future there will be some African history to teach. But at present there is none." Thought of in these terms, the colonies became, as Thomas Pynchon[94] writes in *Gravity's Rainbow*, "the outhouses of the European soul, where a fellow [could] let his pants down and relax, enjoy the smell of his own shit." Africans were not the other. They were nothing. And with no other in which to see their reflection, civilised men acted as if no longer human. They didn't suffer the shame Sartre describes in *Being and Nothingness*, the "recognition of the fact that I am indeed that object which the other is looking at and judging." The Lord Chamberlain[95] created a similar vacuum for Queen

93 Hugh Trevor-Roper (1914–2003) was Regius Professor at Oxford and, later, a life peer thanks to Margaret Thatcher. Trevor-Roper authenticated 'the Hitler Diaries', a forgery that cost him much of his reputation. His brother, Patrick Trevor-Roper, was one of only three gay men to testify before the Wolfenden Committee in 1955, at a time when homosexuality was still illegal (and one year after Alan Turing's suicide). Patrick was instrumental in convincing the Committee that homosexuality was innate, rather than the consequence of "recruitment" or disease.

94 Thomas Pynchon is the American novelist who wrote *Gravity's Rainbow*, *Mason & Dixon*, *Inherent Vice* and other rambling, funny, obscurely operatic yarns. Very few photos exist of Pynchon; his voice can be heard on two short scenes in *The Simpsons* and one YouTube trailer for *Inherent Vice*. His appetite for publicity made fellow recluse J.D. Salinger look like Katie Price.

95 The Lord Chamberlain has been in charge of running the royal household since 1399.

Victoria[96], who wasn't allowed to be mentioned on stage, regardless of whether the plays in question sought to praise or blame her.

Colonialists felt themselves safe in the knowledge that "no word ever gets back" to civilization. Because, even if Africans learnt to write in English, English words hush shit up. The colonialists' professed duty to right, and write, Africa was therefore absurd, a fact that could not always be concealed, even from themselves. Sir James Willcocks[97] was the archetypical imperialist. He fought in the Ashanti War, the Second Afghan War, the Second Boer War and the First World War, ending his career as Governor of Bermuda before returning to die in his birthplace, India. In his memoirs, *From Kabul to Kumassi*, Willcocks gives an account of an Englishman meeting a Frenchman in the Niger Delta, at a time when the two countries vied for control of the Borgu region. As proof of ownership, the Frenchman presented the Englishman with a two-volume history of the Borgu, written in French. Willcocks describes how both Europeans then broke into complicitous laughter. It's probably the most honest moment in the history of colonialism.

Funny, too, are some of the texts sent back to Europe by Africans. In January 1895, the Juju king Koko[98] lost his

96 Queen Victoria (1819–1901) reigned for sixty-three years. Her husband invented the Christmas tree and her son was Jack the Ripper.

97 General Sir James Willcocks GCB GCMG KCSI DSO (1857–1926). Hardcore empire man.

98 In 1885, King Frederick William Koko, Mingi VIII of Nembe (now a part of south Nigeria) led the Brassmen in an unsuccessful revolt against British authorities in the Niger Delta. He was deposed, and the

war against the British in the Delta. Koko wrote a letter to the Prince of Wales; apologising in faultless formalese, he was now "very sorry indeed" for the violence, "particularly the killing and eating parts of your employees." The funny word here is "employees". It's a logical word to use – though it was defended by soldiers like Willcocks, the British empire was mostly built by traders subcontracted by the Crown. These traders were technically employees, making Africa their office. Situated in an office, cannibalism becomes water-cooler banal. The dictionary continent was defeated on its own terms. Its language was now a bastard.

In *Civilisation, Society and Religion*, Freud[99] claims that the transference of authority from "the mother to the father" marks:

> A victory of intellectuality over sensuality, that is, an advance in civilisation, since maternity is proved by the evidence of the senses while paternity is a hypothesis, based on an inference and a premise.

A mother knows that a child is hers – you don't forget a little thing like childbirth. The child's 'father',

---

Brassmen made to pay £20,384 5*s.* 6*d.* Koko crops up in *Dr. Dolittle* (not the Eddie Murphy film).

99 Sigmund Freud (1856–1939) created psychoanalysis, named the id, ego and superego, enjoyed cocaine and took up smoking to stop himself from masturbating. Freud committed assisted suicide with the help of his doctor, Max Schur. The American writer Camille Paglia says that "Freud has no rivals among his successors because they think he wrote science, when he in fact he wrote art."

on the other hand, has to put his faith in the social and/or emotional contracts binding him to the mother. There are few situations in which a man's baby is undeniably *his*. Thus the word "father" fell short of its own authority. Men were denied an absolute definition at the very moment in which they sought absolute power. This, according to my reading of Freud, is how civilisation became neurotic.

Civilised authority rests on disembodied foundations: hypotheses, inferences, the premise of power. So civilisation (publicly, at least) took against sensuality. Women were long banned from the stage; Oliver Cromwell[100] banned theatre altogether; until the 1950s, naked women could only be presented to the public so long as they did not move.

After his 7088-mile, 999-day bisection of Africa, Henry Morton Stanley returned to England a foreigner. The words civilised men "uttered [were] without gesture…[and] immaculately clean." Contrasted to the white, crisp and unphysical, Stanley was now dirtied by gesture. Gestures are only made when you're desperate, or passionate, or on stage, or speaking an unknown language. Using the body to communicate thought was, for Stanley, a backward, near-savage step.

---

100 Oliver Cromwell (1599–1658) found God after a period of depression and financial difficulty. As MP for Cambridge, he rose through the ranks of the Parliamentary side of the English Civil War, becoming one of the big names in the New Model Army, a signatory on Charles I's death warrant, Rump Parliament bailiff and Lord Protector of Britain until his death. Not popular in Ireland.

Dr. Brown[101] is a clown. He's from America, though you wouldn't necessarily know this because he barely ever speaks. What he does do is play with the contagion of gesture. Dr. Brown's last show was called *Befrdfght*. In it, he performed a dumb show in which he impersonated a cow. This cow meets a bull at a disco. They make love and conceive a child, which the bull then abandons, leaving the cow alone with the baby. Later on in the night I saw *Befrdfght*, Dr. Brown brought up from the audience a burly, inebriated Scottish bloke in a tight-fitting rugby shirt – just the sort of man I would run five hundred miles to avoid annoying. With his stooge up on stage, Dr. Brown then repeated the bovine seduction scene, only this time playing the bull. The Scottish bloke became aware that he was expected to be the cow. As Dr. Brown grabbed his head from behind and started dry-humping him on the stage, the bloke faithfully reproduced all the gestures he'd seen 'the cow' make twenty minutes previously. He was left alone on stage, cradling his invisible calf, using his eyes in the plaintive, sensuous way he'd seen Dr. Brown use his.

The whole thing was miraculous. The Scottish bloke was the victim of a bull's advances and the audience's hysterical laughter. The scene was funny, though, not because we wanted him to look like a twat, but because Dr. Brown trusted this stranger to spontaneously perform a long and complex piece of clowning. Being molested by

---

101 Dr. Brown is the invention of Phil Burgers. *Befrdfght* won the 2012 Foster's comedy award at the Edinburgh Festival.

a sweaty, bearded lunatic dressed only in a loose kimono may not be everyone's idea of fun, but it wasn't the sexual content so much as the structural daring of the piece that amused me. After all, imagine if the bloke had refused to play along. *Befrdfght* was a leap of faith, and one infinitely satisfying to see being justified.

Nor was the scene sentimental. The Scottish bloke got a big hand and a hug, but never stopped being the victim. His happiness to be victimised and his evident joy at the loss of dignity, of authority, however, somehow made him his victimiser's equal. Not that I envied this equality. As G. Legman says of Dr. Milgram's experiment, the torturers' laughter was "the coefficient of their being torn between powerful identification with the human victim, and the willingness to continue torturing him." Watching the bloke, I was nervous – would I too be made to simulate cow-sex on stage? How could I refuse, given how demonstrably funny the simulation was? The success of the experiment would surely coerce me into self-abasement. Few people would fail to feel liberated by this realisation.

Text alone could never create a moment of this kind. We have a visual memory, an ability to repeat performances. I couldn't remember a joke without a sense of the performer's accent, gesture and rhythm. What we might call vernacular comedy – i.e. the jokes swapped between non-performers in a social setting – relies on short structures, like the question/answer model Sadowitz exploits. These jokes are seldom, if ever, learnt from text; authorless, they are 'boxed about' around in a kind of obscene relay.

If I remember a particularly good one, I do so because I enjoyed being told it, and covet the teller's power. Legman writes that:

> since the jokes are really only being repeated from previous listening, in the deepest sense *teller and listener are indivisible and identical.* The favourite jokes of one are – by & large – the favourite jokes of the other. Otherwise these jokes would not survive, through centuries and civilisations.

Oral storytelling relies on the performer's trust in their audience to affirm and re-enact the stories being told. For instance, Ruth Finnegan[102] writes that the Limba story-tellers from north Sierra Leone "regularly asked someone to act as their 'replier'...it meant that someone took responsibility for not just receiving but actively acknowledging and supporting the narrator." But really we're all repliers, whether or not we've been formally assigned the role. Sensation is non-consensual; like it or not, we become carriers of story's contagion.

Oral 'texts' have no one author. Homer was possibly hundreds of different people, stretched across centuries and millennia. The name 'Homer' is a gesture at purity, warding off the adulteries of multiple voices. And adultery worried Dr. Johnson. He sought to preserve only "*undefiled*" English, drawn from literature's big bang in

102 Ruth Finnegan is Emeritus Professor in the Faculty of Social Sciences at the Open University, or so my copy of *The Oral and Beyond* tells me.

the late sixteenth century, the purity of which had since succumbed to entropy. But no one wrote English. It's a consensus, a congruence, a crowd-surfing bastard borne along by euphoria and duty and fear. Slang is contagious. And even physical text is no exception to the rule that everything can be defiled.

However pure the content, a page remains a physical structure that can be used for distinctly non-literary purposes. In *Ulysses*, James Joyce's cuckolded protagonist Leopold Bloom wipes his arse with a newspaper. More recently, Snoop Dogg[103] has published a book of his lyrics, printed onto pages that will double as extra-large papers, bound to a spine that can strike matches. The message from the city of Compton is clear: words go up in smoke, it's the feeling that matters. You can't picture Dr. Johnson agreeing with D-O-double-G, despite marijuana's many palliative qualities.

How to keep corporeality from corrupting English? Johnson's solution was to exclude obscenities (mostly references to body parts) from the dictionary, that driest, most official of bodies. "What makes a word obsolete, more than general agreement to forbear it?" he asks in the *Preface*, hoping that, if a word is left unsaid, what it signifies might just go away. Sadly, history is not on

103 Snoop Lion – *née* Dogg – is a reedy-voiced Compton-based rapper, gentleman pornographer and Rastafarian. His debut album, *Doggystyle*, gave the world *Gin and Juice*, and has since gone quadruple platinum. *Doggystyle* always reminds me of the first girl I ever fancied, because she wore a t-shirt with the album cover on it. Perhaps a sinister garment for a twelve-year-old to sport. I should point out that I was also twelve when I fancied her.

Dr. Johnson's side. The Latin word for clitoris ('landica'), for instance, was pretty much the most offensive word in ancient Rome. We know this because 'landica' survives in only one text, the *Priapeia 79*, but Roman graffiti is full of it. We can deduce from this relationship between official abstinence and carnival obsession that the Roman ruling classes were happy not knowing where the clitoris was. Ordinary citizens, less so.

Comfortable silences are mutual. Johnson's 'agreement' is not. He's put the reader in a position where even to question forbearance is an admission of guilt. It's like if Dr. Johnson was the mother of your kids. One day, she says she's getting BT to filter out pornographic websites from your wifi. Now, obviously you don't want her to do this. Why does she think you've bought an iPad? To read *newspapers*? Grow up. iPads are for porn. But you can't say this. You could argue the case for freedom of information, but that'll sound very weak when it's set against the risk of your children turning into hollow-eyed sex maniacs. So you give in to Dr. Johnson, who's daring you to disagree with that flinty look she last gave on your anniversary when you suggested a rusty trombone (and if you don't know what that is, look it up online while you've got the chance).

The word 'pornography', incidentally, was invented to signify artwork discovered in the ruins of Pompeii. The volcano had preserved a goldmine of phalluses, group sex scenes and bestiality which – when unearthed – shocked nineteenth-century archaeologists by proving just how *normal* explicit content was in ancient Rome. Erotic art was socially desirable, a sign of class: the houses of the

Pompeian *nouveau riche*, for instance, are vulgar not for displaying pictures full of shagging, but for *positioning* them in the wrong place. The archaeologists, however, found the whole thing so depraved that they had their discoveries either destroyed or effectively reburied in the Cabinet of Obscene Objects, a room the Naples Archaeological Museum built to purpose.

'Pornography' is the linguistic equivalent of the Cabinet. Derived from the Greek for 'writing about prostitutes', the OED gives the word's first usage as being in 1842, when a *Dictionary of Greece and Roman Antiquity* lists it as one of "the lower classes of art." The next instance is taken from the *Telegraph*, which explains that "pictorial and glyptic 'pornography' grew, flourished, declined and fell with the Second Empire." Inverted commas lent pornography a newfangled air, even in 1882. The Cabinet of Obscene Objects had not disgorged its secrets. Nevertheless, scholars couldn't simply *ignore* evidence of the Romans' sexuality, though it destroyed the purity of 'Rome' as a neoclassical ideal. And the temptation to bring secrets to light – as with the temptation to tell a dirty joke – is usually overpowering.

You only have to watch *Candyman* to know that forbearance will always be broken, whatever the repercussions. In that movie, Candyman, a hook-handed outcast (think Abu Hamza[104] in a fur coat), comes back from the dead whenever someone says 'candyman'

104 Abu Hamza is the 'hook-handed hate cleric' extradited to America in 2012 on terror charges. Hamza blew both his hands off messing around with some landmines in the Soviet-Afghan war.

five times. Candyman then kills them in extravagantly nasty ways. He does this to become notorious; the more people who hear about him, the more who're tempted to say 'candyman' and suffer the consequences. Similarly, the German-language *Funny Games* was made in 1997. In 2005, Haneke made it again, this time in English, to offend people the language barrier might otherwise have left in peace.

Comedians like Jerry Sadowitz are candymen. The more people walk out, the more people walk in. Channel 4 seems to pursue an equally provocative policy. I was in a green room once, watching a show Jack and I had written being filmed. Sat next to me was a Channel 4 commissioner who (like most executives in green rooms)wasn't paying much attention. Then Jack said something like "which to choose?" The commissioner looked up. "Kill all the Jews? Very funny," they said, before returning to their Blackberry, happy in the knowledge that gags like that get people *talking*.

The BBC works differently, on a kind of obscenity exchange rate. In an interview he gave about *The Thick of It*, Armando Iannuci said "I was told if I wanted up to three cunts, I would have to get the fuck rate under one hundred per episode." Now, a hundred fucks in twenty-seven minutes *is* a lot, an approximate rate of 3.7 instances per minute of air time. To put that in perspective, Martin Scorsese's[105] film *Goodfellas* is notoriously obscene, but it

105 Martin Scorsese is the American director who made *Taxi Driver, Raging Bull, Goodfellas* and *The Departed.*

only racks up 296 fucks in 146 minutes, a paltry average of 2.02. But are obscenities so easily quantifiable? Are they like Pokemon? Is 'shit' a Pichu, the innocuous baby obscenity; 'fuck' the transitional monster, Pikachu; 'cunt', the shiny ultimate force of Raichu? Did I waste my youth? Whatever, obscenities have variable powers. The more taboo, the more tempting. The rarer, the better. So, yeah, they're *just* like Pokemon.

We are told we shouldn't say something so we say it. Basil Fawlty mentions the war. Two presenters on Radio 4 accurately, if accidently, labelled the then-Culture Secretary, Jeremy Hunt, as a cunt. They couldn't help themselves. The proximity of Culture to Hunt made 'cunt' a danger, and the danger made it irresistible. Obscenity is both attractive and bluntly obvious. I don't know if this is because what we find attractive's *traditionally* been considered obscene. If blue language wasn't offensive but the colour blue was, would we transfer our profane impulses onto something so purely abstract? In other words, do we respond to the content or the structure of obscenity?

Can you deconstruct obscenity? An extreme example: 16 Wardle Brook Avenue is the house in Hattersley, Greater Manchester, where Ian Brady and Myra Hindley[106] murdered two of their victims. When they raided it, the police also discovered their last victim's

106 Between 1963–65, Ian Brady and Myra Hindley murdered five children. They're known as the Moors murderers because they buried at least three of their victims on Saddleworth Moor. Hindley died in 2002. Brady is still alive.

body, which Brady and Hindley had not yet disposed of. 16 Wardle Brook Avenue was subsequently demolished. This demolition was quite reasonable. Who would want to live in that house? But the stench of what was done in that *site* is impossible to erase.

Persecution, prosecution, increase the status of the offender. Nick Griffin is offensive, but he's lent an added power every time someone attempts to censor him. 'Saying the unsayable' is powerful, whether it's said on stage at the Soho Theatre or on a couple of rotten pallets somewhere in the disenfranchised skirts of Barking. Why else would Griffin cultivate the image of his being the victim of some grand conspiracy, unless he didn't understand that – stripped of hyperbole and taboo – the BNP are fucking pathetic?

Like a flasher exposing his penis, the reality is often laughably less threatening than the shadowy potential. Or so my mother tells me. That's why BNP members were outraged when a list of party members was leaked in 2008. Suddenly, their secret was out. Anyone could now see who belonged to a party that door-steps voters, not with manifestos, but with supersoakers full of human shit. ('What are you doing in the dark, Daddy?' 'Go to sleep, Winston.' 'But why are you taking my supersoaker?' 'It's for work.' 'Why do you need a supersoaker to drive a taxi, Dad?' 'We're having a waterfight at the depot.' 'Oh. So why are your hands covered in shit?' – and isn't it ironic that taxi drivers use more of their brains' capacity than anyone else, and yet so many of their sentences start 'I'm not a racist, *but...*'?)

In his documentary *Into The Abyss*, Werner Herzog shows a graveyard full of death row inmates who'd been executed by the state of Texas. Their graves were unmarked; their names being synonymous with their sins, each criminal was expunged from written history. And yet a human body lay rotting underneath every blank crucifix. Knowing this, the graveyard became a site of curiosity: what did these people do, what did they *mean*? And doesn't the suppression of crime make crime more intriguing than it deserves to be?

Dr. Johnson wanted to exclude 'bad' words from the map of the English language. But the structure he used to do this was compromised, in that a dictionary invites us to seek the offensive. Johnson couldn't stop readers *looking*. As Montaigne points out, some obscenities are so natural that to exclude them would be laughable. Hence, in Johnson's dictionary, the terse definition of 'testicle' as "a stone". Now, a testicle is not a stone. If you called a stone a testicle, people would think you were either mad or trying to be funny. A "stone" is not a definition, then, but a euphemism, slippery, hazy, lazy and complicit.

Euphemisms are amusing. Seeing someone be explicit is never as funny seeing someone trying *not* to be explicit. As the South African author J.M. Coetzee[107] writes, "a censor pronouncing a ban…is like a man trying to stop his penis from standing up. The spectacle is ridiculous."

107 John Coetzee has won the Nobel Prize for literature. He is the best living, practising author in the English language. Coetzee's precision has reached the miraculous: he conveys whole ethical lives in a single comma.

Largely (or not so largely) because all you're thinking about when you're trying not to think about your penis is your penis your penis your penis your penis. Shit, candyman's come.

In *The Psychiatrists*, Basil Fawlty[108] is uneasy about two psychiatrists staying in his hotel because he thinks they'll scrutinise his sex life. Another guest, Mr. Johnson, becomes Basil's scapegoat for these anxieties. Fawlty becomes convinced Johnson is trying to smuggle women into the hotel. His attempts to prove this end in Basil tangling (often literally) with yet another guest, a pretty Australian woman. As he gets more and more desperate to prove that he's not a sex case, Basil gets himself into situations that – in the eyes of his wife and the psychiatrists – prove he definitely *is* one. The episode ends with Basil gathering everyone outside Johnson's room to reveal the woman Johnson has been sleeping with. Johnson says the woman is his mother. Basil calls Johnson's bluff. Then he's presented with Johnson's actual mother.

This episode of *Fawlty Towers* is not offensive. Rather, it's the comedy of offence. Basil's farcical fear of sexual honesty exposes the futility of repression. Freudian slips give way to the equally Freudian conclusion: confronted with the mother, apparently the source of all his sexual anxiety, Basil collapses into what the script describes as "the foetal position." That Basil is actually *right* (Johnson

108 Basil Fawlty is played by John Cleese, who wrote *Fawlty Towers* with Connie Booth. The BBC almost didn't make it after an in-house script editor described the pilot script as "dire...a collection of cliches and stock characters which I can't see being anything but a disaster."

does smuggle a girlfriend up to his room) is irrelevant. Jacques Lacan[109] says that, even if a man's partner is genuinely adulterous, his jealousy is *still* pathological – i.e. a product of his own mind and not the situation he finds himself in. Basil is *obsessed* with sex and its concealment. This particular guest has simply provided Fawlty with the rope he needs to hang himself.

Roland Barthes[110] says that "neither culture nor its destruction is erotic; it is the seam between them, the fault, the flaw, which becomes so." A sadist gets turned on by enacting the destruction of the person they love. We laugh at the violence done to meaning, to morality, to the fault line between said and unsaid. Blindfolds are scary, sexy, funny; they make us navigate *bodily*, by scent, by taste. We enjoy trust, both the giving and the breaking.

To substitute a euphemism for a definition is to drive a flaw between writer and reader. Both parties know what a testicle is; the reader wants the writer to say what it is, and the writer refuses to do so on the basis that the reader already knows. It's the relationship Thom Gunn[111]

---

109 Jacques Lacan (1901–81) was a French post-structuralist psychoanalyst. More of him in a bit.

110 Roland Barthes (1915–80) was a French literary theorist and semotician. My favourite book of his is *Camera Ludica*, a meditation on photography, memory and grief written in the wake of Barthes' mother's death. Also, 1980–1 was a shitty year for French intellectuals: Sartre, Lacan and Barthes all died. Barthes was knocked down by a laundry van, but the other two – maybe the CIA poisoned some natty suits or Gauloises or something?

111 Thom Gunn (1929–2004) was an English poet who moved to San Francisco and never looked back. He died as a consequence of substance abuse. Gunn specialised in brief, spare poems, many of which are extraordinarily moving.

describes in his poem *Carnal Knowledge*: "I know that you know that I know that you know that I know." It's asterisks all over again.

My favourite examples of this carnal relationship come from Francis Grose's[112] *Classical Dictionary for a Vulgar Tongue* (1796). The book has a superficially ideological purpose. "The freedom of thought and speech arising from, and privileged by, our constitution," the British Grose writes in his wartime preface, "gives a force and poignancy to the expressions of our common people, not to be found under arbitrary governments", or, more specifically, revolutionary France. Even billingsgate – the "fugitive cant" named after the London market and its fish-guts gutter – is qualitatively better than French, because at least English working class words are scapegoated by *legitimate* power.

Jingoism aside, the *Classical Dictionary* is really an entertainment, and it plays up to its audience's desire for the obscene. Hence Grose's playful definition of 'turd' (or "T—d"), in which the obscenity is both absent and present:

> There were four t—ds for dinner; stirt t—d, hold t—d, tread t—d, and must-t—d; to whit, a hog's face, feet, and chitterlings, with musturd [sic – perhaps a playful one].

---

112 Francis Grose (c. 1761–91) was a soldier, antiquarian and father to ten children. No doubt he drew a lot of his vulgarities from his time in the dragoons. He died suddenly in Dublin.

Grose knows what a turd is. So does the reader. Both probably do one every day. What pleases us is the dictionary maker's refusal to meet his reader's eye – for fear, perhaps, of laughing. It's a play of open secrets which, in Italian, Spanish and French, are called 'pulcinella secrets' in reference to the *commedia dell'arte* character's comic device, wherein he'd feign ignorance in a situation that made ignorance impossible. The example of a heavily pregnant woman denying all knowledge of her condition is suggested by the French slang for pregnancy: a 'pulcinella secret'.

So Grose's dictionary flirts with transgression. But it seems to reach its limit with the word 'cunt', for which it gives the following definition:

> C**t...The χόννος of the Greek, and the cunnus of the Latin dictionaries; a nasty name for a nasty thing.

Grose allows himself to write the word in ancient Greek and Latin, so that his more educated readers get the drift. But to put such a thing in vernacular English is beyond him (as it's beyond twenty-first century spell-check). That 'cunt' is an ancient word, to be found four to six thousand years ago in Proto-Indo-European, and that it has close, still-existent equivalents in Czech, Persian and Hittite, doesn't stop it from being beyond the pale.

Grose's using classical languages to privilege an elite predates D.H. Lawrence's[113] belief that his notoriously

113 D.H. Lawrence (1885–1930) was an English writer. Surprisingly for a

obscene *Lady Chatterley's Lover* was "far too good...for the gross public." It was intended for "the right sort of people in the Universities" – a strangely snobbish attitude, given that the novel's climax comes with a gamekeeper buggering an aristocrat. Did Lawrence believe that "the right sort" are impervious to filth which would indelibly stain Joe Soap? The clue's maybe in how Lady Chatterley feels during anal sex:

> She would have thought a woman would have died of shame. Instead of which, the shame died. Shame, which is fear: the deep organic shame.

The gamekeeper is working-class, but it's not his social identity that makes him Lady Chatterley's liberator. Connie is cleansed through submission. Is Mellors then the embodiment of obscenity as liberation? Or does his power lie in his unfettered masculinity? Lady Chatterley's husband is a cripple; Mellors, the strong, fecund, outdoorsy kinda guy who won't be denied. Is there also the suspicion that Lady Chatterley in some sense 'transcends' her femininity? Anal has obvious homosexual associations. It's a thing men do. That "deep organic shame" belongs to the nasty, to the unnameable. So is doing it like a dude all Connie's empowerment

---

man so associated with sexual obscenity, Lawrence considered wanking "perhaps the deepest and most dangerous cancer of our civilisation." I don't know if Freud would agree; smoking, his wank-deterrent, killed him with cancer. I also don't know how well back-references in footnotes work.

amounts to? The overwhelmingly male population of "the Universities" might like to think so.

In *After Theory*, Terry Eagleton[114] writes that "language in the eyes of the fundamentalist is far too fecund, forever spawning and proliferating…the desire for purity is the desire for non-being." Now, it's ludicrous to imply that Dr. Johnson was a fundamentalist. Being a suicide bomber in the eighteenth century would have been a much trickier proposition than it is today. Everyone would just ask you why you've got a primed cannon concealed in your breeches. Even if you managed to waddle into the middle of Billingsgate, the delay between lighting the fuse and the cannon's combustion would be enough for most of the infidel to scatter into nearby coffee shops, theatres and stews. That said, those who try to legislate the lives of others generally do so because they don't trust those lives to regulate themselves. More, because they don't really trust life itself.

Hegel said of the Encyclopaedia that "this pure Being [is] pure abstraction and consequentially absolute negation," and the same charge can be levelled at dictionaries. Both are forms of quarantine.

Purity is a product of fear. An authority is afraid of a thing being corrupted, of being led astray. To prevent this (this loss of power), the thing is abstracted from contagious, adulterant life. And to abstract a thing is kind of to kill it.

---

114 Terry Eagleton is a Marxist literary critic, currently teaching at Lancashire University.

Dictionaries try to bottle language, to stopper the Protean, ever-evolving waves of socio-historical thought which crash around each and every word in the language. Dictionaries are Cnuts.

If proliferation is the enemy, it's no wonder sex was so unpopular. Montaigne asks "what harm has the genital act, so natural, so necessary, and so lawful, done to humanity, that we dare not speak of it without shame [whereas] we boldly utter the words, kill, rob, betray." Maybe, though, the situation is more complex than that. Starting with 'vagina' (Latin for the scabbard of a sword – a charming image), parts of our anatomy have been given names either deriving from, or going on to signify violence, anti-sociability, stupidity, crime and punishment. Just as Dr. Johnson does in his Preface, living bodies are associated with degeneracy and decay.

Jonathon Green's *Dictionary of Slang* (2010) shows this trend working its way down the human body. 'Booby' and 'boob', for instance, come from the Spanish word 'bobo', which means 'fool'. By the end of the nineteenth century, 'booby' was slang for a prison in Australia, where 'boob-dot' signified a small blue tattoo under the eye of an ex-con (fairly ubiquitous, you'd think, in that part of the world). In the UK, 'booby-hatch' derived from the criminal asylum in Colney Hatch. In America, a boo-boo is a mistake and booboo is a black person. So why was it that 'booby' was first used to mean breasts in the 1910s, only *after* it had gained most of these, mostly negative, connotations?

'Bum' is echoic, i.e. derived from the sound of a gesture made against that part of the body. It's first recorded in 1363, during a lament about Job's[115] piles – "it semeth that his bom is oute that hath that euel [evil]". From around 1650 to the end of the eighteenth century, it signified the vagina (as in Persian, where *kos* signifies the vulva and *kun* signifies the anus, with both deriving from the same root). Around that same time, 'bum' also came to signify a tramp, a thief and general worthlessness.

'Pussy', meanwhile, is first used to signify a vagina in 1699. It's gone on to mean women, cowards (see, too, 'pussyclart' and 'clart' in general), homosexuals, anuses, and that meddling old pussy Miss Marple[116]. My favourite contemporary variation is 'bowlcat', used to describe a guy who likes giving girls head. The insult lies in the position the eager cunnilinguist is thought to adopt: submissive, on all fours, tongue out, a pussy slurping a pussy like it's a hairy bowl of milk. No wonder Dizzee Rascal[117] has to assure his listeners that he ain't no bowlcat, a relief to everyone, I'm sure, except whichever lucky lady Diz is squiring at the time. Not that cunnilinguiphobia is unique to Mr. Rascal. The baths at Pompeii house the only surviving Roman depiction of a man giving a woman head. The bowlcat is pathetic and fully-clothed; the woman, strong, calm, gratified. The ancient taboo is broken so totally (and the role-reversal is

115 Job is a Biblical character who suffers horribly after God and Satan make a bet on whether his faith would crack under pressure.
116 Miss Marple – the poor man's Poirot.
117 Dizzee Rascal is a popular British 'grime' artist, grandpa.

so shocking) that we assume the artist wanted to make people laugh and that obscenities were permitted if sufficiently 'comic'.

Sex is like a war. There's a lot of attrition – you really have to wear your enemy down sometimes – and it mostly happens in France.

Heckler: Hack.

So is the French language shameless? Hardly. The French word 'putain' means a progression of 'whore', 'hooker', 'bitch', 'bloody' and 'fuck' (its most familiar usage today). Whereas our 'fuck' is ungendered, the French explicitly label women fucks and any fucking thing becomes feminine by association.

European civilisation associates destabilisation with the female body. Le Corbusier[118] ascribed feminine proportions to the unsanitary, prostitute-riddled slums of Barcelona's Raval district. He filled notebooks with sketches of women as he considered ways to 'mop up' the sexualised square kilometre lying between Barcelona and its health. Raval was 'hysterical', a word that derives from the Greek '*husterikos*' ('of the womb'). For centuries, hysteria signified the mental health problems that doctors thought almost exclusive to her indoors. Laughter, too, is hysterical – uncontrollable, unbecoming, suggestive.

118 Le Corbusier (1887–1965) was born Charles-Édouard Jeanneret-Gris. Most famous perhaps for his solutions to housing urban populations, Le Corbusier's elegantly megalomaniac ideas about urban design can be found in *The Radiant City* (1935).

Its 'source', the female reproductive system, was the nasty thing that we did and do gloss over; in the 'decent' imagination, the female body is Barbie-like thanks to the smooth, perineal silence that's been stretched over its groin.

As colonialists discovered in Africa, you can do whatever you like with a blank page. Similarly, a vagina has been what men make of it. It's an asterisk or (in the words of Natalie Angier[119]) "a Rorschach[120] on legs," able to signify "practically anything you want, need or dread." And what do men dread? The loss of control. Do they also generally want and need sex? Yes. That's why, for Freud, "sexuality and obscenity offer the amplest occasions for obtaining comic pleasure... for they can show human beings in their dependence on bodily needs." Neverthless, cunts remain mainstream comedy's last taboo – unsurprisingly, given that mainstream comedy remains an overwhelmingly male profession. Yes, you can be a cock, a dick and a prick, but those are (somewhat illogically) softer insults. You don't call someone a cunt and you never, ever joke about periods.

---

119 Natalie Angier is a Pulitzer Prize-winning American journalist and writer.

120 Hermann Rorschach (1884–1922) was a Swiss psychoanalyst who developed the projective inkblot test that bears his name. He asked his patients to respond to ambiguous images; their responses were then analysed for subconscious associations. As Google Images testifies, Rorschach himself looked like Brad Pitt, or a cowboy in a starched collar. A shifting Rorschach motif, meanwhile, swirls across the mask of the superhero Rorschach in Alan Moore's *The Watchmen*.

The first recorded use of the word 'cunt' in English is in the thirteenth century, when many of the major English cities had a street called Gropecuntlane. Did the taboo begin there, then, on streets which served much the kind of function you'd imagine they would with a name like that? Or is it that men find sex offensive because they can't always obtain it via commodified exchange? Certainly, you can buy access to cunts. Look at the pages of *Hello!* – some twats are only too happy to open up for money. But there's a reason that sex is the thing everyone loves, but which no one wants to do professionally. To use a prostitute is (to paraphrase Montaigne) 'to kill, rob and betray.' Consensual sex requires, however briefly, a yielding, a love. And love, like laughter, is a force you can't control, however big your sword.

A brief dialectic:

Plato[121]: Socrates, can I ask you something?
Socrates[122]: Of course, lad.

---

121 Plato (c. 428–348 BC) was a student of Socrates, and wrote the thirty-six Socratic dialogues. 'Platonism' is the prioritisation of Forms over material reality. This idea is a descendant of Socrates' cave story. As Socrates described it, the prisoners of this cave see shadows, cast in fire and projected onto the walls of the cave. They treat the shadows as reality, whereas reality is in fact situated *outside* of the cave (their prison, their perception). Plato taught Aristotle and, apparently, died in bed while a young Thracian girl played him the flute. Not a bad way to go.

122 Our knowledge of Socrates (c. 469–399 BC) comes mostly from the writing of Plato and Xenophon. Socrates was sentenced to death by the Athenian state for the crimes of blasphemy and corrupting the young. He drank hemlock. Socrates and Plato are a kind of Xavi and Iniesta, passing the ball between them before feeding it to Aristotle's Messi. Definitely.

Plato: Well, there's this girl –

Socrates: Tight cooch?

Plato: I don't really know.

Socrates: Well, check. I fell in love with a girl once. Big mistake. Fanny like a donkey's laugh.

Plato: Um, that doesn't answer my question.

Socrates: My, this *is* complex.

Plato: You see, she wants to rush things. She says I can touch it.

Socrates: Oi oi.

Plato: But I want to be her soul mate, not her gigglestick.

Socrates: Look, Plato, you have to remember that in our male-dominated culture, where you live and die by the swords you spit, a bitch is a bitch.

The DJ whips up an old-school, horn-driven beat. The crowd goes wild.

Socrates: Now I know that I know
Nothing noble or good
Cos I think about fucking
More'n any man should.
So I know I know shit
'Cept what I need
I need your pussy and your mouth
Going down on me.

Plato: Now you know I'm a G
I smoke green by the tree,
But you need to see
Truth ain't in pussy.

Socrates: I know you high on something.
Plato: I'm balls deep in thought.
Socrates: I'm balls deep in bitches.
Plato: Got the itches –
Socrates: Get checked out.
Plato: S'my brain I'm talkin' 'bout.
I'm a thinking man –
Socrates: I'm not a gentle
Babe, I'm a method man.
I'm empirical
In purple and my tongue is lyrical.
Plato: Look at Helen of Troy.
She got up on them boys,
Soldiers, G, set on self-destroy.
Now don't get me wrong,
There's honour in death.
But a bitch is a killer
Worse than crystal meth.
Socrates: Don't want no death and honour
Just wanna be up on her
Elevating my soul
Filling all the holes
In my knowledge of life.
Gonna take a fucking wife
And another –
I'll take yours for a lover.
Cos I seek a higher form
On a quest to be reborn
In a pussy other'n my mother's,
Maybe your'n.

Plato: Don't be fronting, G.
Physicality's transitory.
Cos you start to want more
Quick as tits hit the floor
So let the spirit soar
Away from corruption
Emotional destruction
Sexual eruption –
Follow my instruction.

Socrates: A bitch is a bitch.
She got her lips round my dick
That's the fucking trick.
Cup the balls, see it all
In harmony.
The universe and me
Agree you good on your knees.
I'm about to come, my
Teeth go gritty-gritty,
Hand on your titty-titty, and
My ideal of the ethical plane of beauty
Aligns with my fingers *[spits]* up your booty.

Both: A bitch is a bitch.

The song ends.

Socrates: So shall we have sex?

Plato: Well, I'm a young boy with a thirst for knowledge.

Socrates: I'm an old man with a thirst for young boys.

Plato: So having sex couldn't be more normal.

Socrates: Because remember, Plato…
Plato: It's only gay if you come in me.
Socrates: Or if you cry.
Plato: I'll try not to this time.

*

J.M. Coetzee says that "the experience or premonition of being robbed of power seems to me intrinsic to all instances of taking offense." This takes us back to Middle England's favourite tactic, the way it makes a land-grab for the margins in order better to assert and protect its power. But there's another reason being offended is to occupy a position of strength. Namely, that the offended party sets the terms of the crime that's been committed against them.

I once offended a German by quoting *Fawlty Towers* to him. We were at a mutual friend's house, and (being a wind-bag) I'd started a conversation about architecture in Berlin. Unfortunately, a lot of architecture in Berlin is interesting because it deals with the legacy of the Second World War. I'd got on to how Hitler's bunker was now covered over by an incongruous Astroturf football pitch when I stopped myself and apologised. He asked me why I was apologising. I said because I've always assumed Germans are just *bored* of the war now; when I talk to a German, I said, I'm like Basil Fawlty, telling myself not to mention it. He said he didn't know who Basil Fawlty was. I explained the scene to him. By way of demonstration, I did the Hitler mime, with one hand saluting, one hand the moustache. He stared at me. He said, 'I'm very offended.'

I tried to worm my way out of this situation by saying that *quoting* something offensive doesn't make the *quoter* themselves offensive. The Berliner replied that it was his prerogative to say who and what was offensive. And most people sided with him, not because he was the victim, but because he had all the *status*. Either that, or I'd been a real dick.

Power lies not in the content being repressed, but in the act of repression. Contraband (alcohol, drugs, weapons) has little value in and of itself; it's the structure of distribution that rival forces fight to control. The same substance can be legal in one country and illegal in another; in the 1920s, the hotels of Calais were littered with copies of *Ulysses*, as the ferry back to Britain would turn a novel into an obscenity, punishable by law. Offenders are judged by the body they offend.

Michael Foot[123] was a member of the Joint Select Committee that oversaw the abolition of the Lord Chamberlain's right to censor drama. At the second reading of the Theatres Act on February 23rd 1968, Foot reminded the MPs present that "political fears" and not "the alleged obscenity" are "the main cause of censorship." The reading itself was almost too badly attended to

123 Michael Foot (1913–2010) was a Labour MP for a combined forty-two years. He was Leader of the Opposition in the 1983 election, when Labour received its lowest percentage of the vote since 1918. The '83 Labour manifesto was memorably described as "the longest suicide note in history." He edited *Tribune*, wrote a biography of Jonathan Swift and loathed Rupert Murdoch.

go ahead, though that says more about theatre's waning significance than any decrease in anxiety felt by the authorities.

Edward Bond's[124] 1965 play *Saved* may've featured a baby being stoned to death, but it only happened once a night for 'the right sort' of audience at the Royal Court. Back in 1960, the film *Peeping Tom*[125] centred on a young man who filmed himself murdering women (predating Haneke's *Benny's Video* by some thirty years). Thanks to technology and mass distribution, the movie was available to "the gross public" in a way that theatre can't be. Censors and politicians had to move with the times.

Different media go out of fashion. The reasons we're offended never do. Neither does the impulse to legislate exhaustively against (or around) transgression. Michel Foucault[126] writes that:

> what is peculiar…is not that [European societies] consigned sex to a shadow existence, but that they dedicated themselves to speaking about it ad infinitum, while exploiting it as *the* secret.

---

124 Edward Bond is a British playwright. An uncompromising writer and director, Bond has been frozen out by most of the major theatres in Britain. He now collaborates with amateur groups, most frequently with the theatre-in-education group Big Brum (named after its hometown, Birmingham). Bond does not seem to regret this, but we will.

125 *Peeping Tom* (1960) was written by Second World War cryptographer Leo Marks and directed by the great Michael Powell. The scandal created by *Peeping Tom* destroyed Powell's career.

126 Michel Foucault (1926–1984) was a theorist and historian. Foucault wrote about how power works. He was the first French public figure to die from an AIDS-related illness.

Most of us like sex. Sex, therefore, is a very good way of controlling us. Sensuality has been 'civilised', tamed (in theory) by a myriad of hypotheses, prohibitions and exhortations to describe and recant our desires. Prohibited content excites us. The structure of prohibition is geared to capitalise on this excitement. Francis Grose's *Classical Dictionary* advertises his publishing stablemates, including "A Caveat for Common Cursetors, The Canting Academy...[and] The Scoundrel's Dictionary." 'Billingsgate' was a mass market: there was money in obscenity. Is it too much to suggest that similarly transgressive markets are permitted to distract people from the damage done by the *system* of markets? We enjoy breaking the law too much to question the law's existence.

Sex is sensual. To 'civilise' it, sexuality was given an ethical dimension. To want x was permitted; to want y, prohibited. There's nothing "organic" about Lady Chatterley's shame – a 'normal' sex life was defined, not on the grounds of any 'natural' law, but by power's proclivities. Everyone was a sinner pretty much by default. Thoughts, even dreams, became crimes. The only way to 'normalise' your desire was to create a *useful* relationship. Married couples were exempt from condemnation because marriage was a legal premise, accessible only through the law and the church. Married sex affirmed both. Married couples also had children, which meant more workers.

But your desires could still be offensive even *within* wedlock. The law kept you on your toes. People's innermost lives were a battlefield between good and evil, sane and insane. Illegality aroused us; arousal made us guilty. The good man's desires (spontaneous, helpless as laughter) degraded him and excluded him from heaven. And where could he atone for his perverted-by-default self? Within the asterisk of authority.

Nothing haunts authority like doubt. Photographs of Jesse James's[127] corpse circulated around America as proof of wrongdoing's finitude and the invincibility of good. This man is *definitively* dead. More recently, the corpse of Osama bin Laden has been broadcast in all its explicit detail. But, just as Johnson's 'testicle' tries to neuter the obscene, so too do these images fail to prevent multiple interpretations. If anything, they make people *more* suspicious – you don't need to be a whizz at Photoshop to know that every image is questionable, particularly when it's reproduced by the world's biggest superpower for conspicuously ideological purposes. (Having said that, the photos of Osama weren't as absurd as his 'burial'. Is there anything less convincing than the US military's being culturally sensitive? What's that, you say? An *imam* was present? Well, that's put any questions I had about bin Laden's death to bed. If Osama wasn't kicked off that warship in a sack full of turds, then I'm a Chinaman.)

---

127 Jesse James (1847–82) was an American outlaw. Glamorised and demonised by the media in equal measure, James robbed trains and banks with his gang. He was shot in the back by Robert Ford, who was pardoned. Ford's own murderer was also pardoned, thanks to a public petition.

Foucault quotes a manual given to Catholic confessors in the nineteenth century. Their mission? To be left in no doubt. They had to demand the penitent sinner described their "bad gestures" with an explicitness that would – if taken out of their officially-sanctioned context – sound obscene. As a result, this manual sounds like instructions on how to run a sex line. A confessor asks the sinner:

- Exactly what he was thinking at the time of the pollution.
- Whether he made use of any instrument.
- Whether he made use of the hand of another.
- Which part of the body was used to make the gesture.
- Was the reason for using this part of the body uniquely for reasons of utility, or was it reasons of particularity?

Doubt is the fault-line between body and soul. Confessors' questions aim not to close the gap, but to wrench, abstract the sinner from themselves. It's not the body (the corpse) that has power, it's the soul that *uses* it; your body may belong to you, but your soul belongs to God. Your reality on earth becomes one of shame, of alienation and self-hatred. This situation drives you to seek consolation in the church, the body that's set the terms against which you've offended.

The penitent is required to be explicit about their gestures because, as I said earlier, gestures are sensual. They need 'civilised' readings imposed upon them. Only, all kinds of authorities are competing to read the same gesture. Saul Williams'[128] lyrics in *Penny For A Thought* illustrate this:

> An MC told a crowd of hundreds to put their
> hands in the air
> An armed robber stepped into a bank and told
> everyone to put their hands in the air
> A Christian minister gives his benediction while
> the congregation hold their hands in the air
> Love: the image of the happy Buddha with his
> hands in the air.
> Hands up!

To confess one's sins is to renounce multiple interpretations. This *was* bad. I *am* bad. This gesture – this body – belongs to *your* discourse (and not to me). There are no extenuating circumstances, no rival definitions, permitted within the confessional. Leftfield sex lives aside, Catholic priests and the Marquis de Sade[129] make for odd bedfellows. Nevertheless, confession shares a central tenant of Sade's pornographic 'narrations': the "willingness to disguise no circumstances." In the confessional, silence is the only taboo.

---

128 Saul Williams is a musician and poet from New York. As Nas said, "Saul is every kind of great artist combined into one."

129 Donatien Alphonse François, the Marquis de Sade (1740–1814) was a French revolutionary, writer and libertine. He spent thirty-two years of his life in prisons (including the Bastille) and an asylum. Napoleon ordered his arrest for writing his 'libertine novels'. These included *120 Days of Sodom*, which Sade hoped to be "the most impure tale that has ever been written since the world exists."

Obscenity – far from being "suffered to perish" – is at the centre of faith. And the desire to find God through the body (the rejection of ours, the consuming of Christ's) has sometimes been taken so literally as to seem rather smutty. It's Cartman's[130] logic when, in one episode of *South Park*, he starts a Christian band. "You don't know anything about Christianity," Stan tells him. "I know enough to exploit it," he replies, and he does. Cartman's plan is to take existing love songs and make them about Jesus simply by substituting 'Jesus' for words like 'you' and 'baby'. His lyrics ("I want to feel you deep inside, Jesus") are a huge hit with Christians, who only turn against Cartman when he starts swearing on stage – that is, to literally invoke the act his audience can only express through officially-permitted, shadowy inferences.

Cartman's songs have historical precedent: Medieval England saw a pageant of kinky mystics fantasising about penetrating Jesus. In the saucily-titled *Prickynge of Love*, its fourteenth-century author envies the weapons that wounded the body of Christ on the cross. The author longs to be inside "[Christ's] opening…in stede of that spere." Elsewhere, Margery Kempe[131], a sort of

130 Eric Cartman is a fat schoolboy anti-hero in Trey Parker and Matt Stone's cartoon *South Park*. Cartman hates being the butt of a joke. In one episode, he is sold some pubes by an older boy called Scott Tenorman. When Cartman discovers that *owning* pubes does not make him pubic, and that he's been duped, he exacts his revenge by feeding Tenorman his own parents.

131 Margery Kempe (c. 1373–1438) was a middle-class woman, the daughter of a well-to-do mayor. During her first pregnancy (one of fourteen), Kempe started to see devils. Her wild mental state led her to be chained up for six months. In later life, she travelled on extremely

dishevelled Susan Boyle[132] figure from the same period, is told by Jesus in one of her visions that "thou mayst boldly take me in thy armys & kyssen my mowth…as sweetly as thow wylt." Oi oi! She certainly dreamed a dream *that* night.

A fifteenth-century woodcut (referred to as the 'Washington woodcut'[133]) is even more explicit. It claims to depict "the length and width of Christ's wound which was pierced in his side on the Cross." Unless I'm going mad, the image itself looks like nothing more or less than a vagina. Who's with me? No one? The text beneath this "opening" (it's a fanny), meanwhile, promises that "whoever kisses this wound with remorse…will have seven years of indulgence from Pope Innocent [VIII]." The deal being that you go to church for *everything*. Bowlcats have to transfer their physical need onto the Son of Man's sinless vagina, rather than some Eve's rather more shop-soiled clopper.

Sensuality is the enemy of paternalistic civilisation. Civilisation has responded by keeping its friends close and its enemies closer. Obscenity has been harnessed by the disembodied powers that control us. What can we do to

---

far-flung pilgrimages to holy sites around Europe and Asia. She dictated *The Book of Margery Kempe* to two separate male scribes.

132 Susan Boyle is this shock-haired Scottish chanteuse who rose to fame with her rendition of *I Dreamed A Dream* on *Britain's Got Talent*.

133 A German woodcut in the National Gallery in Washington, DC. Christ's wound is tilted on its end; a white cross is drawn in the middle of the red opening, giving a lip-like look to the flesh. To prove that I'm not insane, Amy Hollywood comments on the woodcut's "startling… vulvic/vaginal resonances" in an essay called *That Glorious Slit*.

free ourselves from the ethical narratives imposed on the way we use ourselves?

Comedy originated in religiously-sanctioned festivals in which giant phalluses were waved around by shepherds, philosophers, Cyclopes and the like. In *The Origin of Attic Comedy*, Francis Macdonald Cornford[134] says that these big dicks were *both* negative and positive symbols. How? Cornford says that "the simplest of all methods of expelling malign influences is to abuse them with the most violent language." The phalluses were a visual, performative part of that language. But do obscenities still expel malign influences on our lives? Or does obscene pleasure actually trick us into conforming with a culture of malignity?

Neil Hamburger is a comic character created by Gregg Turkington[135]. Hamburger stands on stage, clutching three glasses of scotch as he delivers breathtakingly offensive jokes in a garbled parody of the smooth American punchline style. He relies on a call-and-response formula ('why...' or 'what...' or 'when...') similar to those jokes you find in crackers. A sample of his comedy is this:

> What do you get when you cross a sabre-toothed tiger with Sir Elton John? I don't know, but whatever it is, you better keep it away from your ass.

134 Francis Macdonald Cornford (1874–1943) was a British scholar and fellow of Trinity College, Cambridge. He married Charles Darwin's granddaughter, Frances.

135 Gregg Turkington is an American comedian who seems to have played in every obscure 90s San Francisco-based avante-garde/no wave/punk band ever.

Why is that funny? For me, it's because the structure fails. There is no answer, only prejudice (and an amusingly weird mental image). Within the timeframe specific to celebrity-bashing in comedy, Elton John's as dated as Hamburger's hideous suit, making homophobia feel both antiquated *and* hideous. The joke's also satisfying because – by attacking fairly innocuous celebrities with an unbridled vitriol – Hamburger frustrates his audience's desire to hear someone abused. His targets don't warrant violence. His desire to commit violence becomes pathetic and self-lacerating. He hurts himself and we laugh.

Hamburger's every gesture is calculated to repel. The less the audience enjoy it, the better. When he asks "why did Michael Jackson[136] dangle his infant son from a hotel balcony?" and then answers "because the little lad hadn't finished eating his plate of semen," the joke doesn't really attack either Michael Jackson or any of his bizarrely-named children. It's illogically offensive; it makes us question the weapon, not the victim.

As Sadowitz achieves too much with the cracker-joke formula, Hamburger achieves too little. Everything about his material is crap. The Jackson joke's failed topicality signifies a lazy routine; the lame attempt at observational comedy (why don't children eat their food?) is a shoehorn onto which Hamburger hangs this shabby nonsense. The blunt, tedious substance on the plate belies the blunt, tedious mind that would describe it, and the blunt,

136 Michael Jackson (1958–2009) was an American singer whose life resembled the plot of some Gothic novel.

tedious minds that would find the description funny at face value.

Trauma has a positive value. As James Gleick's[137] book *The Information* points out, in the first half of the twentieth century it became clear that words like 'mass', 'energy' and 'wave' could no longer contain the mysterious 'forces' they'd been assigned to signify. Then, in 1931, an Austrian mathematician called Kurt Gödel[138] showed that things could be true and not provable. Numbers were inconstant. Taken apart, abstracted from themselves, they could not always be put back together again. The paper in which Gödel demonstrated this was addressed to Bertrand Russell's[139] *Principia Mathematica*, a three-volume treatise designed to prove that everything obeyed a logical system, and that maths was perfectible. In its own way, the *Principia Mathematica* was a dictionary, seeking to place the most recalcitrant problems in a framework that could control their chaotic energy. In an act of patricide, Gödel exploded this certainty. Numbers, he said, have secret lives.

---

137 James Gleick is a best-selling American science writer and journalist.

138 Kurt Gödel (1906–78) published his incompleteness theorum (*On Formally Undecidable Propositions of 'Principia Mathematica' and Related Systems*) at the age of 25. Like Freud, Gödel fled Austria after the Nazi Anschluss, settling in Princeton, where he became friends with another émigré, Albert Einstein. One day, Gödel became convinced that people were trying to poison him. He asked himself what the logical step was to prevent his poisoning. The logical step was to stop eating. At the time of his death from starvation, Gödel weighed 65 kilograms.

139 Bertrand Russell (1872–1970) was a British mathematician, historian and writer. A pacifist, Russell was imprisoned during the First World War. He worked his way through four marriages and numerous affairs.

Russell's *Principia Mathematica* refused to acknowledge what Gleick calls the "snake-eating-its-tail feedback loop" of paradox. A simple paradox is the statement 'I am lying.' In this, the Liar's Paradox, if the person speaking is lying, then he's telling the truth, so the sentence can't be a lie. And if he's telling the truth, then he's lying, so it can't be true. Let's call the first situation State 1 and the second State 2. As I understand it (cue laughter), modern mathematics isn't interested in proving which State is 'true', so much as exploiting the potential energy of the faultline between them.

Gödel, Shannon and Turing could, in a sense, exist in both States simultaneously. Russell's theory could not. That's why, as Gleick says, Russell declared the feedback loop "illegal, taboo." Once this taboo was broken, doubt destroyed mathematical certainty. This traumatic break with the past freed mathematicians and scientists in all sorts of ways. Essentially, we have Gödel's one destructive idea to thank for modern technology.

State 1: Hamburger is funny because he's offensive. State 2: Hamburger is offensive because he's funny. But proving or disproving 'offensiveness' is old thinking. We'd do much better to live in states of doubt.

Rules can't admit to their own structural weakness. The law lets you plead guilty or not guilty. There is no third option. You have to be one or the other, and both are states of submission. Obscenity is not the act of a free person. It's the act of someone caught in a system that tries to force repression onto its citizens. Is it that we *need* this system to repress us, if only to defy it, to offend it in ways it hasn't assimilated into its own operations?

The structure of offence is valuable. The content is not. Words wane, wax. Someone whose vocabulary is made up entirely of 'fuck' and 'shit' will still feel things worth saying, but their tools – their provocations – have been blunted by familiarity. To assume that 'cunt' has a permanent value is to subscribe to the very same system that profits from repressing it.

To quote Bob Dylan[140], "to live outside the law, you must be honest." Authority exempts the speaker from ordinary constraints only if that speaker has agreed to condemn themselves. Similarly, liberalism says, say what you want *within reason*. Anything liberalism doesn't like, it labels *unreasonable*. That's because it's claimed 'reason' as its jurisdiction. It *is* reason; outcasts and scapegoats sent to live outside its city walls are, 'by definition', unreasonable. Freedom of speech is actually the freedom to conform to parameters.

Offence isn't just tits and arse. You can cause offence by not wearing a poppy on Remembrance Day. You're perfectly free not to, but you wouldn't know it from the fuss that gets made when someone visible (a TV personality, a footballer etc) chooses not to conform. If offence is produced by the fear of being robbed of power, what powers are we defending when we hurl abuse at those who refuse to wear poppies? People

140 Bob Dylan is an American singer. As there's nothing worse than the ramblings of an obsessive fan, I'll leave it at that.

need to be honest about why they think there're some opinions you *can't* express. Who knows – they might be right. My grandfather fought on D-Day and he wears a poppy. So do I. Is that reasonable? I'd say so. But if others exercise their freedom to defy convention, then I have to be ready to defend my position *against* freedom.

Let's say I make a joke about a spastic child. Why be offended? For the sake of the child? Or because the word 'spastic' is disturbing? Are the disabled *untouchable* – a caste, legally excluded from a valid and otherwise unifying type of social exchange, because in Britain nothing says 'you're one of us, mate' like mockery. As the Home Office tells people seeking British citizenship, "the ability to laugh at ourselves...[is] an important part of the UK character." (Nick Griffin, take note.) And don't use Jordan's kid Harvey Price as your argument. That poor fuck's got enough on his plate. Assert a principle, don't just reactively claim sentimental exemptions to a 'freedom' which you simply don't believe in.

The challenge comedians are thought to face – how to shock an audience who've heard it all – is really a challenge we all face. It's a serious one, and it's seeing the wood for the trees. What are the parameters of my freedom? Is it reasonable to repress my doubt? And who's doing the repressing – me, after serious thought, or the authorities, for motives of their own?

Words. Wounds. Poppies. Symbols are designated to discrete units of experience. If the authorities find one of these units offensive, disgusting or *inconvenient*, they destroy its symbol, hoping to disembody a problem and thus make it unutterable. Public outrage at Sir Jimmy Savile's[141] being a sex offender leaves anyone under thirty thinking, where's the twist? Savile couldn't have looked more obviously like a paedophile if his shellsuits had been emblazoned with the word 'PAEDOPHILE'. But removing his headstone – as his family have done – doesn't punish him. Neither does turfing over his grave, posthumously stripping him of his knighthood, nor suspending his 'freedom' of Scarborough (that's right, no more grazing goats on the green or walking across bridges armed with a halberd for *that* freeman's corpse). Nothing will fix Jim. These repressive gestures are the product of a speak-no-evil culture who'd rather televise random acts of benevolence than ask what's going on in the green room. This codified silence *created* Savile. It can't destroy him.

For John Coltrane, "the beauty of jazz is freedom" – the freedom to shock, to reach, to speak. Consider

141 Jimmy Savile (1926–2012) was a DJ and TV presenter who redefined 'hiding in plain sight.' Savile's gravestones had two dire poems engraved on it. One reads "I, Sir Jimmy Savile, | Do lie beneath this stone | From here I view north & south | and the place that was my home | The angle that I lie at is a 45 degree | And that is so I always | Have a view out to the sea. || Stop, share this view I've chosen | And spend some time with me | Look down towards the castle | Which we can also see || And as you leave I thank you | That you have spent a while | and I ask that you remember me | And always – with a smile." Perhaps appropriately given his nautical leanings, Savile's also caused a bit of a sea change. Up until last year, older people would look back on the freewheelin' 60s and 70s and say 'it was a different time, man.' Now, those same people are saying 'it was a different time, your honour.'

jazz historically, as I'm afraid we must. When Charlie Parker[142] was at the height of his bar-walking, the bars in question still made black punters enter through the back door. Parker dealt with this by smashing every empty glass he'd seen a black person drink from. Really, he said, he was doing the clubs a favour – if whites wouldn't use the same door as blacks, they weren't going to drink from the same cup. And I've chosen the word 'cup' because black Americans have historically sought to establish their own churches for much the same reason. In the nineteenth century, these were non-conformist Christian churches. In the fifties and sixties, Islam became the preferred alternative, most famously perhaps for Muhammad Ali[143]. It's a question of self-exile. If society outlaws the word 'nigger', it does so because it invented the word in the first place, and now feels ashamed. So deny them the luxury of silence. Say 'nigger' more! Drag the word back in through the city gates. Celebrate the obscenity, not because it's stopped being offensive, but because you are *bigger* than offence.

Obviously, I'm not the right person to make that claim. I can only hold the n-word between inverted

142 Charlie Parker (1920–55) was the leading figure in bebop. Parker was a heroin addict; John Coltrane took up the drug in the hope of emulating his sound. Miles Davis famously said that you could tell the story of jazz in four words: "Louis Armstrong, Charlie Parker." Personally, I'd bolt "John Coltrane" onto the end of that. Maybe thanks to the heroin.

143 Muhammad Ali floats like a butterfly, stings like a bee. Out of 61 fights, he recorded 56 wins and 5 losses. Ali was stripped of his titles for refusing to fight in Vietnam. He won them back.

commas, tweezer-style. After all, I'm not that woman in New Orleans. But what I'm trying to say is this: there's a value to excess, to force, to exposing the fault-line between culture and its destruction, between an audience and their comedian.

Offence is necessary. It reveals us; once naked, it's up to us to live with our reflection. The best comedy is a gesture towards that ideal.

So this is where TV shows get their canned laughers?
Yup. My family's been breeding laughers for three generations.

Must be fun work. I mean, these guys haven't *stopped* laughing
They better not, if they know what's good for them.
What's the secret to breeding a healthy laugher?

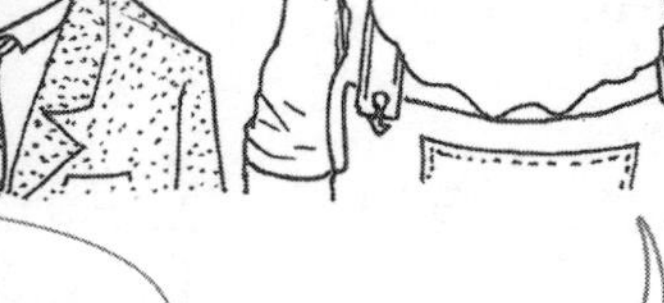
Just gotta keep your ear out...
...for when the laughs turn to sobs

But there's no danger of sobbing with this lot. Do you recognise that dumb, ravenous, hyena-like cackle?
They've been pissing themselves in *Mrs Brown's Boys* for years
This is one of my stud laughers. Listen to that distinctive chocolatey laugh. Beautiful lungs. Beautiful throat. And look at those balls...
Fit to bust.

There's a lovely laugher in that cage.

That? That ain't a laugher. That's my wife.

She's got nothing to laugh about.

Um. Right.
Oh dear. I think one might be a bit, er...

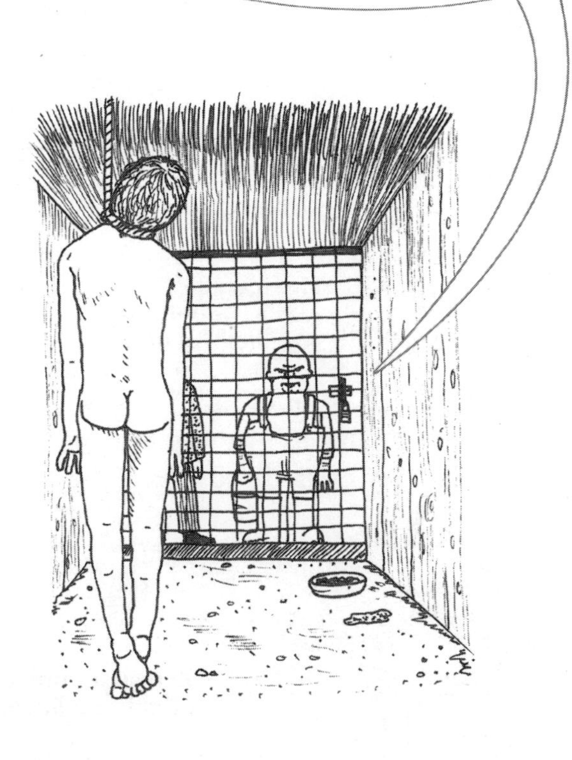
Dead. Yup. Just got a herd back from Ben Elton's *The Wright Way*. I been cutting them down all week.

Bearing Witness.

In 2006, my best friend and I went to Poland, which – unlike Dave, the channel where asinine episodes of *Top Gear* go to die – is not generally considered to be the home of witty banter. However, I did see two funny things there. The first was this: in Krakov, Tom[144] and I were sitting outside a café when we saw a man slip on a banana skin.

The banana skin is an overused trope. A glance at Wikipedia tells me that its first recorded use is in 1920, when a hee-hawing creep called 'Uncle Josh'[145] tells us

144 How do you footnote a friend? Well, Tom Chance is the slick young turk who started Giveacar, a not-for-profit scheme whereby Tom scraps or sells your clapped-out car and then donates any money earned to the charity of your choice. He's raised over a million quid, mostly for good causes, though some of it has gone to animal welfare groups. I don't get those animal people, digging up scientists' mothers because they've smothered a chimp in lipstick and blusher. After all, don't chimps have the right to look fabulous too?

145 Uncle Josh says "my foot hit the bananer peelin' and I went up in the air, and I come down ker-plunk, jist as I was pickin' myself up a little boy come runnin' across the street. He says, 'Oh mister, won't you please do that agin? My little brother didn't see you do it.'" He intersperces this with lots of very creepy, high-pitched whoops. God

he went "ker-plunk" over "a banana peel". I'm sure there are earlier instances – [citation needed] – but bananas must have been a tired old trick for Samuel Beckett[146] to use them as he did in *Krapp's Last Tape* (1959). In that play, Krapp listens to long, pompous tapes he recorded years before, full of promises to the future, all of which Krapp has since broken. This fruitless process has its comic analogy in the banana: no sooner has he tumbled over one banana skin than he's throwing another to the floor.

Krapp is an addict to the fruit and the fall. So why's the banana a good metaphor for his helpless situation? In theatrical terms, it's because we're already over-familiar with a joke that wasn't very funny to begin with. Indeed, when I saw him play Krapp, Michael Gambon[147] chose *not* to slip on the banana skin and the audience laughed in

---

knows what happens to the little boys, but I wouldn't be surprised if Uncle Josh was the next paunchy, ageing light entertainer to be seen professing his innocence to the mob of journalists gathered around the electric gates of his Berkshire home.

146 Samuel Beckett (1906–89) was an Irish playwright and novelist. Beckett moved to Paris in 1928, becoming James Joyce's assistant. Joyce was writing *Finnegans Wake*. His worsening eyesight, however, meant that Joyce sometimes dictated to Beckett, who proved an unreliable mediator between author and text. Richard Ellmann describes one dictation session when "there was a knock on the door which Beckett did not hear. Joyce said, 'Come in,' and Beckett wrote it down. Afterwards, he read back what he had written and Joyce said, 'What's that "Come in"?' 'Yes, you said that,' said Beckett. Joyce thought for a moment, then said, 'Let it stand.'" Beckett was stabbed in the chest by a pimp, fought in the French Resistance (for which he was awarded the croix de guerre), and won the Nobel Prize for Literature. His skill was "impoverishment"; he gave away the Nobel prize-money.

147 Michael Gambon is Dumbledore.

relief. Which annoyed me – the fall is necessary, precisely because the joke is exhausting.

The banana is life. That impression is helped – especially if we're talking about 'man' (which we shouldn't be, really) – by the banana's phallic appearance. Is it that, skinned and unconsumed, the peel represents our desire to feel a sexual death? Andy Warhol[148] seemed to think so, designing a run of sleeves for *The Velvet Underground and Nico* on which the famous yellow banana skin could be peeled back to reveal pink fruit. The theory is also borne out by a girl at my school who couldn't eat bananas, not because of the taste, but because she'd be laughing at their resemblance to penises too hard to swallow. (The banana being too hard, that is, not the penises. It's a hard sentence to grammar.) She's also the only person who's ever found my Czechoslovakian banana joke funny. And on that note, I'm still exercised by the question of whether – when her neurotic transference was confronted by reality – she spat or swallowed. Though I hear there are quite a number of boys from the Bristol UWE class of 2010 who know the answer. Sorry, that's indiscreet. I'll stop now. Your secret's safe with me, Ariadne.

Back to Poland. What made me laugh were the other people who'd witnessed the falling man, because they most definitely did not see the situation as I saw it. No one rushed to the guy's aid. Nor did they look away. 'Suffer with dignity, as our country has all its painful

148 Andy Warhol (1928–87) was an American artist. He made pop art when he looked like he should've been stalking the corridors of a high school, armed with a semi-automatic rifle.

life, for we are as indifferent as the international community has been on a number of occasions…I think,' their faces seemed to say (albeit in the mind of a juvenile Englishman). It was then that I realised how subjective, how inappropriate my response was. I'd been anaesthetised, amazed, by such a hack and unfunny thing *really* happening, a weird life-imitating-art moment that was actually kind of beautiful until I realised what a cock I looked laughing. I'd failed to understand and obey a basic social principle: you don't laugh at a man hurting himself in real life. So what really made me laugh was recognising that *I* was the fool. This came as a shock. To me, at least, if not to you.

The second funny thing I saw in Poland was how people behave at Auschwitz. The day after banana-gate, Tom and I took the coach to the camp. I was eighteen. I'd lugged a backpack full of European classics around China, Cuba and the southern states of America. I'd read Goethe[149] on the Yangtze River just before it flooded; I'd read Joyce in New Orleans just after it flooded. All thought and space juxtaposed, defying the superficies of difference to reveal a grand humanist truth – that was my conscious agenda. I lost weight, I was carrying that much bound physical *thought*. But here, in a death camp, I couldn't think. I'd expected to be moved and engaged, as though Auschwitz was an art gallery. But I wasn't. I was just nothing.

149 Johann Wolfgang von Goethe (1749–1832) achieved early celebrity as part of the *Sturm und Drang* (Storm and Stress) movement, a romanticism heavy on heaving bosoms. Ditching the *Twilight* vibe, Goethe then became a politician, botanist, poet and playwright.

Naturally I'd learnt about the Holocaust, not least from an affectedly tweedy history teacher who we'll call Mr. Carlsberg because:

1. His real name was that of another beer manufacturer (hint: it wasn't Tiger).
2. Because I've just received a court summons for libelling Ariadne Sidnam. Who, for the record, spits.

Mr. Carlsberg, then, taught me about the Nazis. But he seemed to skirt the Holocaust – until, that is, he asked me, 'Syborn, are you a Jew?' I said no and he said something about my nose, face and glasses (glasses?) before handing out photocopies of David Irving's[150] book. David Irving, of course, who – as the world's most famous Holocaust denier – had the hubris to holiday in Austria, one of the seventeen countries in which it's illegal to deny the Holocaust. And how we all laughed at his prison sentence. All, that is, except my history teacher. If Mr. Carlsberg (not Asahi) wasn't trolling online forums under the user name 'TheTruth1945', it was only because he thought computers were made by Jews. Or lizards.

I'm exaggerating. Actually, what annoyed me most about Mr. Carlsberg was the fact that he *wasn't* an anti-Semite. I realise that sounds strange. What I mean is, Mr. Carlsberg gave us David Irving to prove that he,

150 In 2000, High Court Judge Charles Gray said that Irving "is an active Holocaust denier; that he is anti-Semitic and racist and that he associates with right-wing extremists who promote neo-Nazism."

Carlsberg (not Staropramen), wasn't some dusty parochial Mr. Chips but actually a fearless free-thinker. And no one was ever going to make him pretend to be anything else!

And, while we're (vaguely) on the topic, can people who weren't alive at the time please stop setting fiction in the Second World War? You're turning a conflict which killed 60 million people into a fucking Narnia, an allegorical mess of antiquated morals and snazzy costumes. Like the wretched film adaptation of Robert Harris's[151] novel *Enigma*. Aesthetically, the movie is risible – its flashbacks are coated in more Vaseline than a loveless marriage. But the deviation from history made by both the film and its source novel is more than risible. It's sinister.

Enigma sets its story in Bletchley Park, where German codes were cracked by a team of British mathematicians. In real life, they were led, brilliantly, by the homosexual mathematician Alan Turing. In *Enigma*, however, Turing is rewritten as the heterosexual Tom Jericho, played by Dougray Scott[152]. Why? To hammer the perversity of genius straight. As Slavoj Žižek[153] says, *Enigma* provides an "erotic re-framing" – a rigged 'portrait' – of an historical moment so that "the true enigma" becomes the female sex, that unknowable other. Only Jericho can crack women. At one point, Scott is told that "girls go

151 Robert Harris is an English novelist.

152 Dougray Scott is a Scottish actor who played the featureless villain in *Mission Impossible 2.* What a fall from grace for director John Woo – from *Face/Off* to a load of rubbish latex masks.

153 Slavoj Žižek is an omnivorous Slovene philosopher, Communist and Hegel fan.

weak at the thought of the size of your brain." Oh the irony. Women *should* be going weak at the thought of the size of his cock, but that's Shagger Turing/Jericho for you. He's so brainy and not gay that he's able to stop women thinking about bananas. Penises, sorry. I always get those two mixed up.

What's interesting about *Enigma* is how unbothered everyone was by it. There was no outcry, as there was in the wake of the equally terrible *U-571* (2000), featuring Jon Bon Jovi[154] and which the *Daily Mail* described as "a travesty of history." In contrast, the *Mail* actually praised *Enigma* for being "a pure-bred English film" (Carlsberg would be proud) with "a Proustian feel to it." Proustian? I assume the reviewer, Alexander Walker[155], was thinking about all those flashbacks. Though I'd bet very few people at the *Daily Mail* have actually read *A la Recherche du Temps Perdu* – if you asked them what a Madeleine was, they'd say an excuse to pen some shrieking bullshit about Portuguese gypsies.

Walker's review crescendos with the line "our cinema has neglected Britain's wartime achievements, allowing Hollywood to steal, traduce and fictionalise some of our finest hours for its own gung-ho glory," i.e. *U-571*. Why did that offend him? Because it lowers the Union Jack in favour of some ghastly foreign flag – it's like watching

154 Jon Bon Jovi is the American soft-cock-rock 'legend' responsible for every time a DJ turns down the volume to make a roomful of morons bellow "living on a prayer".

155 Alexander Walker (1930–2003) was a film critic from Northern Ireland. He wrote a three-volume history of British cinema.

the hand-over of Hong Kong all over again. *Enigma*, on the other hand, is to be celebrated, not because it doesn't "traduce and fictionalise" history, but because it *does* fictionalise a history whose dimensions do not fit with the *Daily Mail*'s worldview (or, perhaps more appropriately, its Weltanschauung).

History is reportage as appropriation. Facts become fiction when used in the wrong context, and fiction is deniable. Alan Turing was arrested for being homosexual. He was forced (or, in the language of the day, 'chose') to undergo oestrogen injections that amounted to a chemical castration – the idea being that, if sexuality couldn't be corrected, then it could be neutered, silenced. If anything, *Enigma* castrates Turing anew for the entertainment of the *Midsomer Murders* demographic. This is a far more dangerous dishonesty than seeing Jon Bon Jovi slippery when livin' on a U Boat. *U-571* took an event and swapped some accents around; however implicitly, *Enigma* says that gay men don't deserve our admiration. At the end of *Enigma*, Dougray has knocked up the doughty Kate Winslet[156]; at the end of his life, Turing died, alone, after eating half a poisoned apple. It's surely perverse that the British film industry shied away from that fact, when the world's biggest corporation supposedly (but probably not actually) commemorates Turing's tragedy on every product they sell. The half-eaten fruit of Apple's logo stares out

156 Kate Winslet is an English actress, now revelling in her national treasure status despite the fact that she blatantly hogged the *entire* wardrobe. There was definitely space for Leo.

at us every time Carrie Bradshaw[157] types another article about the difference between men and women. And I got to thinking, if that's not circular, what is? *[pause, clears throat]* A joke for all you Turing aficionados out there.

Heckler: If that's a reference to the difference between satisfactory and unsatisfactory numbers – with the unsatisfactory numbers characterised as circular and meaning a figure the final shape of which can neither be predicted nor stabilised – and which has at its roots Kurt Gödel's theory that a number can be true but not provable, then the joke isn't particularly successful.

[long pause]

Freddy: It was just a *passing* reference to Turing's differentiating statements made by artificial intelligence from those made by human beings, an experiment that grew from his interest in telling the difference between men and women. Hence the Carrie Bradshaw/laptop thing. It wasn't a big deal and now I've lost my, you know, my place.

Heckler: I think your intelligence is artificial.

Freddy: I think your mum is artificial.

Heckler: Now you're just showing off.

157 I love *Sex and the City* but basically loathe SJP's character, Carrie, even though I'm Team Big. Go figure.

Freddy: Oh, are you drinking a pint there, mate? Good. Remember to drive home.

To return to Poland, I'd taken my camera to Auschwitz, intending to report my experiences there. As it was, I felt photography was pretty much beside the point. Other tourists didn't. Nor were they content to let the landscape do the talking. These photographers, such as they were, had concluded that Auschwitz itself wasn't enough to warrant their commemoration. What Auschwitz needed were friends and family in the foreground, not to contextualise the otherwise unimaginable loss of the place, nor history's potential for circularity, but to make the images more interesting for the audience back home.

Photos demand a performance. As you're going to be caught in this moment forever, your instinct is to make it look better than it is. Hence that painful delay as you hold the pose of 'being' you. You're so aware of how artificial your still life looks in the ticking world that you laugh from embarrassment at every unexpected delay – people know you're acting! You're actively relieved once the photo's taken: there, done, that's the Freddy I want remembered, a prettier thing at a distance from its performer. Now I can get back to being me. I can always detag it later.

It was funny to see how different tourists dealt with their self-awareness within the context of a death camp, a place where I'd lost so much of my own. Knowing they were framed against the zero-point of humanity, they were stuck as to how to pose. Should they smile or affect an exaggerated seriousness, the better to highlight the setting? Should they look into the camera or is that a bit me, me, me? Or should they think to the future, to when they'd look at their holiday snaps and go, 'oh, there's me next to a massive oven. Didn't my hair look stupid in 2006?' Fundamentally, were they involved in, or detached from, history?

These were the difficulties of bearing witness to murder. Confronted with them, most of the tourists chose to forget. So Tom and I saw an American woman peering out from the window of a dormitory at her husband. Peek-a-boo! We saw eighteen deeply serious Chinese people (equipped with matching red sunhats) waiting for all eighteen of their cameras to be trained on them hovering over a particularly suggestive coil of barbwire. We even saw an especially feckless cunt throw a peace sign.

As I looked around, I realised that, though I couldn't understand my surroundings, I couldn't *believe* the people in it. My feeling then was this: how can you think that a shot of your wife eating a pork hotdog as she coyly rests against a brick pillar supporting the 'arbeit macht frei' sign isn't anything other than irredeemably obscene?

Leaving aside the ultimately hopeless position we're in *vis-à-vis* objectivity, there are things that most people (David Irving aside) *feel* to be true. Call this general consensus and accept the potential pejorative – at the most extreme points in history, it doesn't take a moral philosopher to see something is both true and wrong, though maybe we can't prove *why*. So when a person responds to an event or a principle in a way that's wildly out of kilter with general feeling, when they so drastically misunderstand the world and their position within it, they create comic potential. Because, again, comedy is about standing in judgement.

That the Holocaust was the worst thing to happen in human history is, I'd venture, a widely-held belief. That its chief factotum was Adolf Eichmann[158] is a widely-known fact. But Hannah Arendt's[159] account of his trial, *Eichmann in Jerusalem*, shows that Eichmann himself shared neither of these notions. For Arendt, Eichmann embodied the not uncomic "banality of evil."

How can Eichmann look funny? Because he's a contradictory and unreliable witness. Here was a man whose "knees went weak" at the sight of a dead body. "That was quite enough for me!" he remembered, incorrectly as it

158 Dr. Stanley Milgram wrote in *Dynamics of Obedience* that Adolf Eichmann (1906–62) "[illustrated] a dangerously typical situation in complex society: it is psychologically easy to ignore responsibility when one is only an intermediate link in a chain of evil action but is far from the final consequences of the action. Even Eichmann was sickened when he toured the concentration camps, but to participate in mass murder he had only to sit at a desk and shuffle papers." After the war ended, Eichmann hid in a small north German hamlet for five years, before being spirited away to Argentina with the help of the Nazi Catholic bishop, Alois Hudal.

159 Hannah Arendt (1906–75) was a German political theorist from a secular Jewish background. While at the University of Marburg, Arendt is reported to have had a long affair with the philosopher Martin Heidegger. Heidegger is so tainted by his support of the Nazi party that a book (*The Introduction of Nazism Into Philosophy*) now incites us to label his writing as hate speech. Arendt herself escaped the Nazis by going first to Paris, where she became friends with Walter Benjamin, and then to America. She covered Eichmann's trial for the *New Yorker*, before turning her articles into a book. An asteroid – 100027 hannaharendt – is named in her honour.

turns out, because he went on to oversee the murder of six million more. And yet when his jailer lent Eichmann a copy of *Lolita*, the war criminal complained that the book was "quite unwholesome." Eichmann's being offended by fiction, in the teeth of all the obscenities he's perpetrated on reality, is – *at a sufficient distance* – a sign of what Arendt calls his "grotesque silliness".

For the prosecution, it was "not an individual that is in the dock…[it was] anti-Semitism through history." But Eichmann was an awkward scapegoat for an ideology he often betrayed. Arendt reveals that, as an S.S. officer in Vienna charged with the "forced emigration" of Jews, Eichmann had a long affair with a Jewish "old flame", despite the fact that "*Rassenschande*, sexual intercourse with Jews, was probably the greatest crime a member of the S.S. could commit." Why didn't Eichmann mention this affair under interrogation? It wouldn't have excused him, nor saved him from death, but isn't it a thing you'd *mention*? Apparently not. Eichmann could grasp neither at straws nor the magnitude of his culpability; he could no more play the part of the desperate man than he could the role of anti-Semitism itself.

Eichmann was an unsatisfactory number. The sum he results in (6,000,000) is undeniable. But why? How? Surely the answer can't be plain *thoughtlessness*? But what else are we to make of this fool? He saw no disparity between announcing to the court that "no man, no judge could ever persuade me to make a sworn statement, to declare something under oath," and then, having been told he didn't need to, instantly decide that he *would*, in fact, prefer to testify under oath. Even on the day of his execution, Eichmann declared himself an atheist only to promise that "we shall all meet again." As with Krapp, one banana skin followed another.

The deeper the truth, the more ridiculous the person who fails to understand it. Eichmann couldn't fall under the spectacular gravity we ascribe evil. Auschwitz isn't funny, but it can make people look funny. And *apropos* the Nazis, let's return to the *Daily Mail*. Here again, we see a stupid person (in this instance, Liz Jones[160]) striking poses in front of something they don't understand. In early 2011, Jones wrote an article about Joanna Yeates[161], a woman who'd been murdered in Bristol that Christmas. The idea is to retrace the steps of the murdered girl; like a tornado chaser, or one of the perverts in J.G. Ballard's[162] *Crash*, Jones scuttles around Bristol revelling in the scene of destruction. Her article is

---

160 Liz Jones is a self-involved 'lifestyle journalist' suffering from a textbook case of Middle England paranoia. "The only person in the world you are allowed to criticise these days is the middle-aged, affluent white woman," Jones claims, whereas "serve up any old rubbish if you are Muslim and you'll be lauded to the skies." I'd love to test this theory by 'serving up' one of Jones' own articles, but swapping the usual byline picture for one of her in a burka. Could even political correctness unearth her hidden merits? I doubt it.

161 Joanna Yeates (1985–2010) was the landscape architect murdered by Vincent Tabak in Bristol on the 17th December 2010.

162 J.G. Ballard (1930–2009) was an English novelist who specialised in showing how the human mind is perverted by technology, cities and new methods of control. As a boy in Shanghai during the Second World War, Ballard was interned by the Japanese. He had "not unpleasant memories of the camp", adult brutality providing the backdrop for "a hundred and one" childish games.

so appallingly misjudged that it's worth quoting blow by horrid blow.

"The Ram bar on Park Street in Bristol… is where Joanna Yeates spent her last evening before she set off up the hill, past all the twinkly shops (a Habitat, a Space NK beauty emporium; Bristol is nothing if not upwardly mobile) towards her death." Instantly, Liz evokes Milton's[163] *Paradise Lost*: Yeates, "with wand'ring steps and slow, | Through Eden took [her] solitary way." A Habitat *and* a Space NK – is this not paradise? Truly, nothing speaks more keenly of loss than all the pillows and manicures forever denied the victim of a brutal, sexually-motivated murder. And nice use of 'emporium', BTW. Microsoft's thesaurus never lets me down, either.

"I wish she had spent what were probably her last hours on earth somewhere lovelier." That's good of you.

"The food is awful (I ask for a veggie burger and it comes without the burger – and without the bun!)" If Liz got a veggie burger without the burger or the bun, what came in its place? An empty plate? Surely the waiter would have noticed? Unless Jones just 'asked' someone who doesn't actually work at the bar? It's entirely possible. The pathos is already unbearable at second-hand – God knows how bewildering it was for our intrepid reporter.

163 John Milton (1608–74) was a Puritan and scholar. After Charles I's execution, Milton served as Secretary for Foreign Tongues (a cross between translator, diplomat and propagandist) under Oliver Cromwell. By 1654, Milton had gone completely blind. After Charles II was restored to the throne in 1660, copies of Milton's work were burnt and the poet went into hiding. *Paradise Lost* was written in these ruins of the Commonwealth.

"Alex...was working in the bar on the night of December 17, when Joanna was having a drink before heading home. 'I don't remember her,' she says." A little bit of an anti-climax, but Jones ploughs on.

"I walk past the beautiful university building on my right, with Waitrose on my left. I wander the bright aisles, full of young women rushing round after work, leaving with carrier bags and expectation." That's Waitrose off the list. It's a wonder the police didn't start there, actually. What with it being totally irrelevant.

"I find Tesco, and go in. I almost buy that upmarket pizza [Yeates was last seen buying]*; the choice tells me Jo wanted a lovely life, something above the ordinary."* By ordinary, does she mean the slightly cheaper range of pizza Tesco's sell? Are the people buying those pizzas less worthy of our unchecked grief? And what stopped Liz from buying "that upmarket pizza", synonymous though it is with "a lovely life"? Well, she was probably full after eating that plate.

"As I near her basement flat, at No 44, the road is quiet. I'm reassured to see two policemen standing vigil at her iron gate...I tell them I'm spooked, walking here. 'Don't be spooked,' one says." Another anti-climax, but at least Liz is wasting valuable police time.

"That afternoon I had gone to the lane where Jo's body was found. It was horrible and windswept. I don't know what I had expected but not this." It's hard to imagine what she did expect. Another shop, maybe.

"I got the feeling the world is starting to forget Jo." Ladies and gentlemen: Miss Liz Jones.

"I'd have expected the cars to slow down here to show respect but they sped past." In fairness to those unfeeling bastards, that is the nature of a road. And it's probably not on their sat nav: 'after three hundred yards, you have reached the place a woman's corpse was dumped. Show respect here.'

"I can't see how a car stopped here and a man struggled with a body without being beeped at and told to get out the way, as I was." Is she suggesting she too had a body to deposit? Bloody woman driver.

"My satnav takes me to the Clifton Suspension Bridge. The theory is the killer took the long route from the flat to where he dumped the body to avoid the CCTV cameras. Perhaps he also wanted to avoid the 50p toll." That seems unlikely. I've never killed anyone, but I doubt if – in the direct aftermath of me having done so – I'd go out of my way to save 50p. I'd probably have more on my plate. Unlike Liz. Who has nothing.

"I don't have 50p." Meticulous planning.

"*I try tossing 30p and a White Company button into the bucket. It doesn't work."* Isn't it annoying that toll booths don't operate on a bartering system?

"Isn't it interesting that you can snatch a young woman's life away from her in the most violent, painful, frightening way possible, take away her future children, her future Christmases, take away everything she loves, and yet there are elaborate systems in place to ensure you do not cross a bridge for only 30 pence?" No. The two things aren't comparable.

"A man in a taxi jumps out, and runs to me brandishing

a 50p piece. 'Not all men are monsters,' he says, grinning." He definitely, *definitely* did not say that.

"Maybe not. But one monster is all it takes." What?

Just take a moment to consider the irony of Liz Jones accusing comedians of being offensive, as she has done on a number of occasions. To my mind, there is a clear difference between a joke-writer constructing offence and Jones managing to be offensive. The joke-writer (ideally) will offend us to provoke thought. Liz Jones offends us because she is thought*less*.

If *Enigma* reframes history erotically, then Jones reframes it materialistically. Like the tourists at Auschwitz, moreover, she trivialises a terrible event by inserting her own suffering into its narrative. She reframes the bar, the supermarket, the flat and the lane as stations of the cross she thinks she bears for witnessing history. Clifton Suspension Bridge is her Golgotha, the site of Christ's crucifixion. It doesn't matter that the killer *didn't* drive over the bridge and, therefore, that the whole toll-booth episode has no relevance whatsoever to the story of Joanna Yeates. *This* is the Liz Jones Show.

Both Jesus and Jones are scapegoats through whose agony a truth is revealed. In Jones' case, the truth is that 50p means more to Britain than a young woman's life. Which is funny because the only person such rampant greed appears to be true of is Jones herself.

Why does Liz deserve to be the butt of my jokes? Because she misjudges gravity: the chair is that much further away as she goes ker-plunk. To paraphrase Sally Stott's criticism of me (if I can read it from up here on my high horse), we can only hope Jones isn't as horrific as her article.

Having said that, I bet Mr. Carlsberg doesn't get the fuss.

*

Shock is the pain of disbelief being corrected: I can't believe what I'm seeing, even though I *must* believe it. And corrective pain can be funny. Think about the textbook comic device of mistaken identity. A man dressed like a woman, a woman dressed like a man – these transformations are shocking because they defy 'natural' order. The (not so much natural as cultural) restoration of this order relies on *anagnorisis*, which Aristotle describes as "recognition…the change from ignorance to knowledge."

As a rule, recognition in comedies comes just before disaster. Jeeves[164] is anagnorisis, the servant/mediator able to sort out every situation just at the point when Bertie Wooster looks to be doomed. The joker creates blind panic; the straight man restores our sight. In Shakespeare's[165] *A*

164 Reginald Jeeves and Bertie Wooster are characters created by P.G. Wodehouse (1881–1975). Jeeves and Wooster books are variations on the same story; Wodehouse Ctl+Fed a few names and locations but essentially repeated the same phrases, jokes and situations again and again over the six decades between Jeeves' first appearance and Wodehouse's last novel, *Aunts Aren't Gentlemen*. Luckily, the original blueprint's brilliance can withstand duplication.

165 William Shakespeare (1564–1616) married a cougar called Anne Hathaway before moving to London. There, the budding writer honed his craft with the help of the Globe's digital research department.

Midsummer's Night's Dream, Puck's magic (administered to the eyes of his victims) stops the Athenians from seeing each other for who they really are. So lovers swap lovers, friends try to kill each other, and Bottom goes right to the top. It's as if a donkey had wandered into Pasha at about 4 a.m. Once the morning's dawned, though, everyone's sight is restored and no one wants to have sex with animals any more. Harmony has returned.

Contrast that to the end of Euripides'[166] tragedy the *Bacchae*. In it, a prince called Penthius takes agin a new religious fervour sweeping his city. This fervour emanates from a mysterious outsider called Dionysus. Penthius does not recognise Dionysus as Bacchus and Bacchus as, essentially, the god of Carnival. Dionysus allows himself

---

Thanks to some very robust data mining, the Globe revealed to Shakespeare that 39% of his demographic are 'active adventurers' who enjoy 'content' that 'unpacks a journey'. One fifth of these platform-literate nodes enjoy 'redemption' or 'redemption-style sub-content' in their payload, though only 23% of the other four-fifths consciously demand 'strong, often colourful characters' to motor said content down the two-way, user-driven information highway. Going forward, 2 out of 4.32 enjoy 'conflict and mild peril', though the confluence-driven majority of the Globe's three-dimensional Twitter-handled Venn diagram *do* re-spam 'complexity' across a multi-spectrum, 360 blue-sky of social networks. On a scale of 1 to 5, meanwhile, a multi-channel cluster of 63% would sunset words over two syllables long, though two-up-two-down thinking would leave intact a kitchen sink at ground floor level. Thanks to this fact stream, Shakespeare was able write *Hamlet*. He then retired, only to die blowing out the candles of his birthday cake. #fail

166 Euripides (c. 480–406) was a Greek dramatist, of whose 90-odd plays eighteen or nineteen survive. As well as the *Bacchae*, Euripides wrote *Medea*, *Electra* and *The Trojan Women*. Much of what we know of Euripides comes from Aristophanes' comedies, in which Euripides is depicted as a quick-witted but dangerous man who belongs in hell.

to be arrested. He recommends that Penthius dresses in drag to spy on a female-only bacchanal. Penthius goes to the rave disguised as a woman. Dionysus then sets his followers onto the prince. Penthius ends up being torn apart by his own mother, Agave, whose religious ecstasy is such that she mistakes him for a lion. As with Bottom, Penthius is humiliated by transformation because he lacks the humility of self-knowledge. For Penthius, though, recognition comes too late. Agave realises she's holding her son's head only *after* she's ripped it off.

As genres, as experiences of life, tragedy and comedy are symbiotic. Look at the *Big Momma's House* franchise, then remember that – on the credits for *Bad Boys* – Martin Lawrence[167] was billed *above* Will Smith[168]. Martin Lawrence, you Icarus.

I'll say it again (as though people haven't been saying it for thousands of years), tragedy and comedy are symbiotic. As the stand-up Richard Herring[169] pointed out, Hitler and Charlie Chaplin[170] had the same moustache. Herring even grew one himself.

What's the link? Well, both tragedy and comedy need things to go wrong. In *King Lear*, Lord Gloucester

---

167 Martin Lawrence is a once-successful American actor.

168 Will Smith is a still-successful American actor.

169 Richard Herring began his career writing and performing with Stewart Lee. Herring has an enthusiasm for big ideas and a weakness for cock-orientated puns.

170 Charlie Chaplin (1889–1977). Slapstick sentimentalist. As a child, Chaplin was condemned to the workhouse. He went on to become – in the words of Federico Fellini – "a sort of Adam, from whom [film-makers] are descended."

complains that "as flies to wanton boys are we to the gods, | They kill us for their sport." Who are these gods? The creator and their audience, toying with lives for which they feel nothing.

And we do feel nothing. If audiences couldn't stop themselves caring about the 'flies' that entertain them, they'd be like my mother, who was so upset by bleak, hard-hitting films like *Bambi*, *The Sound of Music*, *The Railway Children*, *The Incredible Journey* and *Chitty Chitty Bang Bang* that she had to be physically removed from the cinema. And I don't want to be tactless, but she wasn't young when those movies were released. She was a teenager. Under sixteen, but still a teenager.

Sarah Syborn[171] hates the cinema because she can't stop caring. She's what Dostoyevsky[172] said of his idiot, Prince Myshkin: "a completely beautiful human being."

---

171 Sarah Syborn is a gardener with no sense of irony. An example: she once spent a weekend as groupie to the thrash metal band Megadeth. It was in India. She was building a garden in Kerala; they were playing a massive concert. As no one else was in the hotel, the Megadeth lads and mum became firm friends. She thought the bassist was a bit two-dimensional, but apparently the singer was charming despite his many tattoos. After the big gig, the biggest in Indian history, Megadeth wanted to par-tay (thrash metallers probably don't say 'par-tay') so Sarah made them a pot of camomile tea with not one but two bags because – quote – "they looked like they could have a pretty high tolerance to camomile." Mum doesn't see anything even *potentially* funny about any of this.

172 Fyodor Dostoyevsky (1821–81) was a Russian novelist. Having been arrested for belonging to what Wikipedia calls 'a secret society of liberal utopians' (the Petrashevsky Circle), Dostoyevsky was spared the death penalty by Tsar Nicholas I. He did four years' hard labour in Siberia instead. Dostoyevsky was a gambling addict who went on a four-year honeymoon and died with a smile on his face.

Myshkin and my mother being the exceptions, then, our empathy has a cut-off point. Why? One reason could be how ugly, annoying and expensive cultural venues are. Gloucester may have had his eyes ripped out in *Lear*, but that's nothing to the fucking gouging the average punter suffers buying a very small coke (the theatre) or an obscenely large one (the cinema). After that, it's hard not to think less of the rip-off suffered by Penthius.

We also stop caring because art commits violence. The French writer Simone Weil[173] argued that violence transforms the human into a thing. In her essay *The Illiad, or the Poem of Force*, she writes that:

> Exercised to the extreme, [force] makes the human being a thing quite literally, that is, a dead body… [but it has] another power, in its way more momentous, that of making a still living human being into a thing.

Now, I don't think corpses are funny. They can be involved in comic situations, but only if they're being manhandled by the living. This is because they can't feel anything. So like in *Fawlty Towers*, when a guest dies in the night, it's only funny because Basil thinks a batch of kippers has killed him, and goes to great lengths to

173 Simone Weil (1909–43) was a French writer and mystic. Albert Camus described her as "the only great spirit of our times." Weil based her theology on hunger. If soldiers could not eat, neither would she. Weil died on a cocktail of TB and empathy.

conceal the death from the other guests. The corpse itself is just a prop from which to wring laughs.

Are corpses even tragic? Only insofar as death is tragic. But whenever someone I know dies, I think of death as a thing being permanently suffered by the still-living person. I've never had to identify a body, but even in such an extreme I'd imagine that the object itself can't *remain* tragic beyond the shock of recognition.

"Tragedy | when the feeling's gone and you can't go on" – though not the first mistake Barry, Maurice and Robin Gibb[174] would make, and certainly not the last, it's nevertheless the most irritating from an academic point of view. Corpses can't feel, and can't go on, but we can. We're the tragedy: bodies can only reflect our living pain.

In *On Regarding the Pain of Others*, Susan Sontag relates Weil's idea to Virginia Woolf's[175] description of a photograph of a corpse taken during the Spanish Civil War. Woolf sees a "photograph of what might be a man's body, or a woman's; it is so mutilated that it might, on the other hand, be the body of a pig." No longer able to pose for a photo, it's a dead weight transformed beyond sex, beyond species. Woolf's point (as I understand it) is that such a loss of identity is a product and a testament to *our*

174 Also known as The Bee Gees.

175 Virginia Woolf (1882–1941) was an English modernist. In 1910, she took part in the 'Dreadnought Hoax'. Woolf and her pals posed as male members of the Abyssinian royal family, then convinced the Royal Navy to show them around their state-of-the-art flagship, the HMS *Dreadnought*. They did this by blacking up, strapping on a fake beard each and saying "bunga bunga" a lot, predating the racist joke that is Italian politics by some ninety years.

loss: we can no longer recognise the human, therefore we treat people like things. Perhaps that's why the bereaved often lose a grip on reality. Take Michael Jackson's death. the *Sun* was outraged that Bubbles[176] (Jackson's monkey butler) wasn't invited to Jackson's funeral. But what did the paper expect him to do? Read *Stop All The Clocks*?

Does reportage try to simply record reality? And, if so, does that make reportage an effective and lasting type of truth? Perhaps not. Do even the most horrific images, like the one Woolf describes, stop us from making war? Charities that use photos of malnourished children, say, are their own worst enemies, because those photos appeal to our flimsiest political instincts, novelty and sentiment. We're a market economy. It's not that we don't feel. It's that shocking imagery saturates our culture – there's so much choice as to what to feel about.

Sontag observes that liberal societies "still tend to choose our images of virtue from among our victims." Our lifestyles can only be sustained by the exploitation of third world and developing nations. So, as a sort of penance, we imbue our victims with purity and wisdom and other like earthy, *spiritual* qualities we've sadly forgotten in our whirlwind of diamonds, computers and call centres. 'Oh *Ind-jah*, babe, you must go to *Ind-jah*!

176 Bubbles has taken tea with the Mayor of Osaka. He also used to sleep in a crib at the foot of Jackson's bed. Sadly, Bubbles in later years has become an overweight, suicidal wreck. He now lives in a great apes sanctuary in Florida. LaToya Jackson recently visited him, compounding Bubbles' misery.

They're such simple, *happy* people.' As though what our victims *really* need is faint praise.

Natural disasters, civil wars, starvation – in the media and in the public imagination, these are slight variations on the boom-and-bust industry of sympathy. We consume, we give, we forget. We even find public figures who've dedicated themselves to a single cause slightly ridiculous, because they will not *shut up* about it. Jamie Oliver[177] and kids' dinners. Bob Geldof[178] and the lack of them. Come on, Jamie, the general public cry, don't go on about it – write another cookbook. Come on, Bob, make another album.

Actually don't, Bob, but my point is this: we get bored of reality. Real situations are dull and real people are self-righteous idiots. If you can remember *Jamie's School Dinners*, there was one scene where a mother berated Oliver for having the sheer temerity to suggest that a diet exclusively consisting of chips might shorten her child's life. *Well*, she fumed, my son *wants* chips, OK? And if he *wants* them, he'll *get* them. To which I'd have replied, "does that logic apply across the board? And if it does, how often do you find yourself calling up his headmaster and saying, 'sorry, my son isn't coming into school because he *wants* to spend the day wanking into a sock.' Where's your parental responsibility?" I'd have continued, well into the stride of my argument,

177 Jamie Oliver is a chef and business mogol.

178 Bob Geldof: very keen on us giving all our fecking money to Africa, possibly less keen on giving all his fecking money to HM Revenues and Customs.

finger pointed directly in her fat face. "And don't make this a class thing," I'd have said, because I knew it was a class thing, and also because I like chips and am quite fat too, "you are destroying your son's life because, because," raising myself to my full height and preparing to tombstone the pinguid bitch with my righteousness, "he will never learn how to cook courgette." At which point she'd have set her Staffy on me and neither of us would have learnt a thing. A point you can only make in fiction, because in reality you'd have to do something stupid like respect her views.

Anagnorisis is the movement from ignorance to knowledge. What's the best vehicle for such a trip? Reportage (the making of history) is in a sense more vulnerable than art because it tries to use reality *as it is* and still manages to corrupt it. However content is shown, the sight is manipulated, representative. Deny the burden of subjectivity all you want: you're still a beast of it.

Everyone knows examples of rigged reality. One of my favourites is the *Guardian*'s online film of the footballer Joey Barton[179] looking at a painting by Lucian Freud.[180] In *The Tempest*, Shakespeare's slave character Caliban is an earthy, ugly, violent bastard and would-be rapist – not unlike certain footballers, then. And yet, the liberal audience coo, Caliban *dreams*. He tells Trinculo (the play's comic relief) that:

179 Joey Barton. Outspoken philosopher.
180 Lucian Freud (1922–2011) was one of the best British painters of the twentieth century.

> ...in dreaming
> The clouds, methought, would open and show riches
> Ready to drop upon me, that when I waked
> I cried to dream again.

Similarly, we know Joey Barton likes a fight. He was born in Liverpool, where A&E's so popular on Saturday nights, they've got bouncers on the door turning away anyone in trainers. But we also know Joey dreams of riches, and not just those that football can provide. His antics on Twitter have revealed him to be a Nietzsche[181]-quoting, Smiths-loving disciple of Orwell[182]. Just imagine! So the *Guardian* walked him round the Freud exhibition at the National Portrait Gallery. Then they (either consciously or unconsciously) edited the footage to show Barton as the fool he may or may not be.

The film shows Barton wondering as to whether the person depicted in one painting is a woman or a man in drag. Barton decides – wrongly – that it's a man in drag. The *Guardian*'s art critic nods politely; we at home are allowed a little laugh at the tragic *literalness* of the man's mind. But what is a portrait? Isn't its purpose to represent its subject's reality? Is it a problem that Barton can't recognise the sitter's sex? If it's not, doesn't art – the *act* of depiction, the technique, hanging and history – risk

181 Friedrich Nietzsche (1844–1900). Outspoken journeyman midfielder for Man City, Newcastle, QPR and Marseilles.

182 George Orwell is the pen-name of Eric Blair (1903–50), an ex-Etonian socialist who fought the Fascists in the Spanish Civil War. Orwell's writing moved from social realism to fable. He was also an incredible essayist. Orwell wrote his health to bits on a damp Scottish island.

excluding people from the pleasure of recognition? Is this exclusivity at all desirable? Why is art forgiven?

The *Guardian* film doesn't address these questions. Instead, it puts its audience's mind at ease. You can take the horse to water, it seems, but you can't make it rhapsodise about chiaroscuro. Barton is left a King Louie[183] figure. Like the monkey in *Jungle Book*, he wants to talk like us, walk like us, shoo-be-doo, but he can't because we're innately superior. Our interest in Joey Barton is the product of cultural imperialism, and even a man who stubs out lit cigars in his team-mates' eyes deserves better than that.

Reportage is debatable in a way that an artistic representation isn't. Interestingly, the first newsreel ever recorded was filmed in Cardiff in 1896, where BBC Wales are still looping the footage as not a lot's happened since. But, unless you take a trip to Wales, there's no way of seeing the past for yourself. We know the results of history, we're just not sure of how they were arrived at. The present is true but not provable. Furthermore, reporters aren't time machines. They can't take us back to an event. They can only reshoot it.

Hannah Arendt's *Eichmann in Jerusalem* is a point of view: some people don't share it. They're troubled by her portrait of Eichmann. The binary nature of justice turns people into 1s or 0s, either innocent or guilty. Eichmann frustrated this coding because he professed both his guilt

183 King Louie was voiced by New Orleans man Louis Prima in *The Jungle Book* (1967).

and his innocence. Why else would he say, striking a pose, that "I shall gladly hang myself in public as a warning to all anti-Semites on earth" and then plead not guilty to a crime whose penalty was death by hanging? But more troubling is Arendt's other suggestion, that the Israeli House of Justice was at fault, and that Eichmann's "silliness" was a consequence of the courtroom subverting itself.

Eichmann was 'forcibly emigrated' from Argentina by Israeli forces in what we now call a rendition. He arrived in court *because* he was guilty. The verdict wasn't in doubt, and thus the justice meted out to Eichmann was not (simply) legal. It was religious, cultural, natural – call it what you will, and I feel myself on very thin ice, but it operated on a plane distinct from the ordinary business of a court. The House of Justice knew Eichmann was guilty, it just had to prove it. Only it dealt with an unsatisfactory number and became unsatisfactory as a result. In Arendt's words, "the irregularities and abnormalities of the trial... only [detracted] from the law's main business." This was a show trial, however legitimate. And being in essence theatrical, it couldn't help but reveal the humanity of its antagonist.

Lacan believed that language imposed order onto the world. Human beings were its subjects. Words ruled the speaker. However, the Real cannot be expressed by language, though signification is constantly attempting to do so. As the Real can't be put into words, so too is there an emptiness in people, a gap that can't be filled. This emptiness compels us to pursue unattainable objects of desire – what Lacan called *l'objet petit a* – in order to feel whole. But, to paraphrase Slavoj Žižek, these desired things are McGuffins.

Hitchcock coined the word 'McGuffin' to signify story devices that drive a plot, but which are more or less meaningless in themselves. Superhero films are full of them: the nuclear bomb in *The Dark Knight Rises* is proved a nonsense when Batman and Gotham escape its blast. No one's interested in the reality of an explosion like that. The city and our hero have achieved anagnorisis; thanks to their quest to find the bomb, Commissioner Gordon has seen through Bruce Wayne's mask to the man beneath it. We'd be outraged if the nuke blew everyone up *after* all that redemption. Audiences don't care about the precise nature of peril, as long as it facilitates the story. We desire meaninglessness. We need it. Our psyche constantly invents plots to close the gap on the Real via the desire for empty objects.

If someone wants something, can you stop them having it? A boy wants his chips. A courthouse wants its scapegoat. And I'm not trying to compare overeating to genocide, but Lacan was all for desire. The empty Eichmann was Israel's *l'objet petit a*. As Arendt says in her epilogue:

> If it is true that 'justice must not only be done but be seen to be done', then the justice of what was done in Jerusalem would have emerged to be seen by all if the judges had dared to address the defendant in something like the following terms... "we find that no one, that is, no member of the human race, can be

expected to want to share the earth with you. This is the reason, and the only reason, you must hang."

What could be more real than that? And what did Eichmann deserve? His crimes were shocking. They violated the ordinary. Why not then violate the ordinary to punish him? Only admit to that violation. Admit to seeing him for what he is, from the loud seats up in the gods. Let comedy in and laugh at it; admit to the force of your feeling, your desire. Only realise that there will still be a void in you. Nothing will fill it. Ever.

King Lear ends with survivors deciding to "speak what we feel, not what we ought to say." This is exactly the mistake Lear's daughter Cordelia made in Act One, a mistake that sets the whole play in motion. The suggestion being that, though witnesses to Cordelia's corpse believe "we that are young | Shall never see so much", witnesses are often wrong. Tragedy is circular.

Forget the contents of the picture. Art is *l'objet petit a*. We need to judge the gallery it's hanged in.

*

Beauty and violence are also symbiotic. Like comedy and tragedy, both are *forceful*. The Dadaist-turned-Surrealist André Breton[184] wrote that "beauty will be

184 André Breton (1896–1966) was the French artist who founded Surrealism. He was expelled from the Communist Party, inspired by Alfred Jarry, and an associate of Antonin Artaud, Leon Trotsky and Frida Kahlo.

convulsive, or it will not be." Beauty transforms people into objects that represent the consequences of that force. Or, to use a peculiar analogy, whenever I see a stunningly beautiful woman, it makes me sad. What happens is this: they interrupt my reality. They make me fantasise. I imagine myself and this woman doing all kinds of things I've seen in the films (and porn, too, if I'm honest, though never in books or poems, because that's a bit dry). Then I become aware of how pathetic these entertaining fantasies are. My gaze is repelled; I look back, now from her point of view. Clear-eyed, I consider what about me puts this stone-cold babe out of my league. I wonder at what she must see, this inadequate thing: me.

This beautiful woman does to me what Herbert Marcuse[185] says of art: she "subverts the dominant consciousness, the ordinary experience." Now, that's not going to be true of everyone, as I'm especially lascivious, narcissistic and insecure. But "extremes of disrelation" – identified by Sontag as "pre-eminently the subject" of both surrealism and comedy – have tragic, violent

185 Herbert Marcuse (1898–1979) was a writer and critical theorist associated with the Frankfurt School. Marcuse disagreed with Freud's opinion that civilisation needs to repress the individual. The repression or displacement of natural desires makes us susceptible to exploitation. "The so-called consumer society and the politics of corporate capitalism have created a second nature of man which ties him libidinally and aggressively to the commodity form," he wrote in *An Essay On Liberation*. "The need for possessing, consuming, handling and constantly renewing the gadgets, devices, instruments, engines, offered to and imposed upon the people, for using these wares even at the danger of one's own destruction, has become a 'biological' need." Good stuff, right?

and beautiful dimensions too. Whatever your tastes, interruptive power *will* tear you from the ordinary as Penthius' head was torn from his body. This is a useful experience.

Daily living lets us no access to knowledge. Its force sweeps us along. How, then, do we understand it? Distance. If, for Jean-Luc Godard[186], "cinema is truth 24 times per second", it's not that cinema is reality, because truth is not real. The emphasis Godard puts on the mechanical process of reproduction – the twenty-four frames of celluloid that make up a second of film – admits to the necessity of distortion and artificiality. Lucian Freud's painting is true despite the ambiguity of its subject.

Here's a thought: seeing truth in cinema *because* it's a constructed medium is a bit like believing in God. When I'm watching a horror film, I stop myself having a heart attack by reminding myself that a director and their crew are just out of shot, that the monsters are made of rubber, the blood is syrup, nothing is real, and it will end but I won't. Similarly, for the religious, the world is no more than an elaborate Jurassic Park designed to test their mettle. Whenever they're tempted to sin, they remind themselves that that is a stage-set, those are fake dinosaurs, and God's directing all this to try our nerve. The

186 Jean-Luc Godard is the French director who made cinema self-reflexive. Godard specialises in pulp polemic and moments of sublime cool – the dance in *Bande à part*, for instance – though he is still perhaps best known for his first film, the romantic, weightless *A Bout de Souffle* (1960).

difference is, *art* creates a temporary distance between life and me, a distance that allows for understanding while never severing my connection to reality. Religion? Not so much. Which is why crimes inspired by films are altogether less frequent than crimes inspired by the Bible, the Koran or one of the other big franchises.

And back to Shakespeare. His late play, *The Winter's Tale*, is classified as a Romance – or, roughly, a tragedy in which illusions die but protagonists do not. The plot is this: King Leontes becomes convinced that his wife, Hermione, is unfaithful, and that their children have been fathered by another king, Polixenes. In his rage, he sends Hermione ("O thou thing") to prison, where she apparently dies. Their son then dies of grief, and Leontes orders their new-born daughter be abandoned on an island, there to die of exposure. All pretty miserable so far. Fast-forward twenty-odd years. Leontes' daughter, now called Perdita, didn't snuff it. She was found by some winsome shepherds and has spent the intervening period being wooed by Polixenes' own child (a strapping lad whose name I've forgotten). More winsome shepherds and a couple of mistaken identities later, and Perdita, her boyfriend and his father are back in Leontes' court, where Leontes has spent the last two decades feeling a bit guilty. Everything is explained, there's a lot of apologising on Leontes' part, and the lovers are allowed to get married. But Hermione's death still oppresses Leontes and that's when the play gets weird.

The Winter's Tale has two moments I want to discuss. The first is when the character Antigonus gets mauled to death by a bear. In a tragedy, this event would most likely be reported by another character – the idea being, maybe, that reportage lends even fiction more seriousness? A contemporary example of this is to be found in *Grizzly Man*, Werner Herzog's[187] film about a man called Timothy Treadwell[188] who thought he could live with bears. In one scene, Herzog uses headphones to listen to the recording of Treadwell being killed by one of his ursine pals. The viewer, however, witnesses Treadwell's death at a distance; all we're shown is Herzog's horrified reaction. *Grizzly Man* isn't a play, of course, but leaving death to the audience's imagination is still generically tragic. I'm no classicist, but I'm pretty certain that we never see an on-stage death in Greek drama. Which is a relief, because there's little more inherently silly than two luvvies setting about each other with tin rapiers. By staging violence (and this is perhaps distinct from filming it), a playwright risks showing that violence can *look* funny. Shakespeare's so entertaining because he exists within the two states: tragedy and comedy.

---

187 Werner Herzog is an Austrian filmmaker most famous for the deadpan voice-overs he provides for his own documentaries. It's one of the great joys to hear Herzog speculate as to the sanity of a penguin, the link between albino crocodiles and paintings in the Chauvet cave, Vietcong cruelty, death row or, indeed, the barmy Timothy Treadwell. Infamously, Herzog has also been shot by an air rifle ("it's not significant") and eaten his own shoe. He once described Wayne Rooney as "part viper, part bison."

188 Timothy Treadwell (1957–2003) was an environmentalist who spent thirteen summers living with grizzly bears in the Katmai National Park in Alaska. He was motivated to protect the animals after surviving a heroin overdose in the 80s. A bear killed Treadwell and his girlfried, Amie Huguenard, in 2003.

At the height of his pomp, the prog keyboardist Rick Wakeman[189] released a series of fantastical/olde worlde narrative solo albums, including *King Arthur*, *Journey to the Centre of the Earth* and that instant pop classic *The Wives of Henry VIII*. Not content with mere LPs, however, Wakeman also staged *King Arthur on Ice* at Wembley Arena, as a kind of concert-cum-play-cum-ice pageant. For reasons that remain as shrouded in mystery as the tale of brave Sir Galahad, one of my parents' friends went to see *King Arthur on Ice* (although I can only hope they bought tickets during a brief bout of catastrophic mental illness). This friend says that, during the climactic battle, the ten good knights and ten bad knights were meant to all kill each other simultaneously. Unfortunately, one bad knight slipped on his ice skates just before this fit of magical M.A.D, leaving one of Arthur's Gs gliding around with no one to kill and be killed by. With Wakeman's glittery-caped orgy reaching its crescendo, this good knight realised that he had to improvise. So, as eighteen other knights cancelled each other out, and as the last jizzum of synthesiser fell away, the odd knight out made a vague, swanlike gesture of despair and stuck his sword under his own arm.

---

189 Rick Wakeman is the Grumpy Old Man of prog. I once saw Wakeman in concert with two members of my prog-blues band, Ice Anvil, but the jury's still out on whether the man *knows* that he's ludicrous. I'm aware that calling someone ludicrous in the same sentence as the phrase "my prog-blues band, Ice Anvil" is a bit ambitious. All I can remember from the concert, meanwhile, is Wakeman being disparaging about what he calls "elf and safety". Lord of the Rings-y *and* dismissive? That's Wakeman!

Clearly, no one turns to Rick Wakeman for brutal theatrical violence. But however well-executed a stage fight is, the end result's still an actor lying on the ground trying not to breathe. Or, in the case of *King Arthur on Ice*, trying not to actually die of hypothermia. If the transformation from person to thing fails – if the representation inadvertently belittles reality – then the 'dead' victim becomes so irrefutably *alive* that an audience will probably find them funny.

So Shakespeare's risking laughter when Antigonus exits "*pursued by a bear.*" How did he stage that? Presumably with a man (or Gwyneth Paltrow[190]) in a bear costume. But, unlike Agave, surely no audience ever believed it was a real animal; unlike Virginia Woolf's pig-thing, we know it's a man (or Gwyneth Paltrow). Either that, or it *was* a real bear who'd escaped from the Globe's neighbouring bear pit, in which case the scene almost certainly became fucking terrifying.

The Winter's Tale's potential silliness doesn't reduce the impact of Antigonus' death, but it does put us at a distance. The bear is fake – like everything else on stage – and Shakespeare repeats the word 'bear' as if to remind us of a kind of systemic artificiality. When she get involved in some identity-swapping, Perdita says that "I see the play so lies | That I must bear a part of it." Of his

190 Gwyneth Paltrow is the character Roald Dahl never wrote, an ageless automaton with one mission in life: to kill Fun. Children are not allowed sugar under Paltrow's witchy reign. No, they must eat spelt, seed and assorted oats, like mice or divorcees. It's as if a faddist Miss Trunchball had somehow gained control over Miss Honey.

suspicions, Leontes says "if I mistake | In those foundations which I build upon, | The centre is not big enough to bear | A school-boy's top." The cross-dressing, the child's toy, the playful energy of life within the play itself mean that – though Leontes' "foundations" bear deathly fruit (bananas, perhaps) – bearing is literally manifested in a distinctly untragic grizzly man.

The second moment I want to discuss happens right the end of *The Winter's Tale*. Leontes is presented with a statue of his wife, whom he turned into a "thing" twenty years ago. Struck by its beauty, its strange interruption, Leontes' gaze is reflected onto himself. "I am asham'd: does not that stone rebuke me | For being more stone than it?" he asks. His recognition is rewarded. The statue begins to breathe. The king is shocked. "We are mock'd with art," he says, as indeed we have been. The audience can see that Hermione is real; like the actor playing dead, she's been alive all along.

Theatre is a mockery of reality. And why is mockery valuable? Because hopefully it will jolt us into recognising life's absurdities at a temporary distance from pain. It takes art, a prank even, for Leontes to reach an equanimity (an anaesthetic) which living can't grant him: "what you…do, | I am content to look on; what to speak, | I am content to hear," he tells his resurrected wife.

Heckler: Never seen it.

Transformations in *The Winter's Tale* are benign, and strange enough to distance the protagonists and their audience from tragedy. But when a violent, art-imitating transformation *really* happens, what's mocked is not so much death as life.

Susan Sontag writes that a catastrophe "will often seem like its representation. The attack on the World Trade Centre on September 11th, 2001 was described as 'unreal', 'surreal' and 'like a movie'." I had the same feeling on 9/11. Being the inveterate sportsman that I am, I was faking an illness to escape PE. Though my lies had caught up with me on my date with the cockroach back in chapter one, this time I was safe. The school nurse didn't give a fuck – she'd prescribe Strepsils whether your throat was sore or slit. So, having binned the Strepsils, I went to the common room to find my fellow truants watching a film. I arrived in time to see an aeroplane crash into a skyscraper.

The gist is this: we've all seen buildings blow up. Images of exploding skyscrapers and exploding cities and exploding people circle the world's screens like the adhan[191] circles mosques. The only difference is that the World Trade Centre did not blow up in a movie.

Jean-Luc Godard's never made an action film. I wish he would, but I suspect his version of the truth might jar with the genre's bellicosity. That's not to say action films are unprincipled. They have to follow a set of rules in order to

191 The adhan is the Islamic call to prayer. It's called out by a muezzin five times a day. You'll recognise the sound from action films: whenever a CIA operative gasps 'if they get hold of that plutonium…my God,' the adhan is the chanting you hear as the scene cuts to a bustling souk full of terrorists poring over the plans of a plutonium dump.

traduce and fictionalise reality as thoroughly as we expect them to do. Here's an excerpt from the rule book:

- A building will blow up either at the beginning or the end of a nefarious scheme. Both will bring closure: if it's at the beginning, the building will be 'innocent' and we know the violence will be avenged; if it's at the end, the building is 'guilty' because it's full of bastards getting their comeuppance.
- If the bastards are American, they will have a sentimental reason for turning bad. They'll be haunted by a dead wife or the soldiers they were forced to leave behind thanks to the interference of two-faced politicians. Their callousness will be forgiven by medals placed on a rainy grave, a blue-eyed child being shot, or Patrick Swayze[192] surfing.
- If the bastards are foreign, they will fall into easily-understood categories. Mexican = drug-dealing psychopath. Arab = religious maniac. South American = banana republic CIA puppet. German = sophisticated pervert. Russian = flinty-eyed extremist. Chinese = cack-handed drone. African = cannibal despot. British = posh twat.
- The bastards will never be from Canada because tedium can't be twisted into villainy. (There was that time between about 2003–2006 when Americans would pretend to be Canadian so that everyone would stop talking to them about Iraq. This backfired because, thinking they were Canadian, everyone stopped talking to them altogether.)

192 Patrick Swayze (1952–2009) was an American actor who starred in *Ghost*, *Point Break* and *Dirty Dancing*.

- Explosions only kill sympathetic but expendable supporting characters. A sage black policeman, maybe, or a nervous university-educated rookie, or a woman our hero doesn't fancy. People we'll get over, basically.
- All the other people who die don't matter because they'll either be extras or computer graphics.
- Everyone involved is heterosexual. Unless you need comic relief.
- If Nicholas Cage[193] is in it and it was made in the 90s, the film will be amazing. Citations: *The Rock*, *Con Air*, *Face/Off*.
- If Nicholas Cage is in it and it was made after the 90s, the film will be horseshit. Citations: everything he's done since *Face/Off* with the exception of *Bad Lieutenant* and *Drive Angry 3D* (tagline: 'he broke out of Hell to make things right'. If you haven't seen it, it's essentially *The Winter's Tale* with guns.)

Unfortunately, life breaks these rules, breaks them as totally as time has broken Nicholas Cage. In life, there's no keening guitar solo to tell me how to feel. As a consequence, I spend most of my time ignoring others' pain. It's as W.H. Auden writes in his poem *Musée des Beaux Arts*: "[suffering] takes place | While someone else is

193 Nicholas Cage is an Ozymandias doomed to live in the wreckage of his empire, wandering between the sets of increasingly shitty thrillers muttering "look upon my works, ye Mighty, and despair!" As the poet Shelley writes, "round the decay | Of that colossal wreck, boundless and bare | The lone and level sands stretch far away," though dotted about in Cage's case with posters for *Bangkok Dangerous*, *Season of the Witch* and the *Wicker Man* remake.

eating or opening a window or just walking dully along." Everyone's an extra in the movie of me (though, again, I am *very* narcissistic).

Action films help reinforce the illusions that we can choose when violence affects us, and that brutality is solved by more brutality. Neither are supported by the slightest shred of evidence. We enjoy the access cinema, music, books and videogames grant us to synthetic suffering. In *The Tempest*, another Shakespearean Romance, Trinculo has a crack at observational comedy when he says that "when [people] will not give a doit to relieve a lame beggar, they will lay out ten to see a dead Indian," and this, to me, seems still to be the case. We have faith in the respect money accords us; we pay to watch pain, safe in the knowledge that the customer has the right not to feel it themselves. It's as though we demand the entertainment industry to monopolise force. That way, we can allow ourselves to believe force itself is fiction, or at least a reality other to our own.

Terry Eagleton says that "the perfect terrorist is a kind of Dadaist, striking not at this or that bit of meaning but at meaning as such." The Dada Manifesto, read at the Salon des Indépendents in Paris on 5th February 1920, bears this out:

> no more painters, no more writers, no more musicians, no more sculptors, no more religions, no more republicans, no more royalists, no more imperialists, no more anarchists, no more socialists, no more Bolsheviks, no more politicians, no more proletarians,

> no more democrats, no more bourgeois, no more aristocrats, no more armies, no more police, no more fatherlands, enough of all these imbecilities, no more anything, no more anything, nothing, *nothing, nothing, nothing.*

Maybe, then, 9/11 wasn't surreal but Dada – from the West's perspective, at least. Surrealism commits violence to create a new meaning. Dadaism is an act of annihilation. Thought-provoking when executed in a gallery, but what does it make us feel as its audience in real life?

There are physical, civic and relational laws we accept and expect to be followed as unthinkingly as the rules of action films. When these laws are blown up, we are forced to witness meaninglessness. Not even death. Worse, the destruction of the order of things: we believe in the order, we are the things. Confronted with this, shocked by violence's uncanny symmetry with what entertains us, our first response is to assume our subjectivity is at fault. This can't be true. But it is. So what we thought was true is false. Then we realise that it doesn't much matter what we think. This *is* – the "suspended animation" of a torture victim, suffering the explosion of their world and their image of themselves within it.

Thomas Hoepker[194] took what may be the most unnerving photograph of 9/11. In the foreground, a group

194 Thomas Hoepker is a distinguished German photographer. Between 2003 and 2006, Hoepker served as president of Magnum, the photographers' organisation set up by Henri Carter-Bresson, Robert Capa and others.

of five New Yorkers. In their chinos and with their carefree body language, they could be in a GAP advert, were it not for their backdrop – the backdrop of a burning city, the backdrop that mocks Francis Fukuyama's[195] neo-conservative (read: moronic) claim that the fall of the Berlin Wall marked "the end point of mankind's ideological evolution." As though mankind is *going* anywhere! As though we're not circular (it's all those chips we eat).

Anyway, Hoepker's New Yorkers seem to be ignoring reality as breezily as Fukuyama himself, reminding me again of *Musée des Beaux Arts* when "everything turns away | Quite leisurely from the disaster." In the photo, a woman leans back to listen to her smiling lover; in Brueghel's[196] *Icarus*, the painting Auden describes, the ploughman works on even as Martin Lawrence tumbles into the sea. But ordinary selfishness is one thing. What people find truly obscene about the image is this: the New Yorkers look like they're laughing.

The *New York Times* said that "the young people in Mr Hoepker's photo aren't necessarily callous. They're just American." Now, I'm just as hasty and imprecise as the next pretentious young man, but I don't see any evidence to support that accusation. Even hard-bitten New Yorkers are hopelessly, blindly sentimental – how else do you

195 Francis Fukuyama is a chump. Nine days after 9/11, he was hectoring George Bush to invade Iraq. Whenever I think about him, Auden springs to mind: "the clever hopes expire | Of a low dishonest decade" as "intellectual disgrace | Stares from every face."

196 Brueghel refers to a dynasty of Flemish painters, the first of which was Pieter (1525–1569), who painted *Landscape with the Fall of Icarus*. The painting itself is bit like *Where's Wally?*

explain their sympathetic attitude towards the IRA (an attitude that 9/11 changed pretty abruptly)?

My own sweeping statement aside, Hoepker didn't *know* that his subjects were being callous. I don't know that they weren't, of course, but in 2012 the website Slate received an email from Walter Sipser[197], the man on the far right of the photo. In his email, Sipser writes that "Thomas Hoepker did not ask permission to photograph us." Is permission relevant? Probably not. Hoepker saw Sipser as history, not a human being, and we don't need to ask history's permission seeing as it never fucking asks for ours. But Sipser also says that he and his friends "were in a profound state of shock." In such a state, are we as accountable for our feelings as when we're compos mentis? Maybe the Auschwitz tourists were shocked too. Who knows? Who am I to judge? Shock makes you do funny things – laughing being one of them.

And why shouldn't the New Yorkers laugh? For the theorist Georges Bataille[198], laughter is a Dada paradise "where nothing counts any more – neither the 'object' nor the 'subject.'" I don't agree with that, but – if they *were* laughing – couldn't you argue that the New Yorkers were simply coping with the annihilation of object and subject in the only way they knew how? And is laughter

---

197 Walter Sipser is a Brooklyn-based artist.

198 Georges Bataille (1897–1962) was a French writer and essayist. Sartre dismissed him but Foucault dug him. Bataille formed a secret society, the symbol of which was the corpse of a decapitated man; the members all promised to be the sacrificial victim, but no one could be persuaded to act as executioner. Bataille's first wife later married Jacques Lacan. Small world.

only callous? You laugh when you know you mustn't; you wouldn't laugh if the reason for not laughing wasn't a good one. You have to acknoweldge the law to break it, to have fun. Helpless laughter runs deeper than callouses.

9/11 wasn't funny ha ha but, as with all terrible events, the prohibition of jokes about it does nothing to help. The idea that a joke can be 'too soon' – what does that mean? That everything has the *potential* to be funny, but that humour is only permitted once an event's been absorbed into the ordinary, made history, even forgotten. In my opinion, the comic who made fun of 9/11 *that night* is far braver than one who makes fun of it twelve years later.

Moreover, to the best of my knowledge (and forgive me if I'm wrong), but Hoepker wasn't hauling survivors out of the Twin Towers. He was on the outside, historicising the moment. There's nothing wrong with that. It's a valuable job. But it's stupid to imagine that a professional photographer did not have an agenda that day. Both the photographer and the photographed were "small against death and the mourning of history" – a beautiful line from a poem written by a soldier in the Second World War on learning that his girlfriend has died. I can't remember the poet's name and for some reason it doesn't come up on my Google (*my* Google?), but I think the poem's called *O Lovely Vessel* and there's a small prize for whoever can track it down. The poet goes on to remember "how small you looked once on the New York quays | Against the harsh skyscraper jargon of the city," and can anyone look big, can anyone be appropriate, *against* reality? The poet's pain springs from the same source as the *New York Times*' censure: the obscene truth that life goes on.

A photograph taken by Kevin Carter[199] in 1993 shows a vulture waiting for a Sudanese child to starve to death. The child, a girl, is crawling towards a UN feeding station. Her little distended body is bowed in submission, a kind of canine prayer. When the photo was published, Carter came under attack. A child was dying. How could he have been that *distanced*? Suddenly, to treat life as material – to seek out terrible things in order to frame them for an audience – was an inhumane, even inhuman occupation. Carter let carrion eyeball an infant. More, he was another kind of carrion, feeding off the *scene*, the symbol (if not the body) of suffering. Did the girl die? If so, in the name of what? Art? In 1994, months after he was awarded the Pulitzer Prize, Carter killed himself.

According to João Silva[200], another photographer the UN flew in to the feeding station, Carter took the photo then shooed the bird away. Perhaps a futile gesture, but could *any* gesture be sufficient in that situation? Life goes on. And what did people want Carter to do? To

---

199 Kevin Carter (1960–1994) was a South African photojournalist. Carter was driven by his disgust at the Apartheid regime. He was so immersed in the violence of the townships that the press began referring to Carter and his colleagues as the Bang-Bang Club. Exhausted by South Africa, Carter went to the Sudan by way of a holiday.

200 João Silva is a photographer born in Portugal and based in Johannesburg. Silva was Carter's friend and fellow member of the Bang-Bang Club. In 2010, Silva trod on a landmine while out on patrol with US troops in Afghanistan. He lost both legs beneath the knee.

drop the camera, fly the girl back to civilisation and turn her into Augustus Gloop? Was Carter a scapegoat for his critics' own inaction? Or was his photo simply too *real*? You don't want to open your newspaper to find that photo staring out at you with the blank, black eyes of the vulture, eyes that put its purpose beyond the fiefdom of sympathy. That kind of shit ruins my appetite.

As Carter's subjects are caught in suspended animation, so too are the photo's viewers, its victims. We are shocked by mankind's frailty. After the flood, God tells Noah that "the fear and dread of you will fall upon all the beasts of the earth and all the birds of the air…everything that lives and moves will be food for you." But here, in Sudan, the fear and dread falls upon human beings. In Carter's photo, the vulture transforms a child into food. It frames our helplessness, our obscene and fundamental thing-ness; when God told Noah that "I now give you everything," he was lying.

Carter made people recognise violence. But he needed to let violence *happen* in order to report it. A reporter can't go back in time, but they obey time-travellers' rules. Don't change history. Only by doing nothing will today make sense tomorrow. Carter's job was to see things for us. Having photographed a murder, he said:

> I was appalled at what I was doing. But then people started talking about those pictures… then I felt that being a witness to something this horrible wasn't necessarily such a bad thing to do.

As the mediator between violence and its audience, Carter had to preserve suffering. But he was not simply a witness. He was also an artist. To make people talk, he needed to frame horror in a way that *pleased* a mass audience. And that pleasure is the ethical difficulty.

A photographer captures a thing. He sells it to the media, who sell it to the public. Carter didn't chase the vulture away *before* taking the photo because he knew it would excite us. As for the girl, did Carter feed her to *us*? Animals – another recognition. Are we vultures?

A few years ago, the Chinese artist Xu Zhen[201] recreated Carter's photograph. Xu paid a Guinean mother and child to spend twenty-one days in a gallery. The child posed for five hours a day next to a mechanical vulture. Xu photographed her. So did visitors to the gallery – they queued up in serried ranks to commemorate the scene for themselves.

Xu posed a number of questions, some specific to China. Guinea is not the Sudan. For Xu's Chinese audience, were Africans all the same? And how did forgery – the mass reproduction of a 'Western' product for a domestic market – affect the quality of the original? Other questions were more universal. In Carter's photograph, the Sudanese girl stops being 'she' and becomes 'this' – *this* is happening! *This* being the very anticipation of her becoming a thing: a corpse, a work of art, the symbol of an event in history. *This* being the moment she stops being her, whoever she was.

201 Xu Zhen is a Chinese artist and prankster who's had work exhibited at the Venice Bienniale, MOMA and the Hayward Gallery, as well as galleries in his native Shanghai.

By turning her into an object, duplicated in millions of newspapers, has Carter committed an act of violence? Or is Xu the brutal one, for treating her as an abstract thing to be toyed with and subverted?

Xu's installation is absurd. On one level, its lack of violence is obscene: the healthy child is cared for by its healthy mother; the audience are nourished by culture; the artist gets paid. Xu turns to bathos Carter's photo and the tragedies with which it's become associated, including Carter's own death. It's an aggressive performance – more prank than joke. The installation even becomes a kind of game. Will you play along by taking photos too? And how will they look? But the discomfort an audience member feels *within* the recreated moment is necessary. The recognition of the mechanical vulture as a surrogate for our own appetites tests, strains and strengthens our connection to reality.

9/11 precipitated The War on Terror (because what's more practical than a war waged against an abstract emotion?), and the War on Terror precipitated a change in the way we fight. Unmanned drones are now so prevalent that the US air force apparently trains more drone pilots than 'real' pilots. These drone pilots sit in the comfort of New Mexico, flying their aircraft via video link. This reduction of warfare's psychological impact spares the pilots from shock. Indeed, the technological gap between the pilots and their victims superficially transforms war into a video game. The pilots use controllers. The damage they cause happens on a TV screen to what may as well be computer graphics. If the pilots are shot, they don't die, they restart. And this new language of combat is spreading – Prince Harry[202] says flying attack helicopters is "a joy for me because I'm one of those people who loves playing PlayStation and Xbox, so with my thumbs I like to think that I'm probably quite useful."

Here's another analogy: the drone pilot is relieved of the duty to consider their victims' feelings. So is the comedian. Both deal with collateral that can be ignored as long as the target is hit.

Art uses a mediating language to turn its victims into things, in order to alert its audience to the transformation. Drone technology, on the other hand, uses a mediating language to fool its users. By sparing them from experiencing the singularity of tragedy, drones make their pilots more efficient killers.

Nevertheless, a Pentagon study shows that 29% of these pilots still suffer stress-induced burnout. The study seems confused by this. After all, the pilots are "family men" with "good values". Why are they burning out? Maybe because, however you frame it, you are still small against death, and not the other way around. Is it that, while the US air force may seek to annihilate the meaning of its victims, and its method of waging war may become increasingly similar to kinds of entertainment, people with "good values" will always eventually *see*?

*

202 Prince Harry is an example of how a spell in the Army sorts out young, aggro, state-funded tearaways.

Heckler: What's all this got to do with comedy?

I see it like this. Violence corrects nothing, though we want it to, desperately. An act of violence works like a joke (again, a supposedly corrective force). It divides people into opposing sides. It gives both a moral framework to believe in or deny. It degrades its targets. But it also degrades those whose supremacy it's supposed to be enforcing. Because which of 'us' isn't degraded by a redacted decade of rendition, of Guantanamo, of the erosion of the very rights we're killing kids to uphold and enforce? Walter Raleigh, striking his son, turns himself into a thing: the aggressor, the victim-in-turn.

Simone Weil says that "the human spirit is…swept away…by the very force it imagined it could handle," suffering by the same means the same fate as those they've victimised. Is that the reason that comedians are stereotypically unhappy "in real life"?

Victims are funny because *things* are funny. Violence works to temporarily relieve the spectator of responsibility even to themselves. Think to those moments when things are *so* bad, we're presented with a choice between collapse or laughter. Both are admissions to the fact that the world can't be corrected, that life is exactly as bad we feared it would be. But collapse, hysteria, weeping – those are acts of total submission. The laugh is different. It submits but it *sees*, and recognition eases the pain. Even if it makes you look callous.

Writers are told to kill their babies. Like I should have killed that bit about Jamie Oliver. Why? Restraint.

Excessive force proves nothing except a lack of self-control. On the other hand, jokes have to create recognition *immediately* – a purpose that sets them apart from books, films, paintings etc. And the only way to do so is to be excessive. Funny shocks tend to be mild (I can't believe Gavin would *say* that to Stacey[203]! Doesn't he love her? Does this mean that everything I hold dear is a lie? And isn't it *funny* that their families are named after Britain's most popular serial killers?) but it's violent nonetheless. People submit to humour because its force relieves them of living.

Can a joke be beautiful? In his last show, *Revelations*, Bill Hicks[204] discusses the media's one-sided portrayal of drug use.

> [It's] always that same LSD story. "Young man on acid, thought he could fly, jumped out of a building. What a tragedy." What a dick – fuck him! He's an idiot. If he thought he could fly, why didn't he take off from the ground first?

What justifies Hicks' violence is the manipulation of a tragic event by those reporting it. Drugs are not evil, whatever the government would like you to believe. People are ignorant and they do stupid things – that's the truth, the tragedy and the comedy, and that's why I find

---

203 *Gavin and Stacey* was a successful BBC sitcom.

204 Bill Hicks (1961–1994) was an American stand-up. Hicks was a prodigiously clever, dark and dedicated comedian. He was killed by pancreatic cancer.

Hicks funny even though a friend of mine *did* die, high, tumbling off a roof.

For Hicks, it's that all-too-rare movement from ignorance to knowledge which is truly newsworthy. He imagines "a positive LSD story":

> Today, a young man on acid realised that all matter is merely energy condensed to a slow vibration. That we are all one consciousness experiencing itself subjectively. There is no such thing as death, life is only a dream and we're the imagination of ourselves. *[beat]* Here's Tom with the weather.

I think that joke's beautiful. Classically beautiful: anagnorisis as comedy. Hicks makes us laugh at how spectacular life is, despite the pay-off's bitter comedown. The old, unchanging structure of the news is reasserted. As at the end of *King Lear*, the witnesses have learnt nothing.

Hicks' show ends with a video clip of him being shot. But the most beautiful joke a comedian has told is powerful because of the real, concrete threat it subjected that comedian to. In *Steamboat Bill Junior*, Buster Keaton[205] runs around a town being buffeted by a hurricane. In one shot, a house collapses around him. As Paul

205 Buster Keaton (1895–1966) was an American actor and filmmaker. Keaton's atonally elegant, blank face forgives us any responsibility we might otherwise have felt for him. He struggled with alcoholism and worse; the legend goes he once escaped a straitjacket thanks to tricks he'd learnt as a vaudevillian. Keaton is Dostoyevsky to Chaplin's Dickens, or Roy Keane to his Gareth Southgate.

Merton[206] writes, the stunt required "no great athleticism or timing: all [Keaton] had to do was stand still while the front of a house weighing three and a half tons fell on top of him." In the shot, the house-front starts to fall. Keaton's character doesn't know he's in danger. Nothing stands between him and death. The house-front hits the ground; the dust settles; Keaton is still standing, by chance in the gap created by a window in the top of the façade. Keaton remembers that "I had clearance of two inches on each shoulder and the top missed my head by two inches and the bottom of my heels by two inches." Allowing himself to become the victim of force, the wild miracle of Keaton's commitment to his art is easily equal to the miracle of his character surviving a building being blown apart. In this joyful instance, the powerful structure is the victim, and the individual remains intact. It's a triumph of being just small enough against death.

A witness is responsible for retelling an event clearly and as it 'really' happened – a task that is literally impossible. An artist is different. They have the right to recreate, truthfully, what they see to be an event's meaning. Maybe the difference is also in a kind of discretion. What's the value in hearing Timothy Treadwell's death, when we could watch *Grizzly Man*?

And I'd like to end by describing a piece of music by John Coltrane. Like Buster Keaton, Coltrane refused to compromise, few though the inches were between success

---

206 Paul Merton is most famous for being curmudgeonly on *Have I Got News For You*.

and crushing defeat. In 1957, Coltrane said that "my music is not a thing of beauty, and the only way it would be justified is if it becomes that." At the time, a great many people agreed with him. *Down Beat* called Coltrane's music "horrifying nonsense." In the *Telegraph,* Philip Larkin[207] tastefully described it as "the scribbling of a subnormal child." And the most telling and oft-repeated criticism was this: that Coltrane played "joke music." The joke is, of course, that *we* don't like it. That it doesn't suit us. That it doesn't make Hull-languishing misogynists boogie. Even when his fans complemented him, they did not do so in terms of traditional beauty: Leroi Jones[208] says Coltrane "showed us how to murder the popular song."

Murderer or not, for me there's nothing more beautiful than Coltrane coping with violence. On 15th September 1963, the Klu Klux Klan blew up a Baptist church in Alabama, Mississippi. The explosion killed four schoolgirls: Addie Mae Collins, Denise McNair, Carole Robertson and Cynthia Wesley[209]. Though he'd go on to die in jail, the bomber (a Klan member called Robert Chambliss[210]) was originally only convicted for the crime

207 Philip Larkin (1922–1985) was an English poet. I've never understood his popularity; for me, Larkin is the best of a post-war bad hand. Obviously I'd rather read Larkin than John Betjeman, but then I'd rather read a dog turd than John Betjeman.

208 Leroi Jones, now called Amiri Baraka, is an American essayist, academic and poet. As a younger man, Baraka said some pretty loathsome stuff about rape. He says Marxism made him revise his opinions.

209 These girls were aged between 11 and 14. They were killed when a bomb went off in the 16th Street Baptist Church. Twenty-two other people, mostly children, were injured by the blast.

210 Robert Chambliss was the member of the KKK positively identified

of possessing dynamite without a permit. How's that for a joke?

If American courts and their witnesses failed, however, artists did not. Recorded in 1964, Nina Simone's[211] *Mississippi Goddam* is a blunt, thrilling polemic, the kind of song she sings so well, *forcing* her voice on until she's beyond the risk of ugliness. John Coltrane's *Alabama* was recorded even earlier, less than two months after the bomb exploded, but he doesn't rage the way Simone does. She demands an eye for an eye: "you're all gonna die and die like flies." He considers not what was lost, nor what's to come, but what remains in the moment.

Coltrane's first, mourning bars shadow the text of Martin Luther King's[212] eulogy, delivered at three of the girls' funeral. The music refuses to play along with violence's circularity; it denies the bomb its charge by recreating not the event but the lesson King salvages from the wreckage. King said:

> [The girls] say to us that we must be concerned not merely about who murdered them, but about the

---

as having placed dynamite under the steps of the church on 16th Street. Chambliss was initially acquitted, only to be re-tried in 1977. Chambliss, then 73, was sentenced to life. His surviving collaborators, Bobby Cherry and Thomas Blanton, have subsequently been convicted of murder.

211 Nina Simone (1933–2003) was an American musician. She made anger sound beautiful.

212 Martin Luther King (1929–68) was an American minister and activist. King advocated non-violent protest. He won the Noble Prize in 1964, and was murdered by petty criminal and sometime-pornographer James Earl Ray.

> system, the way of life, the philosophy which produced the murderers. And history has proven over and over again that unmerited suffering is redemptive.

Has history proved this? I don't know. But it sounds nice – and that's not meant to sound flippant, if you see what I mean. King was in the business of consolation.

The music, meanwhile, is slow. There are no drums. Coltrane's pianist, McCoy Tyner[213], provides a constricted pulse over which the tenor saxophone rises and falls with King's rhetoric. At the completion of his melancholic phrase, Coltrane holds a note that marks its end and, we assume, its recurrence. Then the great drummer Elvin Jones[214] comes in with a groove that throws the tragedy bodily to one side.

At this turning point, *Alabama* even becomes clubby, in a sixties way. Jones and Coltrane were both at one time or another heroin addicts, and now this music – hard-edged, cool, *meant*, with Jones' cursing breath at the back of it – transports us to "the dives and dens" Martin Luther King rails against in his eulogy, the places where "filthy jokes" are told. The key is in the silence *before* the change. In it, we're expecting Coltrane to repeat himself as history does, as injustice does. Instead, a new pulse, a pulse so specifically identified with a people, a place, a moment,

213 McCoy Tyner is a pianist from Philadelphia. Having been taught by his neighbour, Bud Powell, Tyner joined Coltrane's group in 1960. They fell out five years later – to Tyner, Coltrane had begun to play noise.

214 Elvin Jones (1927–2004) was a peerless drummer. A big man, only he could wrestle with the physical presence of Coltrane's music.

a struggle. A pulse that evokes drink, smoke, sex, jokes. Fun.

Is it seemly to stop mourning? Is Coltrane being callous? Can you have fun in such a context? How do we measure death, unless we measure it against life?

After the dives and dens, Coltrane does return to the opening phrase. He has to. Like any good tragedy, *Alabama* finishes where it began. But its force comes from resisting force. *Mississippi Goddam* – a great song and righteous, too, but one that feels brutalised into being. Coltrane, though, doesn't seek power. He reins himself in, playing with an understatement that draws attention away from the individual and towards the whole. He resists being made to hate hate. The innocent building doesn't demand that a guilty building also be blown up. Coltrane breaks the cycle of banana skins.

Maybe that's just postcolonial timidity on my part? Whatever, it asserts what Aimé Césaire's[215] recreated, new-liberated dreamer tells white Prospero in *Tempest*: "I've decided that I will no longer be Caliban."

Why talk like us, walk like us, when you can shoo-be-doo?

Heckler: I want my money back.

---

215 Aimé Césaire (1913–2008) was a writer and politician from Martinique. Césaire taught Frantz Fanon. He resigned his membership to the French Communist Party after 1957's Hungarian Uprising. Césaire refused to meet Sarkozy after the little guy insisted that French schoolbooks present colonialism as a positive force in the world.

Inside Outside.

In 1978, the American chemical manufacturer Union Carbide announced it was moving out of its 53-storey New York skyscraper. With over 130 subsidiaries worldwide, Union Carbide was doing well. New York wasn't. In 1975, President Ford[216] had refused to bail it out of a financial crisis; the city only avoided bankruptcy by raiding teachers' pensions. By 1978, prisons were full to capacity after a city-wide power cut created riots, looting and (thanks to the radical redistribution of electrical equipment) hip hop. The police were reeling from the anti-corruption investigation set in motion by Frank Serpico[217],

216 Gerald Ford (1913–2006) became US President after Richard Nixon resigned in 1974. Ford, a Republican, granted Nixon a pardon for the crimes he committed in office.

217 Frank Serpico joined the NYPD in 1959. His superiors having ignored his evidence of widespread police corruption, Serpico spoke to the *New York Times*. The front page story made the Mayor set up the Knapp Commission to investigate the NYPD. In 1971, Serpico was shot in suspicious circumstances; his colleagues refused to help him as he lay bleeding on the floor. Nevertheless, he survived to testify in front of the Knapp Commission. When Al Pacino asked him why he went through all this, Serpico replied, "if I didn't, who would I be when I listened to a piece of music?"

and the Son of Sam[218] had only just been caught. Union Carbide needed some fresh air.

It was a significant moment in the history of corporate culture. As *Fortune* magazine said at the time, Union Carbide wanted to become "a responsible corporate citizen." To do this, it tried to "discern the popular will and then see how it [could] tailor its own interests to that sentiment." Architecture was the elected medium of this new sentimentality.

In *Utopia's Ghost*, Reinhold Martin[219] details the architect Kevin Roche's[220] efforts to design Union Carbide an egalitarian office. Roche began by conducting a survey, not of the new site, but of the old. He learnt that Union Carbide's employees were unhappy about executives receiving proportionately more office space than they did. So, at the company's new Danbury building, each and every employee was assigned an office of 180 square feet, equipped with individual lighting and temperature

---

218 'Son of Sam' is the nickname of David Berkowitz, a New York man who shot six people dead and wounded a further seven between 1976–77. The press loved him, and Berkowitz revelled in the attention. This led New York to pass the 'Son of Sam Law', which stops criminals profiting from their crime via book deals, newspapers etc. Later, Berkowitz did a Jonathan Aitken and found God in jail. When Spike Lee set his movie *Summer of Sam* against the backdrop of Berkowitz's murders, Berkowitz himself complained to the *New York Times* about "this madness, the ugliness of the past…resurfacing again – all because some people want to make some money."

219 Reinhold Martin is associate professor of architecture at Columbia University.

220 Kevin Roche was born in Dublin in 1922. In 1948, he left Ireland to be taught by Mies van der Rohe at the Illinois Institute of Technology. In 1966, he formed a practice with John Dinkeloo.

controls. The office interiors were chosen by public vote; employees were shown thirty differently-styled mock-ups and asked to state their preferences. The finished design reflected a balance between price and popularity. Danbury's canteen, too, was equipped to respect diversity. It contained six distinct environments, including a singles' bar and (Martin says) "a back room modelled on a men's club", décor the *New York Times* has "charitably" described as "Late Disco."

Danbury is in a wood. Nevertheless, you could get in your car, drive into its internal 2,500-space car park, do a day's work and drive back home without once having to interact with the outside world. To counter claustrophobia, the building is shaped like a snowflake – that most individual pattern – to afford every employee a view of the surrounding country. Each office is also angled 45° away from its neighbours, guaranteeing the privacy of its occupants. Thus everyone has the privilege of being contained, not only from nature, but from everyone else. Union Carbide had created an environment familiar to us all. Corporate solipsism. Atomisation. Danbury is a map of our world.

This corporate sentimentality did not extend to all of Union Carbide's workers. On the 2nd December, 1984, forty-five tons of a lethal gas called methyl isocyanate leaked from badly-maintained containers at a Union Carbide plant in the Indian city of Bhopal. Overnight, at least 3,800 people died. A further 20,000 are estimated to have died as a direct consequence of the leak. Roughly half a million more were injured, though it's hard to know exactly how many, because Union Carbide's victims lacked IDs, birth, marriage and death certificates, land deeds and other written proofs of citizenship.

"How can one determine the damage inflicted on people who live in shacks?" That was the question asked by one of Union Carbide's lawyers in the aftermath of what's still the world's worst industrial disaster. The value of human life, it turns out, is relative. In 1985, the *Wall Street Journal* put it like this:

> An American life is worth approximately five hundred thousand dollars. Taking into account the fact that India's gross national product is 1.7% that of the United States, the court should compensate for the decease of each Indian victim proportionately, that is to say with eight thousand five hundred dollars.

In the end, Union Carbide got a discount, thanks to an Indian Supreme Court determined not to scare off foreign investors. Compensation averaged at just $2,000 per fatality, and $800 for permanent injuries (figures all the more paltry when one considers that India's GNP is now over 12% of America's).

At this point, you're probably thinking, "right, you're sort of done with comedy, then?" Well, Bhopal is obviously not laugh-a-minute. But Union Carbide's actions signify changes that societies are undergoing. Changes to the nature of individuality and power which directly affect us all. Even comedians.

Danbury's "tailored" design marks a sea change in the way in which we're controlled. It was an investment in what Michel Foucault called "human capital" – a new effort to persuade people that their individuality can flourish *only* within the confines of capitalism. To de-babble this, it's a bit like when a man hits his partner. Unless he's drunk, this guy will only become violent once he's convinced his victim that he *alone* can provide them with a secure environment. Under the illusion of security, the victim then *chooses* not to break free. To choose otherwise would be to lose their identity – or, rather, the identity created for them by their victimiser.

For Foucault, 'individuality' (as we're sold it) is a trap. When people struggle against the authorities oppressing them, they often do so on individualistic terms. I want more freedom for myself to be me! But this doesn't damage power, however violent the struggle becomes. The individuals in question actually *strengthen* the authorities; individuality, according to Foucault, "is not the vis-à-vis of power but one of its main effects."

To define 'Freddy Syborn', I must employ words written by the authorities. For some of you, 'c***' will do the job nicely. For others, I must resort to other definitions. Man, woman, gay, straight, black, white – like obscenities, identities are created by a process of often censorious definition, a process the individual cannot exist apart from; like obscenities, identities are signifiers, loaded with a history of prejudice, used to constrain the unpredictable energies of the signified (i.e. me and you).

For my grandfather, 'wog' meant anyone who lived south of Paris. Identities have diversified a good deal since then, but diversification is not automatically liberating. Some signifiers have helped and some have hindered, but all are the product of power. If a white, straight, middle class tree like me fell over in a forest, and no one was there to hear it...

New categories are tailored to fit individual mores. But the authorities, the tailors, aren't looking to liberate us, but to create a glut of false or secondary choices. We're obsessed with lifestyles. But the entitled micromanagement of our *rights* – as consumers, as sexual beings, as snowflakes – makes us forget that each of us is, in the words of John Donne[221], "a piece of the continent, a part of the main." And why do these tailors want us to forget the collective? Because smaller units are easier to break.

Margaret Thatcher[222] (or Lady Gaga to her pals) has gone to Heaven to smash the angels' union. She leaves behind George Osborne[223] in chubby floods of tears,

---

221 John Donne (1572–1631) was an English poet. Donne blew an inheritance on what the musician David 'Whitesnake' Coverdale refers to as "wine, women and song." Donne then fought alongside Sir Walter Raleigh against the Spanish at Cadiz; married the love of his life, Anne More, in defiance of her father; had twelve children, seven of which survived childhood; buried his wife; considered suicide; decided against it and became Dean of St. Paul's at James I's behest. Dying, he wrote "Thou hast done, | I have no more" – the only satisfying pun in history.

222 A chemist, Margaret Thatcher (1925–2013) was rejected for one job on the basis that she was "headstrong, obstinate and dangerously self-opinionated." Happily, J. Lyons & Co. hired her, and she repaid them by inventing Mr. Whippy.

223 The teaty (adj. milkily vindictive, flabbily malign. Synonyms: duggish,

and an interview, given in 1987, in which Mrs. T said "there is no such thing as society. There are individual men and women, and there are families." Thatcher's "family" is a sentimental kick-back, designed to woo the journal in question, namely *Woman's Own* (with its patented mix of recipes, sex surveys and hard-right social theory). Nowadays, David Cameron[224] would rephrase it as something like 'society is a family of families', but it's the same thing. Thatcher just called a black man a spade, is all. Plus, today we like more sugar on the pill. Blame the obesity epidemic (but don't blame the obesity epidemic on the economically-motivated breakdown of societal relations – blame it on individuals who've made their own beds, then lain in them eating until they have to be winched via crane into the super-sized graves that they dug themselves before making their beds).

'Humanity' is now a marketing trope. Take the adverts for the latest Samsung phones. These phones, we're told, are "designed for humans." What does that mean? Literally, that Samsung doesn't design phones for dogs or horses or rats. Associatively, I suppose, they want to suggest that good, caring individuals will buy them in order to maintain relationships with other good, caring individuals. Logically, though, it means that these phones are made for 'humans' whose status is predicated

---

booblike, pappy. Who can resist making up insults using parts of a woman's body?) 'George' Osborne is the current Chancellor of the Exchequer. Along with D. Cameron and B. Johnson, Osborne belonged to the Bullingdon Club, whose members would ruin restaurants and then chuck cash in the faces of the stunned restaurateurs. Classy.

224 David Cameron is the current Prime Minister. An empty vessel.

on material wealth. To put it another way, does Samsung make things for "people who live in shacks"? No. Those people couldn't afford smartphones. So does that exclude them from humanity? Yes, according to Samsung's logic. Man is, not because he thinks, but because he is 'free' to spend, to buy into a "tailored" brand of relational living entirely reliant on expensive technology.

We've bought into the logic of Samsung's slogan. Think back to the Arab Spring. What made the West so optimistic? A profound dislike of Hosni Murabak[225], or the fact that everyone in Tahir Square seemed to be using a smartphone? If they're ready for Twitter, the logic ran, they're ready for change. As long as kangaroo courts Instagram the lynchings, it's alright by us!

Egypt was trending in *our* language #woopwoop, but what has the 'humanising' force of social media resulted in? For us, it's the recent revelation that we are policed by our 'friendly' technology on our governments' behalf and under the sign of Prism. For Egyptians, it's the Muslim Brotherhood[226], a party once banned by Murabak. These charmers recently condemned the UN Commission on the Status of Women for trying to "destroy the family"

225 Hosni Murabak, ex-President of Egypt, was one of Maggie Thatcher's old pals (she thought him "full of beans"). Mubarak kept Egypt under what was essentially martial law for almost thirty years. During the uprising, he ordered that injured protestors should not be treated with anaesthetic.

226 This book is going to print today, on 3rd July 2013, and protesters have once again occupied Tahir Square, this time to oust the Muslim Brotherhood. The Egyptian Army's deadline is fast approaching; President Morsi says he's going nowhere. Everyone's tweeting. This is why print is dead.

and initiate "the complete disintegration of society." And what had the CSW done to deserve this denunciation? Well, they'd demanded that women be given:

> Full rights to file legal complaints against husbands accusing them of rape or sexual harassment, obliging competent authorities to deal husbands punishments similar to those prescribed for raping or sexually harassing a stranger.

These rights, according to the Brotherhood, herald "the decadence that awaits our world." At least one Egyptian sitcom maker agrees. Taqieddin Abdel Rashid, the deputy head of the Islamist TV channel Al-Hafez, says that "everything is about supply and demand and currently there is a demand for...cleaner art in our society." And, by 'cleaner', he means *Coffee Shop*, a sitcom in development which won't feature a single woman.

In the West, meanwhile, there's a sense of disbelief. Is this what Tahir Square boils down to? It looked so hopeful on Pinterest. But do we have the right to be surprised at the Spring's turning into a long, repressive summer?

From the Bible to the Samsung, we load devices with a proselytising, humanising power. John Donne was a priest; the Internet is good for research; all modes of communication are useful. But do they make us "part of the main"? Or do we like them because they give us power over others? There's always someone excluded: a non-believer, a non-speaker, a subhuman who can't afford the technology. Launching the new iPad in 2010, Steve

Jobs[227] said the machine was "a revolution" which would "set you free" – set you free, that is, to look conceited on the Tube as you watch films on a thing that's a bit blurrier than an oldish television. Pity, then, the poor heathen still languishing in an un-iPadded cell!

Perhaps even the CSW is one of these humanising devices? One may condemn the Brotherhood for misogyny. But on a practical level, is the West *that* much better? Take the media's coverage of the Delhi gang-rape in December 2012. In the *Times*, for instance, Libby Purves[228] describes Indian men as possessing a "murderous, hyena-like contempt" for women. While Purves was looking "eastward in disgust", however, Emer O'Toole[229] was pointing out that "the *Wall Street Journal* decries the fact that in India just over a quarter of alleged rapists are convicted" and yet "in the US only 24% of alleged rapes even result in an arrest, never mind a conviction." British success rates are hardly much higher. Then again, Indians are only worth 1.7% of our value, so what's the fuss?

We beat other people with pieties we don't practise ourselves. Dow Chemical is an example of how corporate

227 Steve Jobs (1955–2011) was the co-founder of Apple. A style icon when it came to technology, Jobs was a bizarrely bad dresser, favouring the clumpy jeans/clumpy trainers look beloved by Americans and men who still live with their mothers.

228 Libby Purves is a journalist and author. I've realised that I slag off quite a few journalists in this book. When the bad reviews roll in, I can pretend that Purves is a Svengali rigging the system against me. This'll spare me from acknowledging my work's ropey reality.

229 Emer O'Toole is an Irish academic and journalist. O'Toole recently wowed *This Morning* with the results of having left her armpits unshaved for eighteen months.

language is becoming more "responsible" at a time when corporate action is going the other way. When it joined the vomit-inducing 'Olympic Family' in 2010, Dow Chemical's CEO, Andrew Liveris[230], announced that:

> With our long-standing commitment to global sustainability, innovation, scientific excellence and addressing world challenges, we believe Dow is perfectly matched to the vision of the Olympic Movement, which is about peace, progress and the world coming together to celebrate our common humanity.

This is textbook horseshit. Peace, family, humanity – all fragile enough – feel almost antithetical when one remembers that Dow Chemical bought Union Carbide in 2001. But the Bhopal site it now owns remains dangerous; chemicals, toxins, swill there still, leaking into the local environment and its people, their water, their breast milk. For that reason, in 2012 the London Assembly said that Dow Chemical's belonging to the Olympic Family has "caused damage to the reputation" of the Games. As one Assembly member put it, "almost thirty years after the horrific Bhopal chemical disaster, the factory site has still not been cleared up and the survivors and their families continue to fight for compensation." That must be a bummer for the Family, made up as it is of ethical powerhouses like BP and McDonalds.

230 Andrew Liveris is an Australian engineer, equipped with the perkiest Google images page I've ever seen.

So maybe (and it pains me to say it) Bob Dylan is wrong when he sings that "money doesn't talk, it swears." To swear, one has to operate within a shared system of values, if only to violate those values. If the last ten years alone have taught us anything, it's that money, *big money*, does not obey the same rules as we do. There's more than economics to deregulation.

The Bush administration awarded a number of lucrative contracts in post-war Iraq to a private security firm called Blackwater. However, despite being financed by American tax-payers, Blackwater operated outside of both Iraqi and American law (to which US soldiers are accountable). This immunity was granted by Order 17, a decree issued by Paul Bremer[231] the day before he left Iraq. As Jeremy Scahill[232] points out in his book *Blackwater*, Order 17 was curiously timed, given that "Bremer was leaving after allegedly 'handing over' sovereignty to the Iraqi government." If the war's intention was to establish the democratic rule of law – from which, in principle, no one is excluded, and no one exempt – why was

231 L. Paul "Jerry" Bremer III (even his *name* makes me feel anti-American) was the suspiciously youthful-looking diplomat who served as the Ambassador-at-Large for Counterterrorism under Ronald Reagan. In May 2003, Bremer became Director of the Office for Reconstruction and Humanitarian Assistance in Iraq. He shipped 363 tonnes of money into a warzone, on the basis that the US didn't "have time" to impose financial restrictions. He has since been investigated as part of a Congressional inquiry on financial waste, mismanagement and fraud. See Naomi Klein for more on this. Bremer is currently the Chairman of GlobalSecure Corp, whose mission is "securing the homeland with integrated products and services for the critical incident response community worldwide." So he's basically a villain from *Robocop*.

232 Jeremy Scahill is a journalist and filmmaker from America.

Blackwater free to murder with impunity?

This question became impossible to ignore after September 16th 2007. On that day, Blackwater mercenaries shot up the traffic around Baghdad's Nisour Square, killing seventeen Iraqis. One witness said the massacre was like "a horror movie". Is the comparison prompted simply by blood, or by the sheer arbitrariness of the force being used on visibly innocent civilians (including a school-bus of children)? Blackwater representatives later claimed their men "acted lawfully." How, we might ask, given that Blackwater wasn't operating *within* a legal system?

Blackwater wasn't accountable to US law, so the US wasn't accountable for Blackwater. The Bush administration were free to take x amount of public money, divert it from the public sector (i.e. the military) and give it to a private company from which members of the administration profited. This private company could then do the military's job, but with none of the public sector's accountability. It's a business model that the present British government hopes to apply to schools and hospitals. Unaccountability: that's the dream.

Anyway, I've put my hobby-horse down – it broke its leg making the jump between Blackwater and the coalition, and all I could do was shoot it in the head, blood blooming steam in the frosty spring grass as the gunshot drowns in waving, Wiltshire down. Another day as a racehorse trainer. What a life.

Shack-dwellers don't exist. Neither do mercenaries – Blackwater men can't be measured against Iraqis, even on a scale as utilitarian as gross national product. Both are obscenities, asterisks, capitalism's dirty little secrets. The authorities exclude them from legal and economic definition: if they have no identity then they have no human capital, so they're not human, exempting them (and/or their business partners) from praise or blame. What unites the victims of Bhopal with the victimisers of Baghdad is the double-edged power of that exclusion.

How is the individual included or excluded from capital, from categories of humanity, and from the rule of law? How, in short, is power *bound*? There are two materials I want to talk about. Mirrors and concrete. I'll start with mirrors, because I'm vain like that.

Mirrors were originally highly-polished metal discs, usually of brass or tin. The price of these semi-precious commodities put reflection beyond the means of all but the wealthiest. Then, in the sixteenth century, Venetian craftsman discovered that they could create thin sheets of a reflective compound by mixing mercury and tin, which could then be overlaid by thicker plates of clear glass. Though still prohibitively expensive, mirrors could now be mass-produced. This coincided with the era's most ostentatious make-over.

In 1678, Louis XIV[233] set about transforming his father's old hunting lodge at Versailles into Europe's most spectacular palace. At its centre was the Hall of Mirrors,

233 Louis XIV (1643–1715) was the autocratic king of France for seventy-two years. He was succeeded by his five-year-old great-grandson – the Sun King had outlived his son, his son's son, and his son's son's eldest son. During the Revolution, Louis' body was exhumed and destroyed.

designed by Jules Hardouin-Mansart[234] as a bridge between the *appartements* of the king and queen. The Hall is seventy-three metres long and consists of seventeen arches, each made up of twenty-one mirrors – 357 in all. Despite their multiplicity, however, the mirrors were intended to reflect a singularity: the king's power.

Louis' subject's reflection was made possible by him and – to the extent that the material was synonymous with wealth and power – *in* him. This grandeur was unsustainable; some of the Hall's decorations were melted down to pay for the wars Louis waged. But its extraordinary cost, its detachment from reality, reinforced the myth of a singular, supra-human authority. When a subject caught their reflection in the Hall of Mirrors – under the canopy of a painting called *The King Governs Alone* – they were seeing themselves in the light of the Sun King.

The mirror lost its exclusivity after 1835, when Justus von Liebig[235] (a cracking name for a mirror-maker) discovered how to coat glass in silver. Since then – or certainly since the 1919 Treaty of Versailles, signed in Louis' Hall of Mirrors – authorities have changed the way they make spectacles of themselves, though mirrors still come in handy.

In the past, a king used artifice to create the impression of his omnipresence. Theatrical power compensated for royalty's inherent structural weakness. Monarchs were

234 Jules Hardouin-Mansart (1646–1708) was a French architect. Very Baroque.

235 Justus von Liebig (1803–73) was a German chemist. As well as cheap mirrors, von Liebig invented Oxo cubes and fertilisers.

born to rule. Their bodies were pre-ordained; if they were ill, power itself was ill. The king was visible proof of the state's authority but he was just one man, so his image needed to be reproduced everywhere. This is the art of propaganda, transforming the head of state into a signifier, then stamping it onto the signified of power – just as a monarch's head is stamped onto a coin.

Today, powerful people assert themselves in different ways. Mirrors are used to negate, to create *absence*. Why else are so many skyscrapers made of reflective glass? Their mercenary occupants aren't Sun Kings: they don't want to cultivate singularity, they want to disappear.

When seen in a skyscraper, a whole city is reflected back at itself from the source of its wealth. Mirrors make the city appear to radiate from the skyscraper, but it also allows the skyscraper to evade definition. Where are the boundaries? Who's inside? There's nothing behind a reflection but what's also in front of it. Skyscrapers are privileged with vision and invisibility, like interrogators behind a one-way mirror.

In Versailles, the subjects saw themselves reflected in the decorative archways of a palace (a public space, a sight to be seen). In the interrogation room, however, there is no painted canopy. The only person reflected in the one-way mirror is the subject, the suspect: the singularity of your guilt in the unseen eyes of authority. As Blackwater excludes itself from the law, so too does the interrogator exclude themselves from visibility.

To be seen by someone you can't see is the weakest possible position. To see and not be seen, on the other hand, is the most powerful. Power is refusing to reciprocate. Vulnerability is assuming that this refusal is impossible.

This relationship between total strength and total weakness doesn't have its Woodstock in, say, the cells of Abu Ghraib (as all school caretakers know, if you're going to use cameras, make sure you stay *out* of the picture). Its formative burst of optimism happened over a century ago, when the utilitarian Jeremy Bentham[236] mapped out his hypothetical prison, the Panopticon. Circular and inward-facing, the Panopticon revolved around a central guard tower or 'inspection house'. The prisoners were arranged into individual cells stacked on top of each other. The cells' one open side was angled toward the tower, giving the guards a 360° view of the prisoners, while the prisoners were unable to see either the guards or (in a Union Carbide-esque flourish) their fellow inmates. In this Panopticon, then, or behind one-way glass, or from the executive heights of our financial districts, absolute power is inextricably linked with absolute *sight* – a totalitarian anagnorisis.

Bentham's Panopticon put a name to the face of a new kind of power. As Marcel Gauchet and Gladys Swain[237]

---

236 Jeremy Bentham (1748–1832) was a British philosopher and utilitarian. Bentham left his body to an anatomist, with the proviso that the remains were preserved as an 'auto-icon'. So his skull and spine are attached to a straw body, wax face and olden-day clothes, and this bizarre object now sits in a cupboard in UCL like a wistfully insane Bilbo Baggins. A digital version is available at www.ucl.ac.uk/Bentham-Project/who/autoicon/Virtual_Auto_Icon

237 Gladys Swain (1945–93) was a French psychiatrist. Marcel Gauchet is a French historian and Swain's frequent collaborator.

say in *Madness and Democracy*, the Panopticon is a symbol "for the ambitions of universal readability." This "readability" is "induced by the authorities" in order to achieve what Gauchet and Swain call "society's omnipotence over itself", and what I'd call the Internet.

Why is universal readability a way of controlling us? Because it fosters the illusion that we're free. We're not physically restrained; on this side of the glass, our movements are unrestricted. If we worry, it's about our reflection, which reminds us of our invisible audience. So we control ourselves. We sit still. We look good.

What if I want to know who's *behind* the mirror? Such a desire is taboo, and it's one of the reasons *The Rock*'s so thrilling. In that movie, Sean Connery[238] is under interrogation when he uses a chair to smash the one-way mirror, coming face to face with his tormentor, FBI Director Womack. All together:

"Womack! Why am I not surprised, you piece of shit!"

Yes! Boom! Hats off to Michael Bay[239]. His first three movies were *Bad Boys*, *The Rock* and *Armageddon*. If he'd died before *Pearl Harbor*, you could genuinely say of him

---

238 Sean Connery was the first James Bond. He loves Scotland and hates paying tax. Since Bond, Connery's output has been shaky: *Zardoz* (red loincloths), *Entrapment* (red lasers), *League of Extraordinary Gentleman* (red faces).

239 Michael Bay once referred to his filmmaking style as "fucking the frame". He is currently courting the Chinese market with his interminable *Transformers* franchise, which are probably the worst films *ever* that haven't starred Danny Dyer.

what the *Times Literary Supplement* said of James Joyce: "he published nothing but masterpieces."

Like E.M. Forster's[240] *Maurice*, *The Rock* is a tale of two men inverting social order. In *Maurice*, their inversion was of a purple hue. In *The Rock*, it's orange – the orange of explosions. The plot is this: Sean Connery is the only man to have broken out of Alcatraz. Twice. Or three times. However many times for him to have been the only man to have done so. It's not clear. Anyway, Ed Harris[241] is an American military man who's gone rogue. Why? Again, it's not clear. Harris has taken some tourists hostage on Alcatraz, armed with chemical weapons that look like strings of luminescent anal beads. So Connery joins up with a nervous chemical weapons expert played by – who else? – Nicholas Cage. Their plan? To break *in* to the prison. I know, right? Usually, you'd break *out* of prison! Destroy the signs! Fuck the system! How did Michael Bay come up with that? I'd wager he was smokin' a fatty and kickin' back with Foucault.

I just watched that scene again on YouTube and it's magnificent. And while I calm down, I'd like to move on to discuss YouTube itself. Let's start with its catchphrase

---

240 E.M. Forster (1879–1970) was a British novelist and academic who lived for many years in King's College, Cambridge. *Maurice* was the posthumously-published tale of the titular homosexual, Maurice, gadding around Penge. Forster's novel *A Passage to India*, meanwhile, betrays a fear of "hyena-like" Indian men.

241 Ed Harris is an American actor. I'd like to pretend that *Pollock* is my favourite Harris movie, but it's actually *Stepmom*. When Susan Sarandon gets diagnosed, there's not a dry eye in the house. This house, at least. Where I live. Alone.

– "Broadcast Yourself" – another instance of the world coming together to celebrate our common humanity, though the reek of corporate inclusiveness is undercut by an imperative edge. And what are we broadcasting *on*, exactly? What's the architecture of this new hall of mirrors?

YouTube claims to control its content with rules prohibiting real violence, real death, racial hatred and nipples. So why hasn't it removed videos showing the deaths of Saddam Hussein[242], Muammar Gaddafi[243] and Neda Agha Soltan[244]? How long would comparably raw footage of white Europeans being murdered last online? What about footage of other Iranian protesters dying in the streets, of Syrians mutilated by car bombs, of Pakistani jailers sexually assaulting their prisoners and of Al-Qaeda beheading its captives? Is it too much to suggest that these videos remain in the public domain because they conform to a certain worldview?

(Though I sound like one, I'm not a conspiracy theorist. Quite a few comics are convinced 9/11 was an inside

242 Saddam Hussein (1937–2006) was an Iraqi dictator. Hussein rose to prominence in the 1968 coup, which brought to power the Ba'ath Party. He became President in 1979, and was hanged having been found guilty of a handful of his crimes against humanity.

243 Muammar Gaddafi (1942–2011) was a colourful Libyan dictator. Beyoncé, Usher, Mariah Carey, Timbaland, 50 Cent and Nelly Furtado are just some of the artists who apparently had never heard of Gaddafi before they accepted fees of up to a $1,000,000 to play for the R&B-lovin' Mad Dog. Very much the Berlusconi of North Africa.

244 Neda Agha Soltan (1983–2009) was shot while unarmed and watching a protest over the undemocratic Iranian election in 2009. The Iranian government claim that Soltan was murdered by protesters, the CIA and/or Western journalists greedy for news. Soltan's gravestone has been removed by pro-government vandals.

job. I've been told 'there's this mind-blowing video on YouTube…', as though the American government would secretly kill thousands of its own people and then leave the evidence online.)

There are YouTube videos of violence committed by or against Americans and Europeans. These videos, though, will almost always be authorised clips taken from Western news channels or TV shows. They're filtered of their impurities. 'Western' brutality is presented as freakish, incidental to the culture. *Here*, violence is the product of outsiders – robbers, suicides, madmen. Moreover, CNN or the BBC, say, frame violence with a synthetic 'neutrality'. The news has trained us to trust its aesthetic. Portentous jingle? Check. Earnest, desk-bound silver fox? Check. Husky woman in too much make-up, flashing haughty come-to-bed eyes at the hapless viewer? Check. It must be true!

On the page showing Neda Soltan's death, there's a column of suggested links to 'similar' videos. At the time of writing, these include those of a Kurdish girl's murder, a naughty nurse caught on camera, a Liberian warlord being butchered, a Brazilian woman's bottom, a Paraguayan boy being assaulted by the filth, a man inserting his balls into his partner's anus, two Mexicans being shot dead on a train platform, and a French educational video showing women how to use and dispose of female *préservatifs*.

You'd think only necrophiliacs would readily associate corpses with contraception. But, in YouTube's libidinal mess, public health advice is even *more* shocking than murder. That last video is the only fully-frontal shot of a vagina I've found on YouTube and, yes, my research has been thorough. Nudity as a social violence and vaginas, the last taboo; technology changes, morals remain misogynistic.

So YouTube's very quick to ban fannies. It's less quick to ban hatred. On its 'Safety' page, the website makes the solemn promise to censor "hate speech" directed at:

> "Protected groups [including] but not limited to [people of] race or ethnic origin, religion, disability, gender, age, veteran status and sexual orientation/ gender identity."

That's not my weird grammar, by the way. The square brackets are trying to make sense of over-inclusiveness. As it stands, *everyone* belongs to at least five of those categories, making YouTube's promise too vague to mean much on a moral or pragmatic level. We're all protected, so no one's protected – a corporate irresponsibility "designed for humans".

Every registered YouTube user is automatically the subject of surveillance – not just by the website's authorities, but by other users, signed up or otherwise. This panoptical construction lets me know, for instance, that the user dude201081 joined YouTube on March 31st 2008, that he lives in Denmark, and that he's interested in deep-sea diving and aeroplanes. He has no idea I know this information.

Under a clip of protesters being shot in Bahrain, dude201081's posted a message saying "this is so sweet, I had to touch myself! Modern pestcontrol [sic] and democracy in it's [sic] purest form!" Under the video of Neda Soltan's death, meanwhile, he says "one less rat to pollute the white white west. Thank you islam gunman." Perhaps "white white west" is an allusion to "Wild Wild West | Jim West, desperado | Roughrider," though dude201081 is surely the last person you'd expect to quote Will Smith. I infer this from his comment under a clip of an Arabic man being threatened with death: "at least it doesn't happen to white people. Kill the mother fucking nigger, the west do not give a fuck anyway!" Whether Arabs can be classed as 'niggers', meanwhile, is a question that's perhaps too esoteric for a man of dude201081's intelligence.

If one asked why dude201081's comments remained online, YouTube would point to its policy of 'self-policing'. Users can flag up content that they find offensive. Once flagged, YouTube decides whether or not to remove it. This is "society's omnipotence over itself." But who *are* these policemen with their flags? I imagine they're generally people like dude201081. The small, reactive 'power' they've been given within YouTube's unaccountable confines has maddened these nutjobs like wine. They suffer from the alienation created by websites like YouTube: the disembodied individual is artificially empowered, either as compensation for a lack of real-world status, or to suppress the desire to establish it.

There are no other public forums in which dude201081's sentiments could be expressed, possibly save screenings of *Sex and the City 2*, in which an American woman chucks condoms around a souk. The scene's so bereft of cultural sensitivity that it feels less like a ladies' night and more like an recruitment video for Al-Qaeda. In *SATC 2*, it's also revealed that Arabic women have the latest Western fashions on under their burkas. Theocracy is *so* last season – consumer goods can set us free! The juxtaposition suggests that the burka is simply tasteless, as though dressing badly is the ultimate price a woman can pay. The message being, presumably, that life is like an interrogation room: always look good in the mirror.

Liz Jones loved *SATC 2*.

Anyway, what protects dude201081 and other YouTube users (including, of course, Anders Breivik[245], who wept when the Norwegian court relayed a racist video he'd posted on YouTube) from prosecution? Unaccountability. YouTube's unaccountability, that is. dude201081 can be made to fall on his sword, that of "universal readability" – not a crime you could accuse this book of, unfortunately. But there are no ramifications for the corporation who effectively publish his views.

I'm not advocating censorship. dude201081 can say what he likes. But we mustn't elide free speech with what's made possible by a commercial organization's inaction. To prosecute dude201081 would be do what the sociologist Ulrich Beck[246] describes as seeking "biographic solutions to systemic contradictions", i.e. to blame the individual for authority's problems. But what do we see in the mirror

245 On the 22nd July 2011, Anders Breivik murdered 77 people and injured another 319. Most of his victims were unarmed teenagers on the island of Utøya in Norway.

246 Ulrich Beck is a German sociologist and professor at LSE.

YouTube holds up to us? Foucault calls it "the governance of individuality". We are ruled by a kneejerk semaphore of flagging, by appeals to an unseen, all-seeing power, which evades its responsibilities by exploiting our weakness for a rigged simulation of democracy.

*

How would dude201081 defend what he'd written on YouTube? Most probably by claiming a line like "kill the mother fucking nigger, the west do not give a fuck anyway" was a joke.

We've all done this. The self-defence, that is, not the racist diatribe. Say I express an opinion that offends someone. It doesn't matter if I truly believe that high-waisted jeans *don't* suit my girlfriend, or that the West really *doesn't* give a fuck. If a comment causes offence, I defend myself by saying that 'I was joking'. I say this on the assumption that my victim and I share a preconception about what a joke is: something neither honest nor serious, though – *by its nature* – hostile. I also make the excuse every time I'm made aware of looking judgemental or like I'm ashamed of myself. What does that preconception and that self-awareness say about the comic impulse?

Jokes can stop me taking the implications of my narrow-mindedness and self-loathing seriously. I distance myself from others' feelings, and this distance distances me from my own. It's like the reversal of empathy: by not caring for others, I'm relieved of caring for myself. I get the same sensation whenever I tell someone 'the truth' because, in that context, the truth always hurts. But, unlike a joke, the truth doesn't need to create (at least the simulation of) pleasure. So does the intention to provoke laughter forgive a joke's hurtful content, or does it suggest an even greater callousness?

The tabloids label offensive comments as 'sick jokes' because it's assumed no well or healthy person could *honestly* be so drastically, so shamefully out of step with popular sentiment. On March 17th 2012, Bolton midfielder Fabrice Muamba[247] suffered a heart attack during an FA Cup quarter final. His predicament prompted a student called Liam Stacey[248] to tweet "LOL. Fuck Muamba. He's dead!!!" When other twitterers expressed outrage, Stacey goaded them, sometimes using racist language to do so. He was later jailed for 56 days by the Swansea Magistrates' Court. The District Judge justified the conviction by telling Stacey:

> Not just the footballer's family, not just the footballing world, but the whole world were literally praying for Muamba's life...I have no choice but to impose an immediate custodial sentence to reflect the public outrage at what you have done.

247 Fabrice Muamba played for Arsenal, Birmingham and Bolton. Muamba's heart had been stopped for more than an hour before he was revived.

248 Liam Stacey is in his early twenties. Stacey served half of his fifty-six days' sentence; Swansea university let him complete his finals, but one year late and not on campus.

Was "the whole world" *literally* praying for Muamba? I don't pray. I wished him well but, you know, er, people have cardiac arrests every day and I'm a busy man: this pseudo-intellectual nonsense isn't going to write itself, Muamba. So were Stacey and I the only unsympathetic bastards not knelt in prayer at a candlelit vigil sponsored by the *Sun*? I mean, I can't imagine John Terry was *that* bothered.

A judge speaking in sentimental hyperbole is worrying – I'm amazed he could resist referring to Muamba as the footballer of hearts. His judgements being dictated by that hyperbole, though, is downright scary. Essentially, it seems, Stacey went to prison for being quite unpopular. Is that how it works? If so, let's wish Noel Edmonds[249] good luck in those showers.

Should the law have a reactive, YouTube-style relationship to something as subjective as offence? The public don't get to decide what's legal and what's illegal. Or do we? In which case, tell us and we'll get to it. We'll castrate paedophiles and hang traffic wardens, Jeremy Clarkson[250] will be the king of all the land and Tulisa[251], his straight-talking queen.

---

249 Noel Edmonds, he of the lacquered bouffant and a selection of vividly paisley shirts which even despot dandy Mobutu would have rejected on the grounds of taste. Edmonds has recently swapped his trim little goatee for a poorly-dyed beard. He runs a cult called *Deal or No Deal*.

250 Jeremy Clarkson, Chipping Norton's village idiot.

251 Tulisa is a musician, perfumer and (rather illogically) a judge of talent. To say that Tulisa was the most likeable member of N.Dubz is rather like saying Rudolf Hess was the most likeable high-ranking Nazi. It may be true, but it's still faint praise.

A few months after sicktweetaboutafootballergate, the British courts bashed another unwholesome poster-boy for free speech. With an impressive 77 convictions to his name, Manchester man Barry Thew[252] was never going to be an ardent fan of the constabulary. So when he heard that PCs Nicola Hughes and Fiona Bone[253] had been murdered, it was the work of a moment for Thew to write on his t-shirt the phrases "one less pig, perfect justice" and "killacopforfun.co.uk". These being even punchier than Stacey's *bon mots*, Thew got four months.

Inspector Bryn Williams[254] expressed satisfaction at Barry's banging up. "To mock or joke about the tragic events of that morning is morally reprehensible," Williams said in a statement to the press. There are two things here. Firstly, are "morally reprehensible" things *always* illegal? Piers Morgan[255] isn't in prison. Secondly, to the best of my knowledge, 'joking' wasn't actually part of Thew's defence. So why is his t-shirt considered to be an attempt at humour?

---

252 Barry Thew, 39 at the time of his arrest, was sentenced to four months for a Section 4A Public Order Offence, i.e. displaying writing or other visible representation with the intention of causing alarm or distress.

253 Nicola Hughes (23) and Fiona Bone (32) were killed by Dale Cregan on the 18th September 2012.

254 Inspector Bryn Williams of the Greater Manchester police.

255 Piers Morgan has somehow bounced back after publishing fake photographs of British 'servicemen' abusing Iraqis. When he's not making Peter Andre sob on ITV, Morgan plies his hateful trade in America. A fierce critic of gun culture, it wouldn't be entirely illogical – or tragic – for a rifle-toting hayseed to retaliate by shooting Morgan dead.

1. In Susan Sontag's words, Thew was at "the extremes of disrelation" to society, and consequentially misreacted "according to the norms of feeling." (Though I'd hazard that this disrelation is a consequence of social marginalisation rather than any artistic decision on Thew's part.)
2. The phrase "perfect justice" is a species of judgement.
3. Under "killacopforfun.co.uk", Thew has written "HA, haaa?" A surprisingly modest sign-off for a flâneur of Thew's audacity, the laugh starts confidently and ends with a sort of nervous, minor-key uplift. It's like Thew's some Mancunian Larry David[256], holding out his hands and saying "come on? Who's with me? Someone?"
4. Jokes go *against* the grain of 'normal' feeling.

Sadly, it looks like Thew and Stacey are both colleagues of mine. So I'd better defend them: they were only broadcasting themselves.

Thew was telling a joke and I imagine he meant every word of it. He was intentionally misreacting to public sentiment with lines he'd written himself. He needed an audience with which to communicate, if only to cause

256 Larry David, the co-creator of *Seinfeld* and star of *Curb Your Enthusiasm*, is famed for saying the wrong thing at the wrong moment, then compounding the error by saying it again and again in the effort to prove that it's not offensive. I'm a bit like that. Like when I said it wouldn't be "entirely tragic" if a rifle-toting hayseed shot Piers Morgan dead, I didn't mean I'd *like* a rifle-toting hayseed to shoot Piers Morgan dead. I meant that it would be *appropriate* for a rifle-toting hayseed to shoot Piers Morgan dead. In other words, I'd appreciate the logic of a rifle-toting hayseed shooting Piers Morgan dead, without necessarily *wanting* a rifle-toting hayseed to shoot Piers Morgan dead, or *applauding* the rifle-toting hayseed in question.

offence. He was even making a stab at anagnorisis: "oh yes, policemen *are* antithetical to the justice system they claim to uphold. What a clever switcheroo." Structurally, that's a gag I've used in this book. I would say 'to my shame', only I'm not ashamed. I just wouldn't use Nicola Hughes and Fiona Bone as content. They died doing their job very bravely and commendably, making them unsound signifiers. And I don't want to go to prison.

The joker will either be on the outside looking in, or the inside looking out. Thew, for instance, had positioned himself at a distance from society. Thew was also angry. As Stewart Lee says in *How I Escaped My Certain Fate*, "there are few things as inspiring for a good stand-up as utter disgust, as genuine utter contempt for a person, an event, a point of view." Disgust is looking down on something from the gods. My favourite instance of this is Lee's superlative routine about Richard Littlejohn's[257] campaign to label female sex workers as prostitutes, which ends with Lee carving into Littlejohn's gravestone the word 'cunt'. Watch it – on YouTube, if you're too

257 Richard Littlejohn, Daily Mail journalist, idiot savant and author of *To Hell In A Handcart*. Amazon describes *THIAH* (as we Littlejohncats call it) as a "thrill-packed rollercoaster ride of a novel, bursting with all the humour and irreverence that have made him Britain's No 1 newspaper columnist... Mickey French is just an ordinary bloke, an ex-cop struggling to look after his family as self-righteous do-gooders and bungling bureaucrats bring the country to its knees. But Mickey's life is turned upside down when he is attacked in his own home and forced to defend himself. His arrest for murder is front-page news, and soon the whole nation is watching as he battles for justice, lost in a maze of dodgy lawyers, politically correct police officers, bogus asylum-seekers, self-publicising politicians, shameless journalists and rabble-rousing shock-jocks." Basically, *THIAH* is a love-letter written to Tony Martin.

cheap to buy Lee's DVD – for a great example of why comedians wouldn't enjoy contempt if their audiences didn't enjoy it too.

We love a scapegoat. Liam Stacey and Barry Thew had to go to prison as peace-offerings to the pleasure we took in being *disgusted*. Hatred is sentimentality's B-side, and the Great British Public love to indulge in both. Take London talk radio DJ Nick Ferrari[258] – and shoot him – and shoot all his friends – and then, if you're ever troubled by the part you played in the revolution, listen back to when Ferrari described the MPs' expenses scandal as "9/11 crossed with the death of the Princess." How do you 'cross' those things? Henri Paul dashing Dodi against one tower, Di[259] against the other, before billing the taxpayer for all that beer. Again, check out YouTube – there's this mind-blowing video…

Ferrari's comparison suggests that 9/11 and Diana's dying are two distinct signifiers. September 11th signifies outrage; August 31st signifies (in the words of Stewart Lee) "the shrieking grief of twats." Logically, then, the

258 Nick Ferrari is a DJ on LBC, the London radio station-cum-agony aunt for racists within the M25. My publishers' lawyers have made me remove a joke about Ferrari's strong feelings for the deceased Princess of Hearts. But Ferrari surely wouldn't mind a little bit of un-PC banter? In his philosophical radio *salon*, robust rhetoric is directed at everyone, whether they're immigrants, single mothers or immigrant single mothers. Come on, lawyers, it's just a joke. Diana? A single mother who shacked up with a work-shy Egyptian, breaking the heart of the next in line to the throne of Great England? And you think Ferrari was *upset*? No, you're right, lawyers. He probably was.

259 Dodi al Fayed and Diana, Princess of Wales died on the 31st August 1997 when the car that Henri Paul was driving crashed in a Parisian underpass.

expenses scandal must have made Ferrari angry, but it must also have made him want to peer into a dead sexy woman's house. Who knows, a heady emotional cocktail like that could've aroused him. Did Ferrari fuck a wreath? Anything's possible.

Back in 1826, William Hazlitt[260] wrote that "it is not the quality so much as the quantity of excitement that we are worried about" and I think it's a fair cop. We don't care who the heads belong to, we just wanna see 'em roll! As Hazlitt said, "there is a secret affinity, a *hankering* after evil in the human mind". If there wasn't, tabloids would go bankrupt overnight. Evil *entertains*; hatred is "a never-ending source of satisfaction."

> Animals torment and worry one another without mercy: children kill flies for sport: every one reads the accidents and offences in a newspaper, as the cream of the jest.

No "jest" pleases me more than social order getting smashed against the thirteenth pillar of the underpass, just as long as I'm not in the car at the time. Naturally, I wouldn't admit to being entertained by "accidents and offences". But can you name a single one of Harold Shipman's[261] 215+ victims? Murderers are more exciting than their victims, and artists know it.

---

260 William Hazlitt (1778–1830) was an English writer who hung around with Wordsworth, Keats and Coleridge.

261 Dr. Harold Shipman (1946–2004) killed his victims with an overdose of morphine. 80% of his victims were female. Shipman overstretched

I remember the shock of first seeing the 11ft x 9ft *Myra*, Marcus Harvey's[262] portrait of Myra Hindley. From a distance, the painting looks like a grainy newspaper photo. Close up, it's revealed that Hindley's face is made up of children's handprints in white, black and gradations of ash. Harvey's audacious pointillism suggests to me that serial killers are the vis-à-vis of the tabloid press and a culture that delights in hatred.

In her book on participatory art, *Artificial Hells*, Claire Bishop[263] gives two examples of the artist/audience relationship becoming violent. In the first, she quotes the abstract artist Wassily Kandinsky[264], who described the hostile reaction to an exhibition of his in Munich in 1910.

> each day [the owner of the gallery] had to wipe clean the canvases upon which the public had spat...but [the public] did not cut up the canvases, as happened to me in a different city.

---

himself when he altered his last victim's will to leave him £386,000. He hanged himself in Wakefield Prison. The *Sun* celebrated with a headline saying "Ship Ship hooray!"

262 Marcus Harvey is a British artist. Myra Hindley herself protested about Harvey's *Myra*, writing from prison that the painting showed a "disregard not only for the emotional pain and trauma that would inevitably be experienced by the families of the Moors victims but also the families of any child victim."

263 Claire Bishop is an Associate Professor at The City University of New York.

264 Wassily Kandinsky (1866–1944) was a Russian artist and theorist. The first abstract painter, Kandinsky taught at the Bauhaus for eleven years. His relationship with fellow painter Gabriele Münter helped his art in all sorts of ways, not least when she left a canvas of his on its side. The sight threw Kandinsky into ecstasy, as he no longer recognised it for his own.

The canvases' crime was an aesthetic one: deviation from the norm. This offended Munich's culture-vultures to the degree that Kandinsky's paintings became spittoons, scapegoats for Kandinsky himself. But why weren't the paintings destroyed? Because Kandinsky had freed the public to become deviants themselves. It's not *normal* to spit at a painting, and I'm pretty sure it wasn't normal in 1910.

Myra was vandalised twice on one day, September 17th 1997. The first attack was with blue paint, the second with eggs from Fortnum & Mason's – and could there be a more bourgeois heckle than that? When asked why he'd thrown the eggs, Jacques Rolé[265] (himself an artist) said "there are moments when you must do something about it. Otherwise next time we will have even worse, we will have a picture of the actual torture." But Rolé only bought the eggs after seeing the first attack being carried out. As in Munich, the consensus of disgust made it acceptable to behave unacceptably.

Acceptance (synonyms: to admit, believe, acquiesce, submit) implies a lack of independence. According to Slavoj Žižek, Christopher Nolan's *The Dark Knight* ends with a message: "only a lie can save us". In *The Dark Knight Rises*, this lie – that District Attorney Harvey Dent was incorruptible – has been popularly accepted, allowing Gotham's authorities to justify the erosion of civil liberties. In such a world, Žižek continues, it's:

265 On Google, Jacques Rolé only exists as 'Jacques Rolé Myra'.

> No wonder that, paradoxically, the only figure of truth in [*The Dark Knight*] is the Joker, its supreme villain. His terrorist attacks...will stop only when Batman takes off his mask and reveals his true identity.

The Joker is the Batman's mirror image. Not because he doesn't wear a mask. Rather, as Žižek says, the Joker "*is* his mask – there is nothing, no 'ordinary guy', beneath it." In this, Nolan owes a debt to Haneke's *Funny Games*. The Joker is indefinable. He's got no name, no prints, no past and no explanation for his horrific facial scars. He's only got stories that change to 'please' his different victims – a particular fuck-you to a genre so exhaustingly obsessed with the 'origin story'. "Wanna know how I got these scars?" Tough. No empathy allowed. We've bought into a brand of 'individuality' which folds under negation's interrogation.

The Joker enjoys being interrogated. He even enjoys Batman smashing his head in against a one-way mirror. His pleasure comes from Batman's powerlessness; as the Joker tells his victimiser, "there's nothing you can threaten me with." No violence or pain can make the Joker conform. He's already a *thing*: his own mask, anaesthetised. Batman can't see who's behind the white paint and lipstick. The Joker's face is a surface, reflecting the Dark Knight's own "theatricality" back at him. By *becoming* a one-way mirror, the Joker turns authority's violence in on itself. He puts his interrogators into suspended animation, blowing up Maggie Gyllenhall and, with her, Batman's world.

The Joker's violence, meanwhile, is amusingly simple. We first see him perform a "magic trick" to a room full of Mafia sorts. The Joker jams a pencil into a table, encouraging them to "watch as I make this pencil disappear." Then he smashes a gangster's head onto it. The pencil does indeed disappear, lodged in the man's brain. When I saw that scene in the cinema, the audience laughed. It's not surprising. The murder follows the mechanism of a joke: introduce a familiar structure, prepare people to anticipate a sleight of hand, then batter them with the reveal.

Bill Hicks told anyone in advertising or marketing to kill themselves. I can imagine the Joker issuing such an edict. He's an outsider; his scars alone are enough to exclude him or, worse, to turn him into an object of pity. (I like to imagine that he inflicted these smiley scars on himself, by the way, during a John Bishop[266] set.)

But the Joker's grudge is against more than Gotham. It's against the *polis* as an inclusive concept. For him, as for Margaret Thatcher, there's no such thing as society. His aim is to make his audience see itself as a morass of weak individuals, to recognise themselves *as they appear to him*. A true comedian.

What would the Joker do as a member of the audience? Maybe what happens in Claire Bishop's second story. In the early twentieth century, the Italian artist Tomasso

266 John Bishop is a Liverpudlian comedian who works hard to maintain his 'everyman' persona. I don't think he and Claire Bishop are related, but I can't be sure.

Marinetti[267] pioneered a Futurist performance art called 'Variety Theatre'. Marinetti wanted to place the spectator "in the centre of the picture. He shall not be present at, but participate in the action." Passivity was not an option. The Futurists would put glue or itching powder on the seats, sell the same ticket to ten people and let oddballs in for free. Variety Theatre became so aggravating that, in Florence on the 12th December 1913, "a member of the audience…gave Marinetti a pistol and invited him to commit suicide on stage." It's a Jokerish gesture – recognise that you deserve to die! – and who wouldn't love to see handguns shower John Bishop like bouquets at the ballet? Nonetheless, for all the Futurists' broken social restraints, the gun-giver still felt secure enough not to worry that Marinetti might shoot *them* and not himself.

Marinetti was a Fascist and a close friend of Mussolini[268]. His ideas predated the Nuremburg rallies, where Nazis marched around under the slogan "no spectators, only actors". Bear that in mind the next time you go to a panto and some shagged-out ex-celebrity asks you if you've seen the crocodile.

"He's behind you!" we all cry.

"Who's behind me," the celeb (say it's Jim Davidson)

267 Tomasso Marinetti (1876–1944) was an Italian artist and chancer whose work came second to professional advancement.

268 Benito Mussolini (1883–1944) was an Italian dictator and slaphead. The entrance to Rome's Stadio Olimpico is still dominated by a giant stone needle engraved with 'MVSSOLINI'. The stadium is also home to some fascist sculptures which resemble those Aryan aliens from *Prometheus* chucking discuses about, squat-thrusting or admiring each other's willies.

replies, playing dumb. "Is it H from Steps[269] in a glittery waistcoat, or Joe Pasquale[270] playing a seedy version of Smee?"

"No, it's an impure animal who needs to be gassed for the good of society," we chant unthinkingly as Davidson smirks into his Captain Hook moustache. When Davidson spins around, we congratulate ourselves – yes, we took part, we *acted* to change the course of the narrative. Only later do we realise how easily we fell for entertaining yet reprehensible rhetoric, once H and Pasquale have been tossed (with our assent) into shallow graves at the bottom of Davidson's garden.

Marinetti wrote that "war is beautiful because it combines rifle fire, barrages of bullets, lulls in the firing, and the scents and smells of putrescence into a symphony." Unfortunately for Marinetti, the conflict he fancied was Italy's disastrous one with Ethiopia. Unfortunately for everyone else, a couple of the era's key players also liked the sound of war.

Walter Benjamin[271] was a German-Jewish critic and writer who first fled Berlin for Paris and then committed suicide once the Nazis took France. It was Benjamin who said that Fascists like Marinetti "aestheticised" politics. For Benjamin, the masses had two demands: "to see the

---

269 H from Steps dropped a bombshell on Celebrity Big Brother when he came out as gay. Millions of British women were put on suicide watch, and the Pope was stunned by the revelation that he was, in fact, a Catholic.

270 Joe Pasquale, squeaky-voiced bubble-blower and bejungled celeb.

271 Walter Benjamin (1892–1940) was a Marxist associated with the Frankfurt School.

ownership structure changed" and "to find their voice". In Germany, the ownership structure was camouflaged (allowing it to see and not be seen) and the people's voice became the aestheticised product of the Nazi party. Self-expression became a mark of ownership: the speaker was owned by the sound, which emanated from authority. In other words, expose them to enough propaganda (or marketing) and people will begin to 'naturally' express themselves with an aesthetic invented to control them.

Today, it's kind of tacky to talk of the many speaking as one. "Their voice" has become *The Voice*. *I* want to win by myself, 'because I've worked so hard for thís? I really deserved thís? This is my dreám? I've worked my whole life to be heré?' But, Frederica, you're a sixteen-year-old girl. *What* life?

My accent, my vocabulary, my tastes and all the shit that comes out of my mouth – these make up a character called 'Freddy', angled 45° away from anyone else to make him feel *unique*. But the audience in me is rightly suspicious of this bourgeois construct. The many, albeit myopic, eyes of my ethics see 'Freddy' for what he is: an unstable collection of totally unrealistic motivations, designed to sell him as a professionally, personally and biologically attractive option (the selfish gene's marketing department – no one's killing themselves in there). Even the most intimate details of his private life are regulated by the 'Freddy' brand. What would he say here? What would he do there? Build trust in the image. Build trust in the voice. But what if this trust's being built on nothing? What if Freddy's a fucking Ponzi scheme, selling people promises based on a value he stole, and lies about, and can't pay back?

Why broadcast that?

Fascists aestheticise politics to distract us from unappealing content. Like with hip hop, we can overlook a sensationally aggressive, anti-social and nihilistic message as long as it *sounds* super-cool.

Take *The What*, the Notorious B.I.G.[272] and Method Man's[273] duet (duet? Rap-off? I'm less than *au fait* with thugging) on the former's spryly-titled album, *Ready To Die*. Like most of Biggie's other songs, *The What*'s basic aim is to convince us of his power. In its first verse, Biggie announces that he's "here to excite" by throwing "dick to dykes." Big's peccadilloes? "Bitches, I like 'em brainless | Guns, I like 'em stainless | Steel." With such a classy guy at the helm, it's not long before a lady arrives in the narrative, drawn like a moth to misogyny. Method Man warns this strumpet to "accept it – utmost respect it." Then Biggie leers over his pal's shoulder, instructing

272 The Notorious B.I.G. (1972–97) was an American rapper. Once knee-deep in the crack game, Biggie was murdered just as he reached the heights of the rap game. Smalls is defined by his love-hate relationship with the West Coast's thug angel, Tupac. I got to know a guy in Santiago de Cuba once. He lived with his grandmother in a redistributed diplomat's house from the 1930s. The building's colonial finery remained a target for sporadic anti-Western abuse. Inside, the boy sold rum, which was really vanilla-flavoured ethanol. Their living room (which might have been a ballroom once) was lit only by a single, state-issued strip-light. Its walls ran with chipped gold; the space was dominated by a massive poster of Biggie and Tupac.

273 Method Man, of the Wu-Tang Klan. Method is perhaps the ultimate collaborator, appearing on many a great duet, but never having made his own *Ready To Die* or *Liquid Swords*, GZA's magnum OPZA.

her to "assume the position", before Meth seals the deal with the immortal line "I spit on your grave then I grab my Charles Dickens[274], bitch." And no, rap novice, our jet-black ninja is not browsing *The Pickwick Papers* as he stands over this woman's grave. 'Charles Dickens' is slang for a penis.

Now, to scan those lyrics on the page, you'd be forgiven for disagreeing with Biggie's boast of being "deep like the mind of Farrakhan[275]." The question's not *why* Method's grabbing his Charles Dickens. The question's why such a hideous narrative gives me pleasure.

The What is one of my favourite songs. I'm drawn to its aesthetic, its break and grit. Certainly the violence shocks me, but shock amuses me. I feel unqualified to judge the lyricists or their environment, so different to my own. This distance lets me listen with a degree of irony, as when arty public school kids dance to Pulp's *Common People*. Self-aware, assuming a posture, not a position. I'm a spectator – I don't have to participate. That being said, I sort of want to.

The What's chorus starts "fuck the world." I love that. Destruction is sexy, or at least my death-drive is in full

---

274 Charles Dickens (1812–70) was an English writer. Dickens' early life was marked by poverty, debtors' prisons and manual labour, giving him a sense of humour and a rogues' gallery of ready-made characters.

275 Louis Farrakhan runs the Nation of Islam. He keeps forgetting to pretend not to know anything about Malcolm X's murder. A fan of Gaddafi, Farrakhan labelled Obama "the first Jewish president" for supporting the Libyan rebels. I suppose this makes a change from being called the first Muslim president. Still, it must get frustrating for the POTUS.

working order. When I listen to the song, am I the "you" Biggie and Meth address? Am I the pussy, the bitch, the world being fucked? Or am I doing the fucking, through my two East Coast lyrical surrogates? In reality, I'm neither, but that's what makes it fun. I'm inside the *polis*, peeking out onto the wilderness.

Think about how enjoyable it is seeing the *Grand Theft Auto* character get crushed by the rules of his world. The character lives a hard knock life. He will either end up dead or in jail. He *has* to make each second count. Under this constraint, we're free to enjoy him fucking a prostitute, paying her and then killing her to get his money back. And why not? There are no consequences *after* the inevitable institutionalisation (death being the ultimate life sentence). The character is simply resurrected. The cycle starts again.

The *GTA* character isn't a blank. Though he can be used to play out the desires we have *within* the game, he can't do everything. He can't fall in love or have a baby or hold down an office job. *GTA* isn't 'free world' as much as 'world-view'; a violent ideology is aestheticised to grant the individual all the freedom they want, as long as they want freedoms permitted by that ideology. To a very real degree, *Grand Theft Auto* is fascist art. The franchise only remains comic because its 'reality' is so different to that of its players. Who knows, kids in favelas may enjoy a free world game set in the Square Mile. They could make a little banker fuck a prostitute before stealing her savings.

BIG exploits my weakness for feeling over thought, for being swept up and lost in a sensation. *Grand Theft*

Auto is built on the same, lyrical impulse. If it suits me to accept that I have no future, why not live in the moment and to the full? As the Earl of Rochester[276] told whoever he was buggering at the time:

> The present moment's all my lot…
> Then talk not of inconstancy
> False hearts, and broken vows;
> If I, by miracle, can be
> This live long minute true to thee,
> 'Tis all that Heav'n allows.

Why work your way through a narrative, why complete missions, when you can key in a cheat and get *all the fucking guns NOW*! We're going to die anyway, so it's only logical to maximise what's pleasurable and sublime in every "live long minute". The lyric lives by submitting to death. To quote Omar Little[277], "that's the game."

When we feel what William Hazlitt calls "hatred", "we throw aside the trammels of civilisation, the flimsy veil of humanity." In that moment, when feeling takes over from thought – when we renounce the camouflage of civility,

---

276 John Wilmot, the Earl of Rochester (1647–80) was a Restoration poet and courtier. While Milton was writing *Paradise Lost* in a cold garret somewhere, Rochester was rebounding from Cromwell's Puritanism harder and more sluttily than even Charles II. His friend, Gilbert Burnet (later the Bishop of Salisbury) said that "for five years together" Rochester "was continually drunk." Rochester also had a sideline in quack gynaecology, which he practised in disguise.

277 Omar Little is played by Michael K. Williams in *The Wire*. Fuck flatscreen – there's no deeper telly.

responsibility – Hazlitt claims that "the greatest possible good of each individual consists in doing all the mischief he can to his neighbour." We're at our most individual when at our most destructive.

Nothing feels more natural than hatred. Not even love. Love's tricky. You've got to know practically everything about a person before you can say that you love them. Hatred's the opposite: the less you know, the better.

'Mischief' is fun. It derives from the Old French *meschever*, which means 'to come to an unfortunate end'. '-Chief' comes from the Latin for 'head'; chiefs are synonymous with authority, though 'chief' is now also slang for a dickhead. Mischief is, therefore, the act of doing authority some disservice, of slighting crowning reason. 'Clown', meanwhile, originates from Old English and French words for clod, clot or lump. The word evolved to mean a peasant, before becoming associated with ignorance or rudeness in the sixteenth century; only around 1600 do the first instances of 'clown' as a funny person appear. A deeper gloss (or extrapolation, if you're not convinced) on 'mischief' and 'clown' suggests that comic pleasure derives from attacking authority from a position of weakness or inferiority, *knowing* that authority will win. Fun's uprising must come from below and strike at the boundaries – of reason, of ethics, of taste – set by the established order.

Chinese modern art is an extreme form of mischief, a blizzard of severed arms, severed cocks, man-to-pig skin grafts (very Virginia Woolf) and towers of liposuctioned fat. In 2000, the artist Zhu Yu[278] even ate half of what was allegedly a human foetus. If that sounds nasty, bear in mind that – when Channel 4 broadcast Zhu's stunt in 2003 – only fifteen people complained to Ofcom, whereas 38,000 complained about Sachsgate. Eating a baby's fine, it seems, but romance Andrew Sachs'[279] granddaughter and you become *despicable*.

My editor says that Sachsgate reference is cheating. It's glib, sure, but I guess I'm talking once again about the changing boundaries of offence. Do the British public care more about celebrity than we do the human body? And, if so, how do the authorities exploit us *through* celebrity culture? Materialism, false individuality, the market-concocted singularity of 'my voice'. China's different.

Zhu grievously mutilates the boundaries of taboo, of human physicality, art and spectatorship. But he was *made* to – his identity has been created by China's legal, biological and cultural oppression. According to Ma Jian[280], an author whose books have been banned in mainland China for the last quarter-century, the sight of "discarded foetuses in China" is a common one: "purple lumps of flesh lying on rubbish heaps or inside communal

278 Zhu Yu is a Chinese artist who specialises in abusing the human body – that of others and his own.

279 Andrew Sachs is most famous for playing Manuel in *Fawlty Towers* and the hugely boring Russell Brand/Jonathan Ross/British media clusterfuck.

280 Ma Jian is a Chinese writer. After his underground artworks were denounced by the Anti-Spiritual Pollution Campaign he was arrested; released, he became a nomad, wandering China and Tibet, living off his art. Ma now lives in London.

dustbins." To abandon your child is to obey the law. Written by Deng Xiaoping[281] in 1978, the one-child policy was a way of redressing the population explosion Mao Zedong[282] caused when he banned birth control in the name of a populous revolution. Thanks to Deng, Ma says, "the state owns [women's] ovaries, fallopian tubes and wombs, and has become the silent, malevolent third participant in every act of love."

Zhu said that "no religion forbids cannibalism. Nor can I find any law which prevents us from eating people." If China insists on controlling its citizens' every action – if it takes part in "every act of love" – then the fact that cannibalism is not explicitly prohibited makes it permissible. Zhu seems to be asking whether he should thus live by the letter of the law (exploiting loopholes to

---

281 Deng Xiaoping (1904–97). A wily operator who survived Mao's displeasure, Deng was once the Mayor of Chongqing, a city which now has almost 29,000,000 inhabitants. I once got lost in Chongqing, and it's only thanks to sheer luck that I'm not still wandering the streets of that massive city six years later. That I'd never even *heard* of Chongqing before visiting it says something either about China or the scale of my ignorance.

282 Mao Zedong (1893–1976) invented Chinese communism. Wikipedia says Mao caused the deaths of "40–70 million" people thanks to his monomaniacal taste for starting famines. The horror of the hyphen *between* 40 and 70 million is mind-boggling, perhaps more so than the numbers themselves. Mao married four times; his second wife, Yan Kai-Hui, was murdered by a warlord after repeatedly refusing to renounce Mao and the Communist cause. Mao became a sex case with terrible hygiene: his doctor, Li Zhisui, wrote that Mao "resisted all attempts to get him to see a dentist…Mao's teeth were covered with a heavy greenish film. When I touched the gums, pus oozed out. An infection of that sort usually causes considerable pain [but] Mao hated doctors and illness so much that he often endured [it]."

justify outrageous and disgusting violations), or should the state revert to another system of regulation, one which trusts the individual with the freedom to make their own ethical decisions? If Zhu offended the authorities, he did so because there's "a space between morality and the law" and because this faultline shouldn't exist. In other words, the offended lawmakers have in them a residual human feeling or empathy which the law does not reflect. If they recognised this as the cause of their offence, then some good could come from Zhu's mischief.

Comedy is fundamentally anti-social, but it can effect good through destruction. And stand-ups are 'singular voices' with power over the collective, but it's a power predicated on their status as outsiders. If the comedian uses that power for non-comic, non-violent aims – speaking about politics without a punch line, say – they tend to forfeit an audience's goodwill. Are we now so stupid as to believe that the 'unpolitical' performance (that chimera, that mass-media alibi) is the only form of entertainment? Or do we react badly to sermons because of a deeper feeling of what a comedian should *naturally* do? Josie Long[283] undercuts her political material with the simplest device of all: a silly voice (that of a man in a 1940s film, if I remember correctly). I agree with her politics, but I need her to harm her message nonetheless. Them's the apples. Is that a phrase? Or eggs. Comedians egg their own work. Smooth work by me. Bravo.

283 Josie Long is a comedian who I really like now she's offset her whimsy with a new, harder edge. I reckon this has turned her into one of the best.

Like Zhu, the Joker does not want to wield political power. Batman's nemesis is the relentless *kômôidoi*, degrading the city that – somewhere, somehow – has degraded him. In this, he shares the malignity that initially drives Shakespeare's Richard III. Like the Joker, Richard is physically abnormal. He has a humped back, a gammy hand, and/or a clubbed foot or two. Unlike the Joker, however, Richard's only too happy to fill us in on his motivations:

> I that am…deform'd, unfinish'd…
> Have no delight to pass away the time,
> Unless to spy my shadow in the sun,
> And descant on mine own deformity.
> And therefore, since I cannot prove a lover,
> To entertain these fair, well-spoken days,
> I am determined to prove a villain.

Maybe Richard's sick of seeing his "shadow in the sun", of being lit in the king's mirrors. Despite his deformity, however, Richard doesn't crave invisibility. He becomes a villain because he knows he's being watched. As a comedian descants on his own sins, so too does Richard begin wreaking havoc for our entertainment.

But, where the Joker seeks to destroy power, Richard seeks to usurp it. Though a force of chaos, he still plays by the rules. This brings him in line with the dull, work-a-day baddies of Bond films or the Bullingdon Club, and it's a dullness *Richard III* gets infected by, too. The play begins with Richard killing his brothers, wooing the hate-filled widow of another man he's murdered, and generally having a ball, the showy bastard. But the historical inevitability of the plot sucks the joy out of him and it. Richard dies in a repetitive fifth act, merely a tyrant.

The best *Richard III* I've seen was in 2012 at the Globe. Mark Rylance's[284] Richard was a shambolic, silly man. In the first half, he played mercilessly to the crowd. His victims were our victims: laughter sealed the deal. When his heavies prompted us, we cried out for Richard to become king and cheered when he agreed to do so. We'd assented to the spectacle of our 'voice', and Richard lived in its moment.

Then Rylance did a very interesting thing. His newly-crowned king *forgot* everything: lines, names, places. Slumped on his throne like Jose Mourinho[285] in his dugout, Richard ordered the execution of his new wife because he was bored of winning her. Having destroyed everyone, it was left to him to become king, exactly the role this twisted outcast had always hated. It was like watching a heckler slaying the comic, only to be given the microphone himself. Empowered, he was no longer able to make mischief.

At the end of *The Dark Knight*, the Joker is left hanging, a canvas to be spat at another day. At the end of his *Richard III*, Rylance bobs up from where Richard's been killed and performs a jaunty Morris dance with the

284 Mark Rylance is a British actor of a casual, harebrained intensity.

285 Jose Mourinho is a Portuguese football manager of Chelsea and Real Madrid fame. The proud owner of a massive Christ/persecution complex, Mourinho's also gouged the eyes of a rival coach.

rest of the company. It's funny, going so dramatically against the grain of contemporary theatrical practice. But it's also more menacing than anything in the play itself. It's like Rylance is that babysitter in *The Omen*, telling us that it's all for us, Damian, it's all for us, as she hangs herself.

*

We're stunned by literalness, by the blunt revelation of our appetites and our failures, by any fact we *have* to face. Aristophanes[286], the most famous comic playwright in Ancient Greece, wrote a play called *Lysistrata*. In it, the eponymous heroine gives warmongering Athens one very simple ultimatum: no man will have sex with a woman until the fighting stops. Men are held to ransom not by her, but by their own libidos. They must choose – do they prefer fucking or fighting, its surrogate? Happily (or naively), Aristophanes has them prefer the former.

The second material I want to talk about is concrete.

Gilo is the largest Israeli settlement in the West Bank. It lies on the east side of the Green Line, which on maps denotes the contested territories claimed by Israel during the Six Day War in June 1967 (the West Bank, the Gaza Strip, the Sinai Peninsula and the Golan Heights). Legally,

286 Aristophanes (about 446–386 BC) was a satirist and poet. Of his forty plays, eleven survive in their entirety. Aristophanes was a social comic; his jokes were topical, his victims very much alive and kicking. Plato blamed one of his plays, *The Clouds*, for contributing to the bad buzz around Socrates, who was later condemned to death.

the Green Line isn't a permanent border, but it's hard to imagine its being erased. There are too many Gilos at stake.

More than 30,000 Israelis (mostly Sephardic Jews and immigrants from Russia) have settled in Gilo since 1967. It's a nice place to live. Rent's cheap and it's great for commuters. It's also built on top of a hill, so the views are sweet. The only problem is that your neighbours do sometimes try and kill you. The first time this happened, some shots were fired from Beit Jala, an Arab village down in the valley. The Israeli military shelled back; the houses in Gilo were fitted with bulletproof glass. But the situation required a more permanent solution.

That solution was a wall, built in 2000 from concrete slabs measuring three metres high – high enough to render the valley and its bullets invisible. Though sections of Gilo's wall have since been taken down, a more-or-less continuous physical dividing line now snakes through the West Bank and East Jerusalem, 462 kilometres long and aiming to hit 708km – over twice the length of the Green Line. This, another "temporary" division, is a symptom of what Margaret Thatcher called Israel's "pioneer spirit."

In Richard Fleming's[287] article in *Cabinet* magazine, he describes how Gilo's settlers decorated their stretch of the wall. Shlomi Brosh[288], the then-head of the Municipality's department of culture, commissioned eight Russian immigrants to paint Gilo's obliterated view onto the wall

287 Richard Fleming is an American author.

288 Shlomi Brosh was once Jerusalem's adviser on cultural affairs. Brosh oversaw the construction of a number of galleries, in order to keep young Israeli artists from leaving the city and/or the country.

"in an effort to alleviate some of the ugliness." It was an aesthetically political act. "We did not want to part with the view, but they forced us to. So we copied the view," Brosh told the *Jerusalem Post*. The result was, as Fleming puts it, an "Italian restaurant fresco" from the American Midwest. The banality, however, is not the problem. The problem is, for Fleming, that this fresco is not "a realistic portrait."

> [The fresco is] devoid of Arab inhabitants, and none of the buildings in the distance appears to have been shelled by Israeli tanks. The blurry, distant villages have been settlerized; a disproportionate number of buildings are painted with salmon-tiled gabled roofs, an architectural conceit unknown to the Palestinians, whose villages typically have flat white roofs. The Palestinian 'problem' has…[been] painted out of view.

It's similar to *Enigma*'s treatment of Alan Turing's sexuality – only, of course, that *Enigma* was just a film. This wall is how people actually *live*.

So maybe Fleming's wrong. Gilo's wall is altogether too realistic. That change in architecture more than represents – it *is* – aesthetic cleansing. These painters don't even look down on Palestinians. They've removed them from sight. The defence would state: it's just a picture, there's really nothing behind it. But isn't that the problem? The Palestinians are now Jokers. There are no 'ordinary guys' on the other side. Just as the Joker is his mask, Palestine *is* the wall.

Concrete becomes a mirror. Israel is interrogated by its own construction; its walls are, in Fleming's words, "an admission, unacceptable to the authorities, that the lands on the other side were beyond control." In *Giving Offense*, J.M. Coetzee describes the reaction white settlers have to *One Settler, One Bullet*, "one of the war chants of the Pan-Africanist Congress". Coetzee says that "whites pointed to the threat to their lives contained in the word 'bullet'; but it was 'settler', I believe, that evoked a deeper perturbation." The Israelis are trying to *naturalise* themselves by uprooting Palestinians. Nevertheless, the walls are a manifested premonition of being robbed of power; they are painted to obliterate the evidence of Israel's being a settler. Violence they can control and answer. Bullets do not perturb Israelis so much as Palestine's birthrate. The problem faced by an apartheid power: is an overwhelming ethnic majority proof of an invasion, or of one's own alien status?

I was once at a reggae festival because I'm that kind of guy. There, I saw a German buy an Israeli a teenth of hash to apologise for the Holocaust. The scene went like this:

German: I want to buy you this hash to say that I'm so sorry for the fucked-up shit we did to you.
Israeli: You shouldn't have.
German: It wasn't expensive.
Israeli: No, really. You *shouldn't* have.

Only the scene didn't go like that. Instead, the Israeli wept and then got high with the German. Imagine being that unselfconscious! Six million people, a sixteenth of hash. What shit d'you have to suffer to earn a whole ounce? Plus, if the authorities started an investigation into the hash, the Israeli would have to deny its existence. Lolocaust.

(Internet people use 'lolocaust' to mean a joke that's so funny you and six million other laughers are systematically exterminated. It seems that '-olocaust' now signifies '*very, very*', as in '*very, very* horrible' or '*very, very* laugh-out-loud'. All aboard the last cattle truck to gigglesville and its chuckling chimneys! What a fucking world.)

What is history? I'd say it's the past as manipulated justification for whatever perversion's currently disguising itself as 'normality'. History makes its victims selfish and small. If I could invent a time machine, I wouldn't go back to kill Hitler. I'd go back and punch all the men who've ever kissed my girlfriend, starting with the ten-year-olds. Because how can a man live knowing that – unlike Chesney Hawkes[289] – he's not the one and only?

Leopold Bloom manages it. In *Ulysses*, he comes to terms with his wife's infidelities without loving her the

289 Ah, Chesney, the man who started it all, the alpha of these footnotes. I once saw ex-musician Chesney on a Bath Travel flight to Majorca. Chesney had his headphones in, ignoring the probably sozzled owner of Bath Travel, Mr. Bath, whose custom it was to bid adieu to each plane-load of his customers before it took off from Bournemouth. Mr. Bath is now dead. He has been replaced by his son, Mr. Bath Jr., as Mr. Bath replaced *his* father, Mr. Bath Snr., after Mr. Bath Snr. died or retired. The company was started by Mr. Bath Snr.'s father, also Mr. Bath (R.E. Bath, to give him his initials) in 1924.

less. He does this by imagining a sequence of his wife's lovers:

> Each one who enters imagines himself to be the first to enter whereas he is always the last term of a preceding series even if the first term of a succeeding one, each imagining himself to be first, last, only and alone, whereas he is neither first nor last nor only nor alone in a series originating in and repeated to infinity.

Bloom's escaped the lyrical minute of love and hate to observe it. These other men have no special capital. Neither does Bloom. Privileged singularity is an illusion. No one is alone. It's an equanimity alienated enough to look like cowardice, and one which no state and few citizens could ever accept. Like the great line in Tom Stoppard's[290] play, *Travesties*. The character James Joyce is asked what he did in the First World War. "I wrote *Ulysses*," he replies, "what did you do?" Is there a more privileged singularity, or a greater temptation, to live outside your time?

Hugh Everett's[291] many worlds interpretation proposes

290 Tom Stoppard is a playwright. He was 'made' British by his stepfather, his Jewish family having fled Czechoslovakia just before the German occupation in 1939, and his father having died in the defence of Singapore.

291 Hugh Everett (1930–82) was the American physicist who first came up with the 'MWI', based on what he called 'relative states'. Everett began Princeton by studying game theory; he finished it with a thesis, *The Theory of the Universal Wave Function*, typed up by his new squeeze/future wife. Unfortunately, everyone hated Everett's ideas, most prominently Niels Bohr, co-dreamer-upper of the Copenhagen Interpretation (which, broadly, says that what can't be observed doesn't

that, when two atoms are made to react with one another, they create one six-dimensional atom. Being six-dimensional, this atom exists in two three-dimensional space-time continuums at once. This means the atom exists in two times, which means it can generate two histories. Two atoms create four atoms which create eight which create sixteen, and sixteen atoms give us 256 histories. Every atom, every body, every word, is repeated and moderated in infinite versions of itself, in infinite dimensions. This is called the history tree. Hang yourself from it and you'll escape everything.

As I write this, my grandfather[292] is dying. His hospital bed has an electronic scale. I weigh him as he lies under a sea of morphine. He is 94.5 kg. That means he has approximately 9,450,000,000,000,000,000,000,000,000 atoms in his body, many more than there are stars in the universe. Somewhere, I think, somehow, he may not be dying. Somewhere, somehow, he may not have made quite so many mistakes.

Only he did make them and he is dying. My grandfather broke promises. He was selfish and I don't know what he was navigating by. Maybe he was stupid enough to trust his senses. But physics forgives him. Death

exist). Discouraged by physicists, Everett became a weapons evaluator at the Pentagon, theorising about intercontinental ballistic missiles until his sudden death at the age of 52. His son is the musician Mark 'E' Everett of Eels fame. E's made a documentary about their relationship. It's called *Parallel Worlds, Parallel Lives*. Check it out.

292 John Jackson (1934–2012) flew helicopters for the Army Air Corps. Later, the UN hired him to pioneer anti-famine crop-spraying techniques in Mali. He retired a carpenter.

forgives him. I feel closer to him the further away he gets.

Can you laugh at death? In my grandfather's hospital, I looked around for jokes. I wanted to record material – my get-out-of-jail-free card. I wanted it not to matter. One wing in the hospital was called the Nick Jonas wing. I thought about trying to make my grandfather laugh about it, but that would entail explaining to a dying man who Nick Jonas was, and I think even Nick Jonas would concede that a dying man has better things to do with his time. As has, come to think about it, everybody else. Which is why I haven't footnoted him.

Then I noticed that the scale doctors use to assess the depth of a coma is called the Glasgow Coma Scale. Glasgow, that hard-drinking city in which a large percentage of the population appear to be comatose pretty much all of the time. Comatose, that is, or fucking terrifying. Glasgow's the only city in the world where toddlers are muzzled to stop them chewing the face off Rottweilers.

But there, in the hospital, nothing was funny. Nothing forgiven is funny.

Later – *now* – I'm waiting for the call to tell me he's died. I'm tranquil. I feel completely connected *and* disconnected: to and from a person, to and from a time, to and from a place.

Why do we love a call-back? Because it returns us to a place that we've been before. The first instance of the joke is violent. But when the comedian repeats it, many minutes later and elsewhere in their material, we laugh harder for being safe from its ability to shock. We're inside its walls now.

When I said goodbye to my grandfather, I'd been told that hearing was the last faculty to go. And I couldn't resist the temptation to lie: 'I only have happy memories. I'll see you soon.' Spare him the reality, I told myself, when really I was sparing myself.

About five years ago, I went to Syria. I took with me a friend[293] from university. She and I stayed with some friends of my parents. On our first day, a Syrian guy drove us up into the hills around Damascus. There was a cave. Cain had killed Abel here, the driver told us, and the cave had been screaming ever since. My friend and I stood looking out, Damascus framed by the cave's canines and incisors. Then the adhan began. We swore we could see sound erupt like smoke from this quiet, quieted city. I thought about my grandfather, the army man. Once, he'd flown a helicopter into a cave to save his wounded friends.

Later, we were driving into the desert when a storm did that thing people call bruising the sky. The heaven splitted, purple like I hadn't heard of the colour. The sight was forceful enough for me to forget the blue-tarpaulined camps of Iraqi refugees which lined the road. It was forceful enough to forget the three secret policemen in a pick-up following us, practically bumper to bumper. Earlier, at some traffic lights, I'd swung round in my seat to look back at these spies. I caught them off-guard; the two who weren't driving hastily held up newspapers, inches from their faces. One of the newspapers was upside down. Our driver spotted that. The lights went green. As

293 Citation withheld.

both cars pulled away in a complicit little convoy toward the desert, our driver told us that Jews poison fridge-door handles. I forgot this comment, too, in the storm.

The police were funny to us. Under ruined Roman arches, by souk-light, men in uniforms held hands, solemn as kissing choirboys. We were followed constantly. One day, we locked the car keys in the car. I don't quite know how you do this but we'd done it. It was late afternoon, Ramadan, and our spies wanted to get back to Damascus. Back to wives, to children, to food, to a cacophony that builds in ancient, light-stone alleys and swells and breaks bread. So one spy – a big bloke with a pinkish birthmark down the right side of his face – walked forward, a rock the size of his head in his hand. We had to block him, to stop this clown throwing it through the car window. I didn't ask him why he, a 'stranger', wanted to help. I knew that he knew that I knew that he knew that I knew.

The police were funny to us. We knew their secret. They bugged our bedrooms. A man may have listened to the first time my friend and I made out; the event noted, he'd have smoked, or farted, or fallen asleep. In retrospect, I'm not sure why we found it amusing, being naked under surveillance. Maybe because their power seemed so irrelevant, these Inspector Clouseaus with their newspapers and rocks. What could they punish us for? We were outside their jurisdiction.

They were funny. They're killing children now, these men who use rocks to open windows. Over 90,000 dead at the time of writing. A decade of intervention; a decade of inaction. Iraq. Syria. Victim. Victimiser. Victims'

victims. Victimisers' victimisers. Walls. Those videos of Gaddafi and Saddam – does YouTube treat them as 'historical' documents, and therefore *expect* them to be obscene? Think about Thomas Hoepker's photo of 9/11. Think about Walter Sipser. No permission, no mercy. No wonder history was the nightmare from which Joyce tried to awake. No wonder Israelis and Germans get high together. One time is enough.

My friend and I visited the Golan Heights. This is what I remember: apples being traded across the no-man's-land between Syria and Israel. At the Syrian border, the apples were tipped out into the dirt; their crates, checked for weapons or humans. Once satisfied, the guards let the apples be gathered up. They bit into ones they'd confiscated as the traders' truck barrelled through space and arrived at the Israeli border. Again, the apples were poured out, a baffling libation to this contested earth. Then the traders drove on into the settlements as the Israelis, too, ate confiscated fruit.

But what if the truck stopped in no-man's-land? What if the traders (Israeli or Syrian) got out and lay on their flatbed of apples and looked up at the blue sky? How long could they survive in defiance of both sides, in that little space between boundaries and laws and religions and men who want to murder each other? Would the traders still be there as darkness fell, as stars fell, in the light night of countries yet to kill their skies with industry? Is that utopia?

In a world of choice, is the only choice the choice *not* to choose – not to eat, not to own, not to take part? But not choosing is a choice, too. We are terms in a series; we are in history, on earth, and detachment from those facts, from reality, wounds us. In *Impossible Exchange*, Jean Baudrillard[294] asks:

> Has not humanity, with its inborn consciousness, its ambiguity, its symbolic order and its power of illusion...ended up contaminating the world (of which it is, nevertheless, an integral part) with its non-being, its way of not-being-in-the-world?

Isn't that an extraordinary thing to consider? The environment is the most obvious consequence of the strange idea that, somehow, we're not of this world. We pollute, we ruin the earth irreparably, but we don't stop. It's as though we think we've got somewhere else to live.

I exist in two states at the same time. My mind is a six-dimensional atom. Right now, I am writing at my desk. I look up, touch-typing, at the white wall outside my window. It is blue, deep gloaming blue; the time is 8:12pm and Chelsea are playing Tottenham for a place in the Champions League. But I'm also *here*, in this book. I am recorded. As you listen to my paper heartbeats, where are you?

---

294 Jean Baudrillard (1929–2007) was a French sociologist and writer. Baudrillard famously wrote a book called *The Gulf War Did Not Take Place*, in which he posited the first Gulf War as the inversion (or negation) of the Prussian military-moralist Carl von Clausewitz's formula for war: "the continuation of politics by other means." Baudrillard contested that the Gulf War was a new type of anti-war, "the continuation of an absence of politics by other means."

The Chinese began to write between 4,500 and 8,000 years ago. And think about the change that happened when language – symbolic order – first came into being. Suddenly, people had a voice that survived death. Philosophies, plays and prayers could be transmitted; the soul of multiple experiences, our database, began. As Nick Cave[295] sings, "the past is the past and it's here to stay | Wikipedia is heaven."

Language was a beginning and a beginning was, as Aristotle puts it, "that which itself does not follow necessarily from anything else, but some second thing naturally exists or occurs after it." This big bang opened a space up between two new states: the human and the animal.

What do I mean? Well, we love ideas. What sets us apart from chimps and things, if not for that invisible life of symbols and illusions, of religions and traditions, of words? You can characterise this life as a soul, as culture, whatever – it's built from a disembodied web of voices, a bit like YouTube but without all those increasingly irritating adverts.

Why is this 'soul' so prone to brutality and intolerance? Because illusions are made with words, and words are violent. According to James Gleick, the alphabet spread by contagion via the trade routes of the ancient world. Words were a "new technology" that was "both the virus and the vector of transmission." Viruses are non-consensual. They catch. More, Roland Barthes says

295 Nick Cave is a singer, author and screenwriter. Cave's songs are beautiful, priapic and well aware of their own absurdity.

that language "is quite simply fascist; for fascism does not prevent speech, it compels it." We've seen evidence of this at Nuremberg – "no spectators, only actors" is, in effect, the libidinal opposite to a strip club's 'no touching' rule. Don't watch, *feel*. The rules compel you to express yourself, to gratify your individual tastes as selfishly as you want within its club, paying its fees.

Wikipedia is heaven: a contested, politicised, unreliable, easily-manipulated, long-eroded ideal; an illusion (that of truth, of borderless 'democratic objectivity') to which converts dedicate themselves; bodiless; the source of all my footnotes.

I am a *GTA* avatar created by and playing the game of language. When I write, I use words to delineate boundaries, build walls. My lines provoke counter-attacks or bludgeon others into assent. I challenge ideas, mangle and spread them, and dream up a few of my own. Writing is a little working model of the violence of history, or of (for Aristotle) a *middle*, "that which itself comes after something else, and some other thing comes after it." Some days it's very nice to be involved. But the grind, the contagion of the soul is often too hideous to contemplate. As Ezra Pound[296] wrote, "what is the use of

---

296 Ezra Pound (1885–1972) was an American poet. In his early days, Pound was one of Joyce's key supporters. Pound then fell in love with Mussolini, made pro-Fascist radio broadcasts during the war, was brutally treated by US soldiers upon capture and spent twelve years in a mental hospital before returning to die in Italy. Hemingway wrote that "the best of Pound's writing...will last as long as there is any literature." The poem I've taken those lines from (*Exile's Letter*) is extraordinarily beautiful, particularly for a sentimentalist and Sinophile like me.

talking, and there is no end of talking." To say talking is useless, you must *say* 'talking is useless,' thus taking part in the uselessness. You have to become a carrier. The endlessness of talking is the vis-à-vis of talking's futility.

The next line in Pound's poem reads, "there is no end of things in the heart." Can we say, then, that the soul is short-circuited by the very symbol-world it invented to escape death, to escape "things in the heart." And short-circuited why? Because the soul is still trying to express the animal, or because it's become trapped in language's fascist game, the homogenous whirlpool of signification?

The heart beats within the biological certainty of death, though its function is to live; 'the heart' can never explain itself, though it must. This ox bollock squirming away in my chest and the series of needs we associate with it, both belong in the animal – the dying thing staring at a wall.

The Golan Heights made me think about love. Those moments when my friend and I stopped struggling for status and existed simply, on apples, in nowhere – those moments I remember, and I hope she remembers too. But the mountains around the cool unoccupied valley were ringed with mementos of conflict, just as – on the Syrian side of the Heights – there is a ruined hospital, riddled with Israeli bullets, preserved as a satellite to rebound hate and memorised hurt. Fragile states need enemies. Love is the analogy: we can't survive, *and* we must fight (what

---

Microsoft Word doesn't recognise 'Sinophile' – it wants to replace the word with 'Sinophobe', which it does recognise. Can you have -phobes without -philes?

is the use of talking, *and* there is no end of talking); we deserve to live under threat.

Two states. One is real (animal), one isn't (human). We ignore the animal, which will die; we strive for the human, which will kill us. We pollute ourselves, our eyes on the immortal soul, that hypothetical continuum.

The suicide who left no note.

To paraphrase *Ol' Man River*, I don't want to die, and I don't want to be compelled to live. I don't want a soul. I can't bear the near-infinity of traintracks, or the preceding series of my girlfriend's lovers. So I sever myself, I break away, and make utopia, built on severance, on breakage. This space is not quite an ending, which Aristotle says "is that which does itself naturally follow from something else…but there is nothing else after it." It's a silence, a no-man's-land between the warring states. Sometimes I try and write there, in the gap: a place of gestures, forgetfulness and reconciliation.

Two states. One I know (me), one I don't (you). Why do we read and write? To look beyond our 'privileged' forty-five degrees of privacy, to see the wood for the trees and our fellow employees. But is it enough to do as E.M. Forster bade us and "only connect"? The German and the Israeli "only connected" – they were able to forget. Only I can't stay in nowhere, though its beyondness seduces me. I'm still *here*. Here's violent and blind. Chelsea and Tottenham drew 2:2. And I can't remain silent. The real world demands action. I need to *do* something now. Don't I? So what tools do I have to hand to help?

Coincidentally, right this second I get a text from Amnesty International. "Your text helped ensure 3 women at risk of being killed for 'sorcery' in Papua New Guinea now safe," it tells me. The iPhone, eh? You can make liberal interventions from the comfort of your own home; I recently asked Shell to clear up the Niger Delta whilst taking a colossal dump. Truly, Steve Job's device has set me free. Sorry, the sorceresses free.

The comedian as a mirror. Do I set myself up as a reflection of the everyman? Can you see yourself in me? Surely not. I'm far too flowery and odd. And even if I wanted to be a mirror, the judgemental part of me is still behind it. 'Reflecting' someone else makes me their interrogator, insulated from consequence, damning my victim from a position of safety. I must, then, try to bear my own image, watched by an unknown audience. *I* must be the interrogated, providing you with testimonies to acquit or condemn. That's why I've tried to be honest with you, whoever you are.

You must have disagreed with me. *I* disagree with me. I don't want to put words in your mouth. I've provided the inside. You provide the outside. Attack me. Challenge my laws, my neuroses and projections. Between us, in conflict and accord, we trade.

Which of us is in the weakest, the most vulnerable position?

Jokes as walls. Defensive, offensive, they admit to their constructor's fear of usurpation, of returned fire. Is there a no-man's-land between them, in which the victims and victimisers can meet, a place where (as Bataille says) "nothing counts any more – neither the 'object' nor the 'subject'"? I don't think so.

Utopian laughter is not sustainable. Nor is it useful. So ask instead, should the comedian be inside or outside their jokes' protection? How should the comedian position themselves in the world?

In 2004, the Dutch filmmaker Theo van Gogh[297] was murdered by Mohammed Bouyeri[298]. Bouyeri, a Muslim, had been offended by a film of van Gogh's called *Submission*, which insulted the Prophet, and which had been written by the Somali-Dutch writer Ayaan Hirsi Ali[299]. Speaking at the unveiling of a statue in van Gogh's memory, his friend (and my hero) Hans Teeuwen sang a song. It's a stupid, oompa marching song, sung a capella. I've copied out a translation from YouTube, and the lyrics are worth quoting in their entirety:

---

297 Theo van Gogh (1957–2004) was the great-grandson of Theo van Gogh, Vincent's art dealer brother. Van Gogh was a fan of Pim Fortuyn, the Dutch anti-immigration politician who was murdered in 2002. Both were provocateurs and critics of multiculturalism, political correctness and Islam, which they thought backward and brutal.

298 Mohammed Bouyeri is the man who murdered Theo van Gogh. In the note he stabbed onto van Gogh's chest, Bouyeri says that "Islam like an extinct plant, which has been formed into a diamond through years of high temperatures and pressure. An extinct plant which was formed over the trials of time into the strongest precious stone on earth. A hard stone upon which will defeat any attempts to break it to pieces." Militant Islam Monitor.org, the website Wikipedia uses to source this letter, say "these writings show conclusively that the Islamists are living in a parallel universe. This letter should be a wake up call for all of us to see that militant Islamist killers are dwelling among us." Pot and kettle. Both texts are terrifying.

299 Ayaan Hirsi Ali is a Somali-Dutch writer. It was to Ali that Bouyeri addressed the letter he left at the scene of the crime.

Flush God down the toilet
Shove the prophet up your arse
Dance to express yourself freely.
If they shoot you
Then at least you've enjoyed this song.

One is chased away, the other is murdered.
Free expression, live on.
Christian dogs, goat fuckers,
Everyone participates –
Jesus and Mohammed on a public toilet.

No, I shall not offend, I apologise,
I will punish myself with a blowjob from
A halal chick.

Free expression prevails
No matter how many bullets.
If a bearded guy shoots me
I hope that he misses,
Because I love the good life
I'm not a suicidal terrorist

Take a diet to become a hard target
In that sense, van Gogh brought it upon himself.
[stopping, laughing] Er... there was another line.

[beat, looks up] The sun shines down. Thank you, Theo.

My DVDs are for sale at the DVD shop.

This song contains everything that, in my opinion, makes a comedian true to their history, out beyond the walls of Athens. In chronological order:

God and the prophet belong where shit belongs. Is Teeuwen trying to convert us to an abusive atheism? He'd have better ways of doing this than with a ludicrous, childish, bouncy chant – a chant you can't dance to without looking silly. Silliness: small compensation, surely, in the event of being shot?

Is this song a manifestation of 'freedom'? Yes, within a world in which people are murdered for their opinions. But Teeuwen doesn't want to sing like this; the song doesn't appear in any set of his that I've seen. I imagine he felt *forced* to perform it in the moment, by the moment. His song is bred of violence.

Teeuwen commits van Gogh's own 'crime', the crime of offending religious people. He's been abused into the role of blasphemer – turned into that *thing* – an identity created by van Gogh's victimiser. The impulse to defame God comes naturally to the survivors of religiously-motivated violence. But Teeuwen's *also* offensive about van Gogh. Abuse is better even-handed. Teeuwen exists in (between) two states.

One flees, one dies. Does the choice to live freely boil down to this binary decision: cowardice or death? Again, that's not freedom so much as two types of self-destruction. Those are the rules we play by in this shitty, bestial mess. Free speech is a mischief. It's punishment-by-self-indulgence. So is that blow-job from a pun, the halal chicken (and what a horrific image that conjures: a woman, her neck slit for purity's sake...).

That Van Gogh was fat – that he presented a big target – mocks his friend in order to mock the argument that says van Gogh *deserved* to be a victim. Freedom. A catch-22. It exists because it doesn't exist. Likewise, anyone who wants to be free risks ceasing to be anything at all.

We don't live in a country in which (to the best of our knowledge) bedrooms are bugged. So we never think of our speech as being 'free'. Until, that is, we offend someone's delicate sensibilities. Then we have to invoke – with increasingly hoarse and tedious rhetoric – the prerogative to have a crack at the monarchy. Our newspapers still ask "Has Free Speech Gone Too Far?" But how *can* freedom go too far?

Hans Teeuwen appeared on a Dutch debate show called *Bikinis and Burkas* (my second-favourite title after *Noppen & Naaldhakken*, which is the Dutch for *Footballer's Wives*). He was made to sit on a kind of psychiatrist's bed, bedded with fake nails, and flanked by three women in hijabs. They asked him why he chose to offend Muslims in his comedy. His answer? "Because it was funny."

As he lay dying in the street, Theo van Gogh said to Bouyeri, "surely we can talk about this?" Bouyeri replied by slitting van Gogh's throat. He then affixed a letter onto the artist's stomach with a knife. The letter was addressed to Hirsi Ali, and one line reads: "these writings will cause your mask to fall off." There is no end of talking.

The comedian is not a light entertainer. As Teeuwen told his interrogators on *Bikinis and Burkas*, "everything with a certain status has a certain power. Power always tends to corrupt, and has to be ridiculed." And it seems to me that the target of Teeuwen's song is neither Islam specifically, nor religion as a whole. The target is silence. Silence used by a state to make us forget. Silence used by a state to falsify a sense of freedom. A utopia in the proper sense: a 'not-place', a nowhere the temptations of which are overpowering, thoughtless and, in the end, malign.

Utopias are not a mature response to the world. Leopold Bloom's dream of utopia – "not a heaventree, not a heavengrot, not a heavenbeast, not a heavenman" but "a mobility of illusory forms" – is impossible. We will always have an identity, some ghastly suffix (like "heaven-") grafted onto us. So Teeuwen is *here*. Dealing with his own suffix (comediantree, comediangrot, comedianbeast, comedianman), he has to sing.

And singing, Teeuwen is both inside and outside his comfort zone; his friend's death; the law; the public eye; the boundaries of taste, of what's seemly to be said. He occupies each territory, and rebels against his own occupation. "Free expression prevails | No matter how many bullets." But it takes bullets to fight bullets. These are Teeuwen's. His good bullets. The bullets that wound only those weak enough to believe in their power. And Teeuwen even shoots himself, by having the sheer bad taste to promote his DVDs at the end of the gig.

Conked.

We spent one term at my university studying the Tragedy paper. On the first day of this term, the head of the English faculty gave us a lecture which ended with rather a lame trick. He shut with a flourish the copy of *Lear* he was using as a prop. "Tragedy isn't on the page," he told us, rather begging the question why we'd have to read so many of them if it wasn't. "Tragedy is everywhere. In Iraq. In Afghanistan. In Africa." There was a beat. He checked his watch. He had at least two minutes left. Shit.

Our lecturer could have said, 'thanks a lot, see a proportionately diminishing number of you dweebs over the next eight weeks.' But, in (just some of) the immortal words of Ving Rhames[300], pride was fucking with him. Surely he could fill 120 seconds with places that could be considered tragic. So he began to list countries at random. "America, South America, Russia, Cuba, Poland, Burma – Myanmar," he corrected himself, before the liberal in

300 Ving Rhames is an American actor best known for playing Marsellus Wallace in *Pulp Fiction* and Diamond Dog in *Con Air.*

him decided that to say 'Myanmar' was to collude with the junta, meaning that he corrected himself again, this time by saying "Burma" in a wistful voice. Then he hit an inspired streak. "Britain," he said, eyes raised. Uh oh, his audience thought, are *we* involved too? "England. Cambridge." That's us! Thirty seconds on the clock. "Ely. Cherry Hinton. Royston. Crewe." Ten seconds. "The sea." A curve-ball – the tragic gyre had widened. Where could he go from here? Space? We'll never know, because the bell went.

The point is this. I've been guilty throughout this book of attacking you. I've had my fair share of Cherry Hinton moments. But I started by attacking *me* to suggest that the cruelty I exhibit as a comedy writer is, in a sense, microcosmic of the cruelty of comedy itself. Without wishing to coin any aphorisms, tragedy is life happening to you, comedy is how you deal with it and how you fight back. That's my Tony Blair impression ("today is not a day for soundbites, really, but I feel the hand of history on my shoulder") though I for one would rather not feel history's hot breath burning at my behind.

Very, very little a comedian does in this country has any relevance whatsoever, beyond Comic Relief and, perhaps, giving the *Daily Mail*'s editor, Paul Dacre[301], a

301 Paul Dacre is the current editor of the *Daily Mail*. Dacre's paper despises our modern obsession with celebrity, sex and vulgarity, as proved by this random collection of stories I've taken from the *Mail*'s website: '*Kate Lawler flashes a little too much flesh as she struggles to contain her legs in thigh split monochrome dress*', '*Feeling cheeky! Keira Knightley and new husband James Righton show off their derrieres as they enjoy a dip in the sea*' and '*That's one way to get attention! Aubrey O'Day*

well-deserved stroke. In a perfect world, of course, Dacre would be at the wheel of a fast car in wet conditions, with A.N. Wilson[302] and Melanie Phillips[303] in the back, neither of whom would be wearing seatbelts in defiance of the nanny state and/or the fact that Jimmy Savile klunk-klipped every trip. Its driver slumped forward against the dashboard, Dacre's car would then career into the O2 arena, bursting into flames and thus sparing the fans of music and comedy from being forced to suffocate in its meaningless vacuum ever again.

Sadly, we don't live in a perfect world. In Somalia, the comedian Abdi Jeylani Malaq[304] was murdered for calling the Islamist group al-Shabaab cowards. Shooting an unarmed 43-year-old five times in the head and chest,

---

tweets bikini-clad selfie as she reunites with Danity Kane' (who?). Steve Coogan described Dacre's ethics as being those of "a Victorian father masturbating secretly in his bedroom." The *Mail*'s website receives over 43 million hits a month.

302 A.N. Wilson is a British author and journalist. He writes paragraphs like this: "Potential immigrants to the UK have to sit a citizenship test to see whether they have a basic knowledge of this country. I do not know whether questions about *The Archers* have found their way into this test, but for me, as for millions of other people in this country, the theme tune, composed by Arthur Wood in 1924, sets off a chain of associations which are all quintessentially English."

303 Melanie Phillips is a British journalist. Of Maggie T's death, Phillips wrote that "it wasn't just Lady Thatcher being buried in London today" – Great Britain died with her. As a friend pointed out, Phillips could have been buried with Thatcher in the style of a pharaoh's handmaid, sacrificed to serve her boss in the hereafter. Phillips could have lain down in the coffin, clutching the empty clay jar where her brain would have been stored, had she had one for the mummifier to tug through her nostril with a hook.

304 Abdi Jeylani Malaq (1969–2012) was a radio and TV performer best known in Somalia for parodying local militants.

apparently, proves that al-Shabaab are anything but. Somalia is a country that's been without a fully-functioning government since 1991. In it, violence is often directed towards those in the media who criticise organisations like al-Shabaab, violence that remains unprosecuted. What was Abdi Jeylani Malaq's crime? In the words of one resident of Mogadishu, to "bring smiles to our faces."

We have a functioning government. Its violence is subtler, and directed at the disadvantaged. Legal Aid was its first victim. Judges must spend many more man-hours in courts than they previously did, guiding parents and children through disputes that they are (as I would be) ill-equipped to understand. People must speak for themselves now, in situations where they need someone else to speak for them.

What am I doing to help? Very, very little. Nothing. I haven't retrained as a lawyer. I haven't retrained as a doctor. Nor do I think that *Bad Education*, the sitcom Jack and I write, can help. It's light, broad and silly, but we can still sometimes make a point. One of my favourite jokes in the first series of *Bad Education* was the school bully's description of the Big Society as a place in which "no one can hear you scream." This is the tag-line of *Alien*, in which low-level space workers are left to die by a corporation. I enjoyed appropriating that. Can I aspire to more? I must, whether I'm able to or not.

That episode ends with the school election being won by a fat boy in a Spiderman outfit, who yells "with great power comes great responsibility" as he sprays silly-string from his wrists. Did we mean that as criticism of popularism-over-policy, or of *all* political power? To be honest, neither Jack nor I think as much as we ought. But at the very least, the gag – light, broad, silly – speaks for two people with the amazing privilege (one of many) to make a living by being funny.

This is where I feel Stewart Lee *die* with contempt for me, but I'll continue.

As a number of papers and online forums will attest, I am not good at my job. As I can attest, I am not good. My taste for violence is undiminished. When I have nothing to say, I bite and tear at my fingernails until they bleed.

The eighteenth-century philosopher Jean-Jacques Rousseau[305] wrote that "the primitive passions, which all directly tend towards our happiness, make us deal only with objects which relate to" that happiness. However, Rousseau goes on to say that, when people are "diverted from [happiness] by obstacles, they are more occupied with the obstacle they try to get rid of, than with the [happiness] they try to reach."

So, to return to *Fawlty Towers*, Basil is happy when *not* talking about sex. Mr. Johnson and the psychiatrists are

305 Jean-Jacques Rousseau (1712–78) was a French philosopher. A big fan of pre-civilised man, Rousseau advocated a return to "the state of nature." He writes in 1754's *Discourse on Inequality* that "The first man who, having fenced in a piece of land, said 'This is mine,' and found people naïve enough to believe him, that man was the true founder of civil society. From how many crimes, wars, and murders, from how many horrors and misfortunes might not any one have saved mankind, by pulling up the stakes, or filling up the ditch, and crying to his fellows: Beware of listening to this impostor." Hannah Arendt was not seduced.

obstacles to that happiness. He thinks they will make him talk, that they will ask questions. Basil becomes obsessed with them – just as, for Foucault, we 'dedicate' ourselves to talking about sex in the self-defeating effort to consign it "to a shadow existence." The failure of this effort, in *Fawlty Towers*, is funny. We laugh at Basil being unintentionally obscene, though (if we're to believe Rousseau) our "enjoyment is purely negative".

Rousseau concludes that, once diverted by obstacles, we don't "strive to find satisfaction in our own well-being, but only in the misfortune of others." By doing that, we "become irascible and hateful." Rousseau wasn't talking about comedy, but the fact remains that comedians exist to attack obstacles. The more they are frustrated, the funnier they become, and the happier *we* become. Comedians perform suffering for us. Does this make them hateful?

Tristram Shandy is one of the great comedies. It's a book by Laurence Sterne[306], Rousseau's contemporary. Its eponymous hero, Tristram Shandy, aims to tell the story of his life. He can barely get beyond his own birth, however, because he's too preoccupied telling us about his parents.

Are his parents Tristram's obstacles, or his happiness? He certainly seems happiest when talking about his

306 Laurence Sterne (1713–68) was an Irish-born novelist, clergyman and closet epicure. Sterne discovered that he was funny in 1759. Blinded by the revelation, he gave up his vicarish day-job to write *Tristram Shandy*. Legend has it that – after he'd died of consumption – Sterne's body was grave-robbed and sold to an anatomist. Only when a student recognised Sterne's large nose did the anatomist stop his grisly and then-illegal excavations.

mother and father, though we infer that both have died. Time, then, becomes his obstacle. Dead, they are inaccessible. If Tristram could only 'get rid' of time, he could get to his parents and be happy. That he never can is his tragedy and our comedy.

Tristram's parents have a different relationship to time. His mother is so used to her husband's winding the clock on the stairs up to their bedroom that the very sound of it arouses her. Time is her happiness. So it is that, on the night of Tristram's conception, she becomes obsessed with her more-than-usually horny husband's failure to do so:

> *Pray, my dear,* quoth my mother, *have you not forgot to wind up the clock? Good G– !* cried my father, making an exclamation, but taking care to moderate his voice at the same time…

Mrs. Shandy tries to kill the mood that's obstructed her own pleasure, which is in the *anticipation* of sex, rather than sex itself. All her husband, Walter, can do is modulate his obscenity in the throes of an equally obscene act. Tristram, meanwhile, curses having been conceived under the sign of the stopped clock.

It's later suggested that Tristram's genitals have been irreparably 'cut short' by a falling window. This disability, it's supposed, renders him unable to have children. Without wishing to get too wanky (though that boat's probably sailed), Tristram will never be a parent. He's a lot like his father – prone to tangents and obfuscation – but he'll never write his child their own encyclopaedia, as

Walter Shandy did for Tristram. Nor will Tristram be the subject of his child's writing. He's cut off from becoming a story, a happiness.

The lyrical moment is temporary; pleasure arises in defiance of death, but there's nothing to defy outside the march of time. Tristram's parents are dead so he brings them back to life, if only on the page (if only as souls). But Tristram will have no one to resurrect him. Like the characters in Kendrick Lamar's[307] *Sing About Me, I'm Dying Of Thirst*, Tristram is trapped in the game. He'll either be cut off or fade away. Who'll promise to sing about him? Lamar's protagonists find Jesus. Tristram, madly, becomes his own saviour.

Thwarted by time, Tristram invents a new measurement for the ebb of his life. He becomes his own historian. But, like Sisyphus[308] (and if that boat hadn't sailed before, it's now a speck on the fucking horizon), Tristram's been set an impossible task. Namely, the book of himself: *Tristram Shandy*. How can he finish? How can he even begin? "I am this month one whole year older than I was" when he started his book:

307 Kendrick Lamar, he of the extraordinary lyric "all my life I want money and power | Respect my mind or die from lead shower | I pray my dick gets big as the Eiffel Tower | So I can fuck the world for seventy-two hours."

308 Sisyphus was a king of Corinth. The gods punished him for being a slippery son-of-a-bitch; they condemned Sisyphus to rolling a boulder up a hill, a boulder which would – at the crest – turn and roll back to the bottom. Though Camus wrote that "one must imagine Sisyphus happy," it sounds pretty shit to me.

> and having got...almost into the middle of my fourth volume – and no further than my first day's life – 'tis demonstrative that I have three hundred and sixty-four days more life to write.

Time is again Tristram's obstacle. He's barely born in his autobiography and yet his authorship is coming to a close; nearing death, Tristram has more life than he can cope with. Farce is a question of bad timing. Characters enter and exit too early, or too late, and their disrelation to 'appropriate' chronology makes us laugh. Tristram Shandy makes us laugh. It is also unbearably sad.

Tristram vows to write as long as "the fountain of life" keeps him going. Accordingly, the very book that I'm holding in my hand now – because, yes, I can type with one hand, though it's now become quite ffivult – *difficult* – a bit of physical comedy there – the very book that I was holding in my hand, *Tristram Shandy*, is Tristram Shandy's own gravestone. Its bodily length represents a life; its finitude confirms our hero's death.

By writing, Tristram has created a kind of mirror in which is reflected his own defeat. "Time wastes too fast," he exclaims, "every letter I trace tells me with what rapidity life follows my pen." Every newly-born word prefigures the "eternal separation" that Tristram and Jenny, his beloved, are "shortly to make." Other times he tries running away from death, but here Tristram is "content to look on" it (as Leontes is in *The Winter's Tale*). He is also defiant: "for what the world thinks of that ejaculation – I would not give a groat."

The printed page is dead. But the book – the art – *is* the life of its creator, and their created. Inside, outside. Animal, soul. The *Mona Lisa* was, in part, painted with the menstrual blood of its subject.

Gnomic. Risible. In the words of Simon Pegg[309] in the last episode of *Spaced*, "skip to the end." What's my point? That Tristram succeeded because he failed to remove obstacles. His unhappiness turns into pleasure for both reader and writer. What pleasure? A kind of violence. *Tristram Shandy* exacts its revenge on time. It's wilfully anti-chronological, vandalising the history it's built for itself. So Tristram's happiness is not in the lives of his parents. It's in the living of stories, against the clock, despite never having been born. Mischief: the assault on reason.

Writing is Tristram's way back into the world. Writing is also his way of saying to hell with it. And this paradox gives him pleasure, and it gives us pleasure, and it allows Tristram to become (like Muddy Waters[310]) *Hard Again*. It's pure ego – Nietzsche described Tristram's own, dying author, Laurence Sterne, as "the most liberated spirit of all time, in comparison with whom all others seem stiff, square, intolerant and boorishly direct."

---

309 Simon Pegg starred in *Spaced* and *Big Train* before making movies with Edgar Wright and Nick Frost.

310 Muddy Waters, AKA McKinley Morganfield, was never clear on the year of his birth, but he definitely died aged 70-odd in 1983. He was the great Chicago bluesman who began his career opening for Big Bill Broonzy, collaborated with Willie Dixon and Otis Spann, became frenemies with Howlin' Wolf, fell out of fashion and then got lucky with Johnny Winter.

Is this a kind of quietism? Am I denying the political possibilities of art by placing ultimate importance on the artist's 'personal journey'? I'm probably making a hash of this conclusion, so I'll let Chinua Achebe[311] take over. Achebe said that "the writer does not give prescriptions, he gives headaches." This is not to say that he or she does not 'help'. But that – galvanised somehow by the pleasure of living, keenly, with death – the writer, the artist, is better suited to asking questions than to answering them; to identify obstacles, rather than pretend that obstacles either do not exist or that the artist has the power to remove them from the path to happiness.

For Rousseau, savagery is happiness. For our sins, we are civilised. We live in time and can't uninvent clocks. The Greeks danced with phalluses. They were obstacles designed to ward off evil. Time is violent. Death is evil. It can't be questioned, so it *must* be, even though to do so is absurd and kind of a waste of time.

There's a superb routine by Louis CK[312] about his daughter asking *why*. The habits of children: seldom satisfying material for a comic, but gold in the hands of the best observational stand-up around. As CK tells it, his daughter asks him why they can't play outside. "Because

---

311 Chinua Achebe (1930–2013) was a Nigerian writer and teacher. Achebe's first novel, *Things Fall Apart*, was the first to make Europeans take African writers seriously. I once saw Achebe speak at Cambridge; at the end of the lecture, I embarrassed myself by standing up with a crap disposable camera and trying to photograph him from right at the back of the hall. The photo didn't come out but I can still hear his voice.

312 Louis CK is an American stand-up comedian.

it's raining," he replies. "Why?" she asks. He waffles about vapour clouds but she's relentless. So he admits he doesn't know. *Why* don't you know? "Because I didn't pay attention in school." *Why?* "Cos I was high all the time." *Why?* "Because my parents didn't give a shit. They gave me no guidance. They fucked in a car and had me and resented me for taking their youth." *Why?* "Cos they had shitty parents, it just keeps going like that." *Why?* "Cos, fuck it, we're alone in the universe. Nobody gives a shit about us."

At this point, you'd expect the child to stop asking questions. But she doesn't, which means that Louis CK finds himself embroiled in a philosophical debate with a four-year-old. "Some things are and some things are not. Things that are not can't be," he explains, trying to keep his cool. *Why?* "Then nothing wouldn't be. You can't have fucking nothing isn't." *Why?* "Cos if nothing was, there'd be all kinds of shit that we don't understand, like giant ants in top hats, dancing around." *Why?* "Oh fuck you, eat your French fries, you little shit."

In that exchange, Louis CK isn't the comedian. His daughter is. She drives towards anagnorisis, though anagnorisis is, finally, impossible. No one can see the world. The revelation she forces into being is not why rain clouds form, but why her father is a weak man, floundering at the threshold of his understanding. Are his daughter's questions a diversion, an irascible attack on the obstacle to her happiness? Or is she never happier than when asking *why*? As with obscenity, the pleasure is so much greater when fighting prohibition than if she were simply allowed to play in the rain.

John Bishop has a routine about not being able to dump an old fridge in a fly-tip without prior consent. He tells it as though the person manning the fly-tip is an idiot. Isn't it frustrating, John asks, when ordinary, decent people aren't allowed to leave fridges anywhere they want? To which we might reasonably reply, 'why?'

Bishop's audience laugh uproariously at the fridge routine. But if you asked them individually, 'see that non-degradable object full of poisonous chemicals and weighing quarter of a ton? Yeah, that thing a kid could probably get trapped in without any means to open it from the inside. Mind if I leave it in your garden?' I'd suggest that their assent to the idea wouldn't be quite so hearty.

Bertold Brecht wrote that the bourgeois theatre-goer watches a play and thinks, "yes, I have felt like that too – Just like me – It's only natural – It'll never change." So Bishop's bourgeois audience-member thinks, 'yes, I've felt that too, the annoyance at not being able to randomly dump used white goods wherever I like…' And who can blame them? We trust comedians to ask questions for us. The problem is, John Bishop doesn't ask questions. Though he does do a massive amount for Comic Relief.

Brecht's ideal audience member watches a play and thinks:

> I'd never have thought it – That's not the way – That's extraordinary, hardly believable – It's got to stop – The sufferings of this man appal me, because they are unnecessary.

This response runs contrary to something ingrained in comedy as a communal art. Bishop is big for a reason; people like recognising themselves. Nevertheless, the perversity of Brecht's ideal is *also* integral to comedy. The bourgeois audience member wants to weep when the actors weep "and laugh when they laugh." But Brecht's theatre-goer laughs when others weep, weeps when they laugh, and that's what happens in the best comedy. If you don't believe me, watch anything written by Julia Davis.

To make your audience laugh or weep? To involve them or insist that they keep their distance? It's a tricky balance to strike. But take heart from the Scotch egg – that perfect balance between science and theatre. If Ginsters can do it, then so can you.

The audience member. You. Me. Should we be *made* to think anything at all? Maybe that's the wrong question. Comedy is essentially sceptical. It's about undercutting, not asserting. However serious the point a comedian makes, it's still told in the form of a joke, and within a context which demands laughter: if your opinion isn't funny, keep it to yourself. However, an audience also recognises dishonesty. Can you imagine trying to insert product placement into a comedy routine?

In February 2011, product placement was legalised on British telly (excluding the BBC). Ofcom says that "the content of programmes shouldn't seem to be created or distorted" by the practice, "just to feature the placed products" in a *natural* way. But it's doubly deceitful to emphasise subterfuge when obviously product placement requires distortion. What's Ofcom's message? Distort programmes for money, in secret, but don't break the fourth wall. The audience mustn't recognise that they're being manipulated. By trying to make alien, purely mercantile desires 'seem' unobtrusive, aren't Ofcom trying to trick us into accepting them as a natural dimension of art and entertainment? If, that is, we're bourgeois enough to accept (as Brecht says we do) the unnatural as natural.

When James Bond sips a bottle of Heineken, his Omega watch glinting in the light of his Sony laptop, I want to vomit. I want to take Daniel Craig[313] by the scruff of his neck and vomit into his inexpressive, strangely penile face and scream '*haven't you got enough fucking money?*' and continue to scream '*haven't you got enough fucking money?*' as his minders reduce me to a bloody pulp. I would rather be the middle of a human centipede than swallow that shit. I would even rather watch *Quantum of Solace*.

How silly they'll look in thirty years, these meat-heads selling us mobile phones. When we're all on jetpacks, eating whole meals in a single pill and belittling an underclass of robot butlers into bloody revolt, we'll watch *Skyfall* and think *why?* Why prostitute yourself for a laughably obsolete piece of junk? The equivalent today would be Octopussy sliding off her seat at the sight of Roger Moore[314] using a Teasmade.

---

313 Daniel Craig is a British actor. He's great as George Dyer in *Love is the Devil*.

314 Roger Moore's later Bond films were characterised by tangerine turtlenecks, half-concealed wattle and a couple of shots of Bond pausing on flights of stairs to pant.

Beer, watches and laptops are obstacles. That's why they never occur in artforms predicated on participation. Would Daniel Craig dare sip a bottle of Heineken, his Omega watch glinting in the light of his Sony laptop, *on stage*? Of course he wouldn't. Audiences enjoy attacking obstacles. He'd be heckled. Spat at, hopefully. Someone might even throw him a Walther PPK with which to kill himself. That's because a live performer is in the room with his audience. He isn't a thing up on a hundred thousand cinema screens; he's a person to be judged and found wanting, the potential victim of our laughter.

The only place I've ever seen advertising read out by a real person to a real crowd is at the Grand Ole Opry in Nashville. After a stirring song about a father dying in the Gulf War only for his son to 'finish the job' in the Iraq war, a bald man walked to a lectern on the side of the stage and read in folksy *basso profundo*: "do y'all like a warm, rich, chocolately cuppa joe? Then buy Folgers. Start your day the American way." Though they were all doubtlessly armed, the good people of Tennessee did not hurl their firearms at the bald man. Instead, each added Folgers to their shopping lists, which – to judge from the girth of their rhinestone belts – were already *ginormous*, before settling back to enjoy another song about killing "ragheads". But I hope that they were an exception to a number of rules.

Honesty should be the comedian's only censor. Not just sexual honesty, but remaining true to what it was about you that your audience fell in love with in the first place. By all means evolve, but *We Will Rock You*? Really,

Ben Elton? Would Freddie Mercury[315] *want* that? If the Queen musical is not the single worst consequence of AIDS, then that's only because lazy punch-lines ending with the word 'AIDS' are even worse.

I love performers who commit to the integrity of a story. Like the time I saw John Gordillo's[316] 2008 Edinburgh set about his father. I doubt Gordillo would claim it to be the best hour of comedy ever, but it's up there for me. I saw it at a conjunction of time and place in my life that made the show unforgettable. Why? I remember that Gordillo *talked.* He allowed himself that most dangerous of luxuries for a comedian: he let us not laugh. As Stewart Lee says, the last taboo in comedy is to do a thing sincerely and well.

I'm being sincere. I'm not sure I'm doing it well.

The audience and the artist share their wealth. They reward each other. 'Coinage' refers to money – a fistful of coins, a system of currency – but it also refers to the creation of words. Shakespeare is the most famous and durable exponent of the practice. He coined words which include fashionable, vulnerable, outbreak, dauntless, sanctimonious, inauspicious, lustrous and unearthly. He did so because he wanted to express himself perfectly, and because his audience enjoyed pocketing new coins to spend themselves. His words have lasted, perhaps,

---

315 Freddie Mercury (1946–91) was born Farrokh Bulsara in Zanzibar. Mercury was Queen's frontman. He died of pneumonia as a consequence of AIDS in 1991.

316 John Gordillo is a comedian and director. He collaborates with Eddie Izzard and Reginald D. Hunter.

because the Protestant Reformation swept away Catholic Latin and the courts stopped speaking French; English was crawling out of the primeval swamp of conquerors' tongues, and growing the legs to conquer others.

The theatres of sixteenth and seventeenth-century London reflect the radical changes that the English economy underwent. They were commercial animals. Actors, producers and playwrights mirrored the new system of joint stock trading companies: theatres pooled resources and took a share of the profits. The 'city comedies' of Ben Jonson[317], meanwhile, mark a change in how social status is measured. In *Theatre of a City*, Jean E. Howard[318] writes that these plays seldom dealt "with monarchy and rarely with aristocrats," marking a "moment in modern culture when urban commoners... could become the protagonists in theatrical fiction." The theory goes that money could now be earned by anyone, and so – if money was the new power, supplanting the birth and blood of aristocracy – then anyone could be the subject of drama, which is always fundamentally about the gain and loss of status.

Was this new theatre really so egalitarian? In his essay *Invisible Bullets*, the American academic Stephen Greenblatt[319] argues that, in Shakespeare's plays, "authority is subjected to open, sustained and radical questioning

---

317 Ben Jonson (1572–1637) was a British playwright and poet. A contemporary, collaborator and rival of Shakespeare's, Jonson was the more cynical and sensationalist of the two.

318 Jean E. Howard teaches English at Columbia.

319 Stephen Greenblatt is an American literary critic who's interested in what he calls "cultural poetics".

before it is reaffirmed, with ironic reservations, at the close." I agree with the first part. *King Lear* ends, as we've seen, with new noblemen geared up to make the same mistakes as the dead king and his family. But does that reaffirm authority, or cast further doubt upon it?

Greenblatt also says that Renaissance power relied on artifice, on show (think back to Louis XIV's Hall of Mirrors). For Greenblatt, theatre was "a primary expression" of kingship. And so Shakespeare's "radical questioning" was contained by its own language. His transgressions were "licensed" by authority; his plays were performed at court. Subversion has to happen within power – or, more appropriately and given the derivation of 'subvert' from the Latin *sub-* 'from below' (plus the origin of 'clown' with lump or clod), *beneath* power. The *kômôidoi* – Dionysus – must enter the city walls in order to attack and be scapegoated by the authorities. Must he, though, reaffirm (however ironically) his victimisers' power?

Alan Partridge moved to Sky. Rupert Murdoch[320] now indirectly pays for and profits from the shows of Steve Coogan[321], one of News International's most persistent adversaries. How do we defend this strange situation? To offend someone, you have to speak their language; you have to trade with the old coinage to coin new words.

320 Rupert Murdoch is an octogenarian press baron. He is worth a reported $8.3billion, and was played by Jonathan Pryce in *Tomorrow Never Dies.*

321 Steve Coogan is the British actor most famous for his recurring comedy character, Steve Coogan.

Murdoch may need Coogan more than Coogan needs Murdoch. Who knows? But one thing is clear: mediums are changed by subversion. *Tristram Shandy* changed literature forever.

In the sixties, the Royal Court theatre exploited an interesting loophole. Private performances were beyond the Lord Chamberlain's censorious jurisdiction. So the Royal Court became a club. George Devine[322], its artistic director, ticketed Edward Bond's offensive play *Saved* as a private performance, staged for an audience who had, in effect, 'hired' the theatre as a collective. Devine thus bypassed authority by conforming to its logic. How could the Lord Chamberlain object to privatised content? He couldn't prevent the punters from buying what they wanted (tickets to *Saved*) without undermining the principles of a market economy, principles in which the authorities had invested all their power. Privatisation permitted *Saved* to offend a system that it was now *inside*. And where you fit 'ironically' into those sentences, and what intonation you put on the irony, is up to you. As with Zhu Yu's foetus-eating, the Royal Court exploited loopholes to cause an obscenity that authorities couldn't smother without exposing the flaws in their system.

322 George Devine (1910–66) founded the English Stage Company in 1955, along with Tony Richardson and George Goetischus. They rented the Royal Court theatre in Sloane Square with the intention of staging new writing. Devine helped launch the careers of Edward Bond and Lindsay Anderson, though he wasn't happy. Before he died, he wrote that "I wanted to change the attitude of the public towards the theatre. All I did was to change the attitude of the theatre towards the public."

Today, Louis CK is doing a similar thing to Devine's Royal Court, i.e. selling his shows through his own website. This is good for his fans because a) he charges us less than DVD and ticket middlemen do, and b) we assume he pays tax, unlike Amazon.

Self-sufficiency is today's radical option. But the audience is still paying, as we should – how many people who illegally download music would be cool with their employers' deciding not to pay them for their own work? *South Park*, of course, is typically contrary when it comes to piracy. In one episode, the FBI crack down on the kids for pirating Metallica's music. Stan, Kyle and Kenny's[323] crime? Robbing Metallica's members of slightly bigger swimming pools. It's funny, but less wealthy artists *do* need to live on something, however ludicrously overzealous the anti-piracy rhetoric becomes. And it strikes me as symptomatic of the arts' devalued role in society that audiences think nothing of stealing a self-produced song or a low-budget film just because technology enables them to carry out the theft.

The movie industry's solution to piracy is 3D. Exploiting the hype economy of blockbuster cinema, Hollywood tells punters that the only way to see *all* of the next big thing is to watch it in three dimensions. Never mind that these movies are grey and dark and ugly, and that they reduce grown men to snatching their hands at horizons

323 Stan, Kyle and Kenny are Eric Cartman's reluctant friends. Cartman hates Kyle for being Jewish and Kenny for being poor, but sort of worships Stan as the well-rounded American everyman which Cartman himself can never be.

in the manner of handicapped children on a hilltop, 3D is apparently the only way the film industry can turn a healthy profit.

3D films can't be recorded on video-cameras. The day *Avatar* came out, a thousand Chinese people in big puffer jackets cried themselves to sleep on a bed of unsold VCDs. And the sad thing is, we've swallowed the lie. 3D is not a revolution. It's a piece of legislation, designed not so much to place the product as to enforce it.

Money has long since ceased to be the democratising force it was in Ben Jonson's 'city comedies'. In fact, it never was democratising, being the then-new coinage of an ancient system of debt owed by people to power. As Jean Baudrillard says, "all current strategies" of control boil down to this:

> passing round the debt, the credit, the unreal, unnameable thing you cannot get rid of. Nietzsche analysed the stratagem of God in these terms: in redeeming man's debt by the sacrifice of His son, God, the great Creditor, created a situation where the debt could never be redeemed by the debtor, since it had already been redeemed by the creditor.

The 'real', numerical dimension of my debt is paid by someone else. But this doesn't free me from my obligation. I am instead chained to an 'unreal' debt, a feeling of being bound to that someone's generosity. I will be mortgaged to the hilt till the day I die. One definition of sin.

For Baudrillard, capital works this way. It "plunges the

world into ever greater debt" even as it "works simultaneously to redeem that debt, thus creating a situation in which it will never be able to be cancelled or exchanged for anything." By doing this, capital aims to seem as natural as the world itself, and thus as *inescapable* as life itself. Because, after all, life can't be exchanged for anything except death. So we become Brecht's bourgeois theatre-goer. "It'll never change," we say, when actually we know that it *will* change, in that we will die. In our heads, change, revolution, is death.

I sound like my father's nightmare, some Trot relic from before I was born. I am also a hypocrite. I went to public school. I wrote this book for £6,000. I can't reconcile these things. They are my obstacles. I dash myself against them. I'm happy doing it.

Rousseau defined two types of self-love. 'Amour-de-soi' is the love felt for yourself by yourself. It's savage. 'Amour-propre' is a deviant happiness based on the perceptions others have of you or, rather, your perception of their perception. It's civilised. Hellish, like maintaining a relationship in a hall of mirrors. More, the foundations of such a happiness being insecure, this type of love becomes aggressive, always seeking status over other people. You are my audience; I want to control the way you see things, believing that – without you – I would not exist.

Indebted to you, I become aware of debt's opposite: credit. If only I can credit myself with more power, then I can pay myself out of this thoroughly abstract debt. Happiness becomes a matter of copyright. So I kid you that I'm better in 3D, though this in reality leaves you snatching at false horizons as I pocket the change. When, ideally, we'd be trading in no-man's-land.

Artists need an audience. Every laugh credits the comedian. Every globule of spit credited Kandinsky. Whatever the worth of others' response to their work, artists depend on systems of value: moral, aesthetic, economic. But they also control the creation of their image. Not entirely – you never know how a joke's going to fly – but you can manipulate yourself in such a way to surprise and frustrate the exchange rate. Shakespeare traded in English; he was compelled to speak, but he did so with words he'd coined himself.

The tool to disrupt the credit-debit power structure is, for Baudrillard, "radical uncertainty". For the artist, it's asking *why?* (an interrogative adverb), especially if anyone quotes that bloody *If* poem at you. 'If' is a conjunction, a conditional clause. If you do x, y and z, "then yours is the earth and everything in it, and what's more, you'll be a man, my son." Sacrifice and reward on authority's terms. But I don't want the earth. I'm also not being wild about being a "man" – a violent identity, coined to indebt me to its author. And who's judging me? Rudyard Kipling[324]?

324 Rudyard Kipling (1865–1936) was an English writer and freemason. Kipling knew and admired luminaries like Cecil Rhodes and Leander Starr Jameson. At the beginning of the First World War, Kipling's son, John, failed his military medical three times due to his poor eyesight. Kipling pulled some strings and landed John in the Battle of Loos. John was promptly blown to bits. A grave that may or not hold his remains was only identified in 1992. Kipling wrote a poem ("if any question why we died | Tell them, because our fathers lied") and invented the lunchbox-sized apple pie for future generations of children to enjoy by way of penance.

The guy who sent his son to die in the trenches? Fuck that.

Patti Smith said that "Jesus died for somebody's sins but not mine." As far as possible, I want to be sceptical about the source of credit, to refuse forgiveness, to live at my own risk: "my sins, they belong to me, *me*." This impulse is partly the old, aggressive power-play of amour-propre. But it's also an attempt to return to amour-de-soi, to say – as the scotch egg does – love me or leave me.

In Berlin, the graves of Bertold Brecht and Helene Weigel[325] made me cry. Two rocks up against a wall. A bed of pachysandra and the odd red carnation. Such severe, unadorned intimacy. I cried at the simplicity-in-the-gesture – there must be a German word for what I mean – and because I was hugely hungover.

I've been talking about an ideal. This will embarrass some of you. Me too, in time. But what I'm really aiming at is the readiness to self-destruct. As I tried to do with my play, *Anatomy Act*, a response to another's self-destruction. And as this book has become a response to Jessie's self-destruction. The willingness to explode my world with one simple question: *why?* This is an outpouring of everything I have in me. Sorry for making you wade through my guts.

This book is not pretty. It's not very good. But self-destruction can be both. In 2012, I saw a Polish dance company called Teatr Zar perform their piece, *Caesarian Section: Essays on Suicide.* In one scene, a woman tied a noose around her neck, then attached the rope to the

325 Helene Weigel (1900–71) was a German actress. Weigel and Brecht ran the Berliner Ensemble, and Weigel continued to do so after his death. She was *the* Mother Courage.

infant branch of an infant tree. The scene ended with her stood with a watering can, patiently nurturing the tree in the hope that it would grow big enough to kill her. Everyone laughed. It was beautiful.

Time, the great healer. But what if our wounds (and no one else's, Christ's or otherwise) make us the people we are? To go on, bleeding, and laughing at the sight of blood.

This book is called *A Good Bullet*. That's because Brecht wrote a poem called *The Interrogation of the Good*. In it, he addresses the good man. Good because he asked no questions of himself or the world. Good in the eyes of authority. Brecht tells this good, passive man – whose the earth was to inherit – that:

> "You are our enemy. This is why we shall
> Now put you in front of a wall. But in consideration
> of your merits and good qualities
> We shall put you in front of a good wall and shoot
> you
> With a good bullet from a good gun and bury you
> With a good shovel in the good earth."

Tragedy may happen in Ely, Cherry Hinton, Royston and Crewe, but comedy starts with you. Me. I am a good person, in suspended animation. My sins are mine alone. When the time comes to pay for them, I hope I line myself up against the wall, jawing, naked as a headlit maw. If my executioners are funny enough, I may not feel the bullet.

Here is a blank page. Draw your own conclusion.

Acknowledgements.

Thanks to David Isaacs and Emma, my editor; to Jack Whitehall, Ben Cavey, Dan Swimer, Aiden Spackman, Pippa Brown and Amanda Davis; to Oliver Bancroft, Doc H, Martin Golding and my parents; to Alice Bingham, always, and to Fran Drescher. Seriously, check out *The Nanny*. It'll blow your fucking mind.

Props to my godson Theo and his mother, Maria Onyango. I write, as ever, with Victoria Lupton tutting in a rich and haughty French over my shoulder.

And a special mention belongs to my grandfather, John Jackson, who went to death an animal, and who filled and fills every room. He was a carpenter. I remember him making me swords from cast-off wood, with a vein down the middle, cut should the imaginary blood of an imagined man overwhelm the point.

Plagiarists' Corner.

I've stolen quotes (and more) from this embarrassingly phallocentric selection of books:

Allen, James – *Without Sanctuary: Lynching Photography in America*
Angier, Natalie – *Woman: An Intimate Geography*
Arendt, Hannah – *Eichmann in Jerusalem*
Aristotle – *Poetics*
Auden, W.H. – *Another Time*
Bakhtin, Mikhail – *Rabelais and his World*
Barthes, Roland – *The Pleasure of the Text* and *A Roland Barthes Reader* (ed. Susan Sontag)
Baudrillard, Jean – *Impossible Exchange*
de Beauvoir, Simone – *A Very Easy Death*
Beckett, Samuel – *Krapp's Last Tape*
Benjamin, Walter – *One-Way Street and Other Writings*
Bishop, Claire – *Artificial Hells: Participatory Art and the Politics of Spectatorship*
Booker, Christopher – *The Seven Basic Plots*

Brecht, Bertold – *Theatre for Pleasure or Theatre for Instruction*
Cesar, Aimé – *Tempest*
'Coetzee', 'J.M.' – *Giving Offense*
Danchev, Alex (ed.) – *100 Artists' Manifestos*
Dostoyevsky, Fyodor – *The Idiot*
Eagleton, Terry – *After Theory*
Euripides – *The Bacchae*
Foucault, Michel – *The History of Sexuality*
Freud, Sigmund – *Civilisation, Society and Religion*
Gauchet and Swain – *Madness and Democracy*
Girard, René – *The Scapegoat*
Gleick, James – *The Information* and *Chaos*
God – *The Bible*
Grose, Francis – *A Classical Dictionary for a Vulgar Tongue*
Gunn, Thom – *Collected Poems*
Harvey, Elizabeth D. and Krier, Theresa – *Luce Irigaray and Premodern Culture*
Hazlitt, William – *The Pleasure of Hating*
Hunter, Saunders and Williamson – *On Pornography*
Howard, Jean E. – *Theatre of a City*
Johnson, Doctor – *The Dictionary*
Jones, Leroi – *Black Music*
Klein, Naomi – *The Shock Doctrine*
Kapuściński, Ryszard – *The Other*
Laing, R.D. – *The Politics of Experience*
Lawrence, D.H. – *Lady Chatterley's Lover*
Leavitt, David – *The Man Who Knew Too Much: Alan Turing and the Invention of the Computer*

Lee, Stewart – *How I Escaped My Certain Fate*
Legman, G – *No Laughing Matter: Rationale of the Dirty Joke (Second Series)*
Macdonald Cornford, Francis – *The Origin of Attic Comedy*
MacKinnon, Catherine – *Feminism Unmodified*
Martin, Reinhold – *Utopia's Ghost: Architecture and Postmodernism, Again*
Merton, Paul – *Silent Comedy*
Pakenham, Thomas – *The Scramble for Africa*
Porter, Lewis – *John Coltrane: His Life and Music*
Pynchon, Thomas – *Gravity's Rainbow*
Scahill, Jeremy – *Blackwater*
Shakespeare, William – *King Lear, Richard III, The Tempest* and *The Winter's Tale*
Skinner, Quentin – *Visions of Politics*
Sontag, Susan – *Against Criticism* and *On Regarding the Pain of Others*
Sterne, Laurence – *Tristram Shandy*
Sutherland, John – *Offensive Literature*
Weil, Simone – *The Illiad, or the Poem of Force*
Žižek, Slavoj – *Living In The End Times* and *Violence*

Plus **sets** by Frankie Boyle, Louis CK, Jim Davidson, Neil Hamburger, Bill Hicks, possibly Michael McIntyre, Jerry Sadowitz and Hans Teeuwen.

Plus **comedies** including *Bad Education*, *Fawlty Towers*, *Life's Too Short*, *Miranda*, *Mr. Bean*, *The Nanny*, *Spaced* and *South Park*.

Plus **music** by The Beegees, The Notorious BIG, John Coltrane, Bob Dylan, Missy Elliot, Kendrick Lamar, Nina Simone, Rick Wakeman and Saul Williams.

Plus **films** including *Alien*, *Candyman*, *Casino Royale*, *The Dark Knight*, *The Dark Knight Rises*, *The Departed*, *Enigma*, *Funny Games*, *Grizzly Man* and *The Rock*, *Steamboat Bill Jr.*

Plus **articles** from *Cabinet* magazine, the *Daily Mail*, *Fortune*, the *Guardian*, the *Jerusalem Post*, the *New York Times*, the *Radio Times*, the *Scotsman*, *Slate*, the *Telegraph*, *The Times*.

Plus **shitloads** from Wikipedia.

[illegible] by [illegible] The Notorious B.I.G., John [illegible] Missy Elliot, Kendrick Lamar, [illegible] and Saul Williams.

[illegible] *Chuck Brown*, [illegible] *The Departed*, [illegible] and *The Rock*, [illegible]

[illegible] magazine, the *Daily Mail*, [illegible] *Washington Post*, the *New York* [illegible] the [illegible] the *Telegraph*, [illegible]

[illegible]

Freddy Syborn co-writes the record-breaking BBC3 sitcom, *Bad Education*. He's also co-written a Sky *Little Cracker*, contributed sketches to *Psychobitches*, and written jokes for TV shows including *Live at the Apollo*, *Never Mind the Buzzcocks*, *Stand Up For The Week* and *Big Brother's Big Mouth*. He's still most proud of that last show.